Praise for *18 & Out*

"With not so much as a nod to the "Greatest G
a fascinating story of his growing up during Wo...
was dirt poor and his parents preternaturally indifferent to him, yet he was endlessly curious and creative: he drew, played the violin, started little businesses, mastered his school work, climbed tall mountains and worked on expensive racing cars. He neither liked nor respected his mother and his father, but thrived anyway under circumstances that today would be called child neglect. Funny, candid, idiosyncratic and full of surprises—you won't put it down."
— **JERRY BROWN**, Governor of California 1975-1983 and 2011-2019

"This riveting memoir is what you get when a great sociologist turns his ethnographic eye and sharp pen - now generous, now acid - on his own mid-century upbringing on the Pacific. Short of food and parental love, the young MacCannell, an endlessly curious and self-reliant gearhead with enough caring mentors and a talent for drafting and reading with purpose, finds beauty in bricolage and life lessons in sudden epiphanies.
— **IAIN BOAL**, Social Historian, co-author of Resisting the Virtual Life: The Culture and Politics of Information City, and co-founder of the Retort Collective

"MacCannell describes a childhood that is anything but idyllic with such generosity, tenderness and humor, that it will cure you of any lingering self-pity. As a fairly recent immigrant, I learned a lot from it, not only about life and how to live it, but about an America I never knew existed."
— **MILENA MOSER**, Best-selling Swiss novelist author of more than twenty German language books with several translated into French and English.

"This is a difficult book to put down! It is a very lively romp through MacCannell's life from birth through college, touching on family, school, work, play, sex and education. ... His independence from his parents allowed to him unusual hobbies, including racing sports cars, mountain climbing in Mexico and entertaining his own friends."
—**NELSON GRABURN,** Distinguished Professor Emeritus, Anthropology, University of California Berkeley and Co-Chair, The Tourism Studies Working Group

"As a refugee woman, Dean MacCannell's memoir will deeply resonate with many such as myself who have had to overcome adversity to find one's own path, with love and support from the few who see their potential."
— **MAI-NHUNG LE**, Professor & Chair, Asian American Studies, San Francisco State University

18

&

OUT

An Average Boy's
Childhood and Youth in
Mid-Twentieth Century America

Dean MacCannell

BONGO BOOKS

Cover Drawing: Mark Primack
Production Design: Brian Shea

Bongo Books
P.O. Box 162096
Sacramento, CA 95816

ISBN: 978-1-7375065-6-0

Table of Contents

A note on the cover drawing.

Artist Mark Primack drew this version of the 1942 photograph of two-year old Dean found on page 15. Mark writes:

"[We] can all see ourselves in your photo, in that reverie. A child is born de-centered and breathes in the world, moment by moment.

And Tourism is the promised re-enactment of that wonder and sensation of seeing the world anew."

"Dean, young," graphite drawing by Mark Primack 2022

Introduction

The following incident happened when I was twelve, about half grown. In the early 1950s, Gilbert Chemistry Sets still contained vials of potassium nitrate. The two other ingredients of gun powder were easily sourced. A neighbor named Phil Freeman showed me experiments I could perform well beyond the Gilbert instruction book, like creating an epic stench. Phil was a graduate student in physics, and he grinned the whole time he taught me how to grind charcoal into fine dust and the most effective ratios of sulfur to use. He cautioned me not to ignite my black powder in any closed vessels like screw-top Mason jars and left me to devise my own applications of my new power.

Mostly I liked to amuse other children with the intense white-light flash of a teaspoon of powder. We were living in Union Bay Village Projects in Seattle and there were hundreds of baby-booming kids to impress. Before long I hatched more malevolent schemes. When you are twelve years old and can make your own black powder, it is hard not to let your imagination run away with you. In the 1950s every other adult smoked cigarettes and every other ashtray in public places was filled with sand. Black powder mixed with grey sand is impossible to discern. And a lighted cigarette is an effective ignition device. WHOOOOM! A few people in the North End of Seattle may have considered giving up smoking that year. Especially if they had been drinking as well as smoking.

I didn't try for a big event until I used up about half my supply of potassium nitrate. I thought, "Instead of making a lot of little flashes, why not make one really big one with everything that's left?" My parents and youngest brother, John, were gone for the weekend, camping with a neighbor family who had a car. We didn't own a car; few of the families in the projects did. My parents left my brother Bill in my care because two whole families with their camping gear did not fit into one car. Bill and I liked staying home alone because we could eat as much sugar as we wanted, spread thick on slices of Wonder Bread. We set ourselves to grinding a large supply of charcoal dust.

My plan was to mix about a half-cup of powder, put it in the bottom of our old coal scuttle, throw in a match and stand back. I had never tried to scale up production before. Without precise measuring instruments, getting the exact ratios of chemicals and charcoal wasn't easy. But after about a half-day of work, we thought we were good to go. I took the scuttle out onto the back porch and looked around carefully in all directions. Bill, not quite ten years old, stood beside me with his fist pressed against his chin, shivering with anticipation.

It must have been a holiday weekend, probably the Fourth of July, because not a soul was stirring in the common area between the row houses. This is great, I thought. I did not want any witnesses. I waited. There was still no one around so I lit the match, tossed it in the scuttle and stepped back, pulling Bill with me.

Nothing happened.

Oh, crap! It's a bad batch. This had happened before on a smaller scale. Instead of a big flash, there were a few sparkles on the surface of the powder. The ratio was off. Maybe it could be saved and adjusted.

Bill and I were standing by the scuttle observing the sparkles, disappointed, when a man came into the courtyard between the houses. "How are you boys doing?" he called out in a friendly way. It was the manager of the Project. I don't remember his name. We were frozen in fear that he might see or smell the slender columns of blue-green smoke rising out of the scuttle. "We're fine," we said through gritted teeth. He passed by and was a few steps away with his back to us when the scuttle went off.

The flash made a horrendous WHOOMPH sound and shot up to the eaves of the house. Even though we were in full sun, the intense flash caused the houses across the way and the project manager's back to lose their color for an instant. Everything reflected brilliant blue-white light. The manager spun on his heels. We were half-hidden behind a grey mushroom cloud that was spooling up about thirty feet into the air. Our eyebrows, lashes and the front of our hair was burnt into little brittle brown curly wires and smoking. But we suffered no injuries or burns that might require treatment.

"What was that?" the manager demanded, more frightened than angry.

Without hesitation and in unison, Bill and I answered in a sing-song, "We don't know."

"Well, whatever it was, don't do it again. EVER!" he said. He turned away quickly and left the scene at a rapid pace. Like he was the perpetrator, not us.

*   *   *

The delayed ignition in the scuttle happened just past the mid-point of this memoir. An editor asked me to bring it forward to the beginning. I think he wanted my story to start with a bang. At first, I resisted. It's not my style. But I relented. It does contain several portents about the overall design of my childhood and youth. Already my reader may have correctly surmised that we were poor to the point of food deprivation and living in public housing; that my parents sometimes left me to care for myself and my younger siblings; and that our poverty did not prevent me from coming up with interesting things to do. Usually, something interesting to do was predicated on my parents' not knowing about it, as it certainly was in this flash-in-the-scuttle incident.

The big flash occurred when I was about half-way toward working out for myself what is right and wrong, and good and bad. I knew not to look to my parents for advice about these important matters. According to them, whatever they did, no matter how sketchy, was right; any suggestion that they might not be right was wrong; bad behavior was anything that annoyed them or cost them money. The one thing that was guaranteed to annoy them was questioning authority, starting with their authority. Good behavior meant never challenging their word, staying quiet, and making no demands for their attention. I suspect I am not alone in having role models like these.

While this is the story of my childhood, it must not be read as a parenting book. There is only one lesson here for parents. If you have as little regard for your children as mine had for me, one of them might put you in a book like this someday.

Throughout my childhood and youth, I could do pretty much as I pleased so long as my parents didn't catch wind of my thoughts and actions. There were risks involved. When you have a good imagination and you are dirt poor, curious, and possess only a half-formed sense of what is right and what is wrong, almost every scheme you come up with exposes you to danger. You, and sometimes your little brothers. Hardly a month went by that I didn't try something that might have literally or figuratively blown up in my face. You name it and I probably got up to it.

By seeking alternatives to parenting outside the home, and education outside of my schools, I was eventually able to arrive at my understanding of right and wrong, and good and bad. No matter how great our schools or families might happen to be, none of them provides every answer we need to get through life. In this book I tell of large and small events and moments in my life that turned my thinking on its axis, fundamentally altering my understanding of the world, my family, and myself. The main theme of my story is how I learned to rely on epiphanies—revelations about life and human character that came to me in a flash, that altered my way of thinking and kept me searching and curious about the world beyond my immediate situation. I may have had more than my fair share of revelatory moments. Hopefully, very few of my readers will have had a father as creepily instructive as mine, or a mother as self-centered.

If there is any "use value" in the following it will be in my invitation for my reader to revisit similar potential life altering moments in your own past. Do some of these need to be re-evaluated? Are the true heroes of your childhood who you think they are?

Those familiar with my other writing who look here for social or cultural analysis and critique will search in vain. The connections between my childhood experience and my later work are more suggestive and episodic than direct. There is one area of strong continuity, however.

From early childhood to the present moment, I have had a relaxed, almost friendly acquaintanceship with danger. This does not mean I am attracted to things that are dangerous. Danger itself does not interest me. What I enjoy is avoiding or thwarting danger that stands in my path. My relationship to danger is as much aesthetic as ethical. I love certain loud noises--the unmuffled exhaust note of a twelve cylinder Ferrari, the fulminations of an infuriated bureaucrat.

My favorite uncle, Eddie Meskimen, warned me not to pick up a firecracker that failed to detonate. "It might be smoldering inside and explode after a delay and blow your fingers off." I applied his warning to my black powder mixture in the scuttle. Concerned about our safety, I had already passed along our uncle's advice to Bill, warning him about the possibility of delayed combustion. If we had been bending over the scuttle when it blew, it might have burned our faces off and blinded us. When it happened we were both standing a half-step back, our heads tilted slightly away. Small precaution, but enough to avoid harm while being able to experience a "thump," a flash, and a sulphurous stench that might have come straight out of hell itself.

Life is mostly about caring and taking care of oneself and others. Extreme care is paradoxically at the heart of the two sports I pursued seriously as a teenager. Expeditionary mountaineering and car racing are ideal arenas to learn not about the avoidance of danger, but necessary care, caution, and preparation at the edge of danger.

Metaphorically, I never stopped enjoying making and igniting black powder. It has been my pleasure to bring a few explosive research findings to light. In the 1980s, digging through recently declassified government files, I discovered that the 1950s and '60s abject degradation of the inner city was the intended result of US strategic nuclear defense policy. When I published my findings I drew quite a bit of negative attention from the State Department. When my research on the causal relationship between industrial agriculture and rural poverty was used to shape federal reclamation law and water distribution policy, the California Westside Farmers Association demanded that I be fired from my university position. When I gave a lecture in South Carolina arguing that Southern plantation tourism should fully acknowledge slavery, I received death threats. As an adult I have spent quite a bit of time "on the carpet." No one who came for me succeeded in bringing me down, slowing me down, or stopping me from taking future risks. My numerous adult brushes with anxious or enraged authority all played out like the flash in the coal scuttle, with the project managers cutting and running, not me. A close reader will see how my childhood was perfect preparation for this important aspect of my adult life.

A secondary but important goal of this memoir is to give close attention to material culture that is lost in the advance of technology. I have witnessed life-altering shifts in dominant sources of power— external combustion (steam and coal), internal combustion and petro-chemicals, electricity, and renewables. A vast culture that formed around coal-fired steam power died during the first decade of my life. When I was very young, anything that required a great deal of force was done with steam under pressure. Ocean liners were called "steamships." Heavy building equipment was generically called "steam rollers" and "steam shovels." Jackhammers were "steam drills." Railroad locomotives were "steam engines." My maternal grandmother and grandfather were both members of the Boiler Makers Union well after there were no longer any boilers to make.

As a teenager I was singularly focused on preparing myself for respectable blue-collar work. I entered the labor force and became self-supporting, at age fifteen. At the time I was preoccupied with automobiles powered by state-of-the-art internal combustion engines, racing engines. I did not know then that internal combustion of fossil fuels was destroying the planet. No one did. I hope my memories of my late teen years may help explain the mystique of those technologies—and how humans can, and very often do, fall in love with something that's killing them.

We are still doing this. The current direction of the lightning advance of information technology seems designed to distract us from the only real problem we are facing as a species. Artificial intelligence and virtual reality may effectively do some tasks previously performed by humans and provide new forms of entertainment, but they are not cleaning up the deadly messes left by the last technological revolutions. Playing cute in a Metaverse mocked up virtual heaven on earth may become profitable escapist entertainment, but it won't prevent us from burning in the hell of our own making in the real world.

a

ACKNOWLEDGEMENTS

This book would not have been written without the encouragement of friends and relations who have responded with more than polite interest to my telling of these stories. Most demanded to know more about how I coped with my peculiar parents and early family life.

My childhood feels more challenging from my current vantage point than it felt as I was living it. Day-to-day I mainly stayed out of trouble, had fun, and never wanted for interesting things to do. My mother and father succeeded in mocking-up a version of ordinary everyday life that allowed us to go through the motions of being a family without appearing especially strange to outsiders. They strained to keep up appearances, to lean conservatively across the line into the seemingly normal. For this, for the cover they maintained, I thank them without equivocation.

My behavior as a child was sufficiently standard that I could expand my social circle without arousing confusion, pity, or fear. Against large odds, I had clothes on my back, a roof over my head, and I got off to school on time every morning. They often could not afford to meet our minimal nutritional requirements, but we were always fed something. Without irony I thank them for the energy and imagination they put into maintaining normal appearances. Their greatest gift to me was a well-formed negative mold for pouring a beautifully positive family and professional life into.

If the life portrayed in the following account is turned on its axis 180 degrees it would accurately reflect the primary family I collaboratively created as an adult with Juliet Flower and our two sons, Daniel and Jason. Every moment of our lives together, they have given me their unforced love, shared intense involvement in, and support for, our collective creative works, collaboration, non-stop conversation, all punctuated by peels of laughter. Juliet, Daniel and Jason knew my stories before I began writing them down. They assured me that an account of my strange childhood and youth could be of interest to others. Without their encouragement I would never have undertaken this project.

Janie Augustson, Judith Adler, Iain Boal, Bernie Lubell, Milena Moser, Mark Primack, Achva Stein, and David Stein read part or all of the manuscript in serial form as it was being written. They asked the kinds of questions and supplied comments that made me want to keep at it.

Acknowledging everyone else who worked with me after I turned eighteen, who powered me to where I am today, would be longer than the current book. It would include some super professors and even more super students and colleagues from near and far, assistants, collaborators, artists, curators, conference organizers, editors, many of whom became as much or more friends as professional associates. Thank you for everything we were able to accomplish together and please accept my regret for what we left unfinished.

Special thanks are owed to my friend Mark Primack, an extraordinary artist and architect who provided the graphite drawing for the cover of this book. He read an earlier draft in its entirety and selected the photograph he made the basis for his portrait from the many I provided him. It connects several key themes in my narrative.

My story requires me to explain how deeply in love I fell with a certain kind of automobile in the 1950s. Mid-twentieth century cars had not become the globally homogenized appliances they are today. Alfa Romeos, Jaguars, MGs, were different from everything else then and now in ways that resist words.

Marc Vorgers very generously granted me permission to use his sensitive photographs of the cars I drove and worked on in period, i.e., before they became "classics": MGTC (p. 164); XK 120 Jaguar (p. 220); Porsche 356 (p. 229); MGTD (p. 228); Alfa Giulietta (p. 228). Copyright Marc Vorgers, ClassicarGarage.com. The photo on p. 249 is of a Fiat Abarth Zagato, one of the cars that most engaged me at the time. Paul Combes owns this particular example and supplied me with the photograph and permission to use it. I thank both Marc and Paul for their lively correspondence and their enthusiastic support for this part of my memoir. See photo credits at the end of this book.

Most of the other photos that accompany the text are from my family archive. My parent's lifelong hobby was amateur photography. No matter how poor we were, they spent money on paper, film, and chemicals needed for a makeshift, at-home photography lab, set up in our bathroom every two or three months to process photos for the "Family Album."

They did not regard photography as an art form. Taking snapshots was merely something they did for fun. They purchased a basic enlarger and chemical trays for developing their photos, not to exercise artistic control over the process. It was simply cheaper than commercial finishing, permitting them to take as many pictures as they wished. They always owned slightly better than the most basic cameras and they took on average about 200 photos a year. My childhood was documented almost as thoroughly as childhoods today by parents wielding smart phone cameras. I now possess 25 years of these Family Albums with a location and a brief comment written by my mother for each picture. As each Album begins on January 1 and ends on December 31 and the pictures are displayed in the order they were taken, it is easy to establish the date of each photo to within a few days.

These Albums have been indispensable to me as I write, permitting me to verify the dates of all my memories. I regard them as a valuable archive, not just of my early life, but of my family's slow and painful movement through and eventually out of poverty in the second half of the 20th century. Excepting a very few taken by other family members, every unattributed photograph in the following was taken by Earle H. MacCannell and Helen Frances MacCannell.

1

My Birth and its Lesson

1,500 BABIES, GIVE OR TAKE, were born in the United States on Saturday, May 25, 1940. This was toward the end of the week the Nazi German infantry blitzed across Europe and established its beachhead on the English Channel. I was one of those babies. My childhood memories were of living in a world at war, not the kinds of wars we have today, but total war, shaping every detail of life on the "home front." My mother had just turned 19 and my father was 22 when I was born. It is often said that the birth of a child causes a young parent to reassess everything and mature quickly. That did not happen. Both my parents had recently been teenagers during the Great Depression. They had big dreams, but they were also habituated to live day to day on almost nothing and without expecting anything positive to happen.

There is photographic evidence that I brought them some joy for the first few months. I hope so. But by the time of my earliest memories, about 18 months after my birth, I had become just another mouth to feed.

I do not remember my birth, but I can reconstruct it. I had just spent months enclosed in a

Helen Frances and Earle H. MacCannell, early May 1940

soft, dark, hot, wet, sack inside my mother. My arms and my legs were tight across my chest like a cleverly folded figure in a pop-up book. For some time I had been aware of movement and sound, mainly muffled voices. And the monotony of the constant "lub-dub, lub-dub, lub-dub," of my mother's heartbeat. I hadn't been bothered by any need to eat or breathe. My mother was doing all that for me. There were no smells, no tastes, and if I opened my eyes, nothing to see. My brain had been developing for some time along with the rest of me. It wasn't equipped with a master switch to turn it on and off. Though my senses were limited, I was already quite aware of my surroundings. When my mother moved, I felt it. When she spoke or was spoken to, I heard it even though I did not understand. And when she was emotionally upset, or delighted, the cortisol, adrenaline, endorphins, etc. that coursed through her veins coursed through mine as well. Occasionally, I felt like kicking or punching and I did.

From Day One, I Was Not A Perfect Fit With The World I Was Born Into. Nobody Is

Then, during a particularly intense chemical storm, I was pushed out through an impossibly small opening. It was a very tight fit and took several hours. Toward the end, according to eye- witnesses, they called a doctor to the house who reached in with forceps, grabbed my head and yanked me free.

Gosh! What just happened? I was born.

I emerged into a world of bright lights and colors, noises, cold drafts, smells, and hunger. I was surrounded by enormous beings hovering over me taking turns making incomprehensible noises. What had been soft murmurs in the womb became loud, ugly strings of noun-vowel-noun-vowel,—pause, noun-vowel, pause-vowel-noun-vowel, pause—the ack-ack of articulate English speech. I shivered all over and everything stank of medicine and bodily fluids. One of the giants wrapped me in a warm blanket. I guessed they were going to protect and care for me, not continue trying to squeeze the life out of me. I could tell that I was the focus of attention, and they appeared to understand and respond to each other, but it was impossible for me to know what they were saying or had in mind.

Birth powerfully validates the idea that all matter and being is susceptible to instantaneous total transformation, to absolute change that comes from deep within. Birth is the first total change. Then comes life.

In life, we are taught something quite different: that change comes incrementally; that who we end up being is a result of addition and subtraction. We are admonished to add up years of education, Sunday School attendance, Little League home runs, college entrance exam scores, months of sobriety, degrees earned, starting salaries, calories consumed, hours of exercise, numbers of promotions, increasing wages, quarterly sales, real estate appreciation, retirement savings. We are told to believe that these things are the building blocks of human life—bit by bit by bit. And some, perhaps most of us, believe this.

No wonder we have childhood amnesia. We must deny the initial truth of our being. We must forget the lesson we learned at birth: BLAM! Everything is different now and life will be a series of crucial transformations. Instead, we join the grand illusion and start to believe in continuity. And progress.

Sequential transformation has always seemed to me a much better fit for what happens on history's stage, and personally on an intimate scale. The main problem is that none of us can plan or schedule when transformative causality is about to hit us or to recognize it as it happens. You never know when you are about to overhear a life-altering secret. Or get turned down for the job that would have made all the difference in the world. A desire that has taken precedent over all others suddenly gets replaced by a completely different desire.

Everything becomes its opposite in its own time and at wildly different rates of speed. One part of the economy transforms overnight, while the other parts take a hundred years to catch up. A solid can turn into a liquid in twenty minutes as the ice cube in the bottom of my glass proves, and the liquid becomes a gas a week or so after that. But it took several million years for a dinosaur to become a hummingbird. We are all about to happen every moment of our lives until we become fertilizer. Actually still happening as and after we become fertilizer, but it does not much matter anymore—to us. We continue to make a life and death difference to the flowers we nurture and the lives of those who remember us.

It is difficult for nicely socialized adults to accept the possibility that an individual's life, and even human history, might be changed by a single small object or event, by a single word, or glance. Or, by silence when the right word would have meant all the difference; by a moment of stupidity that required a moment of sentience. This assumes more responsibility, or as we now say "agency," than most adults are willing to bear. It is easier to follow formulas even if none of them have a better than 50/50 success rate.

Born-Again Christians believe in total transformation. But they think there is only one big one in life and that everything that went before doesn't matter and can be erased.

Wouldn't that be great? The problem is this: even if everything changes completely, nothing ever gets erased. After an epiphany, after a life changing event, marks and traces remain of every former state of being. Early childhood amnesia is proof that children refuse to accept the compact with society that is initially thrust upon us. We do not start to remember things until we either accept the definition of the situation that is imposed on us, or we begin to make our own unique sense of it.

Life began to make sense to me at an early age, but not arithmetically. Not by addition and subtraction. As I acquired language, the nonsensical babble I had been hearing all around me became my most powerful tool for learning about and understanding my surroundings. When I started to crawl, total dependence on my caregivers for movement from A to B became a giddy sense of independence and freedom. Did each of these transformations bring with it a completely new way of being in the world? No. Each total change is haunted by the older conditions that gave rise to it. Yes, language gave me much greater insight about life. But when I began to speak and eventually to read, I continuously discovered there are great tracts of language and life that I did not understand. Language-based knowledge only brought me to the frontiers of the unknown. When I started to crawl, I had enormous new freedom, and I quickly learned that I was not free to stick my little fingers into the electrical sockets. Freedom only brought me to the frontiers of danger and the forbidden. I do not think I am alone in these realizations. I suspect every human infant deeply understands and embodies the unity of opposites.

As infants, however, we are surrounded by powerful beings who are empiricists and logical positivists. Most popular parenting advice assumes that childhood is a matter of incremental growth and development: i.e., if given age-appropriate instruction and learning toys one by one by one, if manifestations of negative character are effectively subtracted as they occur, it will eventually add up to a well-adjusted, functional young adult. No one's life actually unfolds like that. Life outcomes are more about how we deal with expressions of love that are either too large or too small, instances of hypocrisy, dislocations, luck, inconsistency, unfairness, undeserved good and bad fortune, contradiction, opposition, simmering and open conflict, accident, and sheer absurdity.

In the last few years I witnessed mass resistance to the knowledge that our entire earth is warming to the point where it will soon become uninhabitable. In the course of my lifetime, Christian love and charity turned into racial hatred and impotent rage against secular humanism and science. In fewer than ten years Maoist Communism became a ruthlessly effective form of State Capitalism. Emotional fragility and masculine insecurity became macho gun-toting rugged individualism. Men with no character, and negative character, amassed huge fortunes. This list is as long as anyone would wish to make it. Do not imagine for a moment that your children aren't noticing, especially during their teen years. I doubt that anyone completely shakes the lesson of their birth.

Large and small transformative moments are occurring constantly. We may wish many of them did not happen, and they are repressed. Sometimes we see them coming a mile off, sometimes they hit us out of the blue. The test is whether we face them, learn from them, and build upon them, grow out of them. Or do they knock us for a loop and cause us to spiral down into existential confusion and self-pity. Mostly it hinges on whether or not someone loved us enough to give us permission and confidence to navigate these turbulent waters. I was fortunate to have been loved enough—just not by my parents.

2
Three Transformative Events

AS I SAID, MY STORY is not a linear progression of experiences, way-stations along a path of increasing maturity. I am not entirely certain that I ever "matured." My childhood and youth were more like the action inside a pinball machine: random collisions resulting in new directions, lights going off, bells ringing. Moments when the ball goes down the hole and a new ball is needed. Other moments when a purposeful and productive new trajectory is occasioned by a well-timed strike with the flippers. Here are the three most transformative moments in my early childhood: I learn about *"18 and out"*; I receive proof that I have a mediocre intellect; and I start to read.

My Mother Tells Me About *18 and out*

Late summer, 1946 just before I entered first grade, was when my mother told me of "18 and out." My father was in the military in Europe, and we were living in Enlisted Men's Family Housing on the Fort Lewis Army Base, a government housing project in Washington State between Tacoma and Olympia. I remember the conversation well. My mother's serious tone marked the moment for me. She spoke in a professional manner, framing her directive in legal terms. There was no emotion.

She explained that in the United States of America all parental responsibility legally ends at age 18, and that it was her duty to alert me well in advance that she and my father would be exercising their legal option. She did not want it to come as a shock to me later. She calmly went into detail about what it meant. On my eighteenth birthday, I would pack my personal belongings and leave their house. They would not help with rent or my other expenses and there would be no support for college. She added that it was possible, even probable, that I might not be mature enough to take this big step on my own. But that didn't change anything. If I was not ready, or if I could not find employment sufficient to support myself, "That's what the United States military is for. You can volunteer to join the Army or some other branch of the service at age 18 and they will house, clothe and feed you, and even train you in a vocation, until you are mature enough to be on your own."

It is important that my younger readers know that learning about "*18 and out*" did not come to me as a shock. I had no way of knowing that this wasn't something every six-year-old boy was told by his mother. It was not even the slightest bit frightening. It felt somewhat liberating; like something to look forward to; like getting out of jail. In the moment, I felt closer to her because she was taking me into her confidence, addressing me as though I was an adult.

She, or my father, or the two of them in concert, reminded me of "*18 and out*" periodically throughout my childhood and into my teens. My brother Bill was included in the "*18 and out*" directive. My youngest brother John would be the only child slated to go to college with their support. Almost every reminder was calm, and matter-of-fact. I remember only one occasion when it was done with strong affect. I don't recall exactly what we had done to set her off, but once when she was telling us that she would not have to be putting up with us for too much longer, she hissed, "Nobody really wants children. They are only an unfortunate byproduct of sex."

"*18 and out*" was simplicity itself; easy to understand and execute. Neither my mother nor my father ever pushed me to succeed at anything. To the contrary, they emphasized there was little likelihood that I might succeed at anything--so why waste time trying? This freed me to think of my life in easy, neutral terms. The idea of failure never entered my mind. If no one puts a goal in front of you, there is no possibility of failure. Consequently, I was able to go through each day doing pretty much as I pleased, unconstrained by judgment, the need to please someone, or trying to meet some preparation criterion for future "success." I simply did what I enjoyed doing. Why not? We were below the poverty line poor but, on the whole, I was cheerful, as happy and having as much fun as any other kid. My youth was certainly more fulfilling and enjoyable than it would have been had my parents tried to leverage me onto some middle-class fast-track.

My parents crafted an ideology around their children's competencies and futures that lowered their expectation for me to zero. They never once speculated or expressed any interest in what I might do as an adult. "It's your life and your choice," they told me. Their only additional requirement was that until I turned 18, I should stay out of trouble with the law. If I was arrested, "We won't be there to bail you out." They ranked the three of us by intelligence and spoke openly and often about our limits. John was a genius like them and would be recognized for his brilliance in whatever field he decided to pursue. Bill was the "dumb one." I was "average," or slightly above average. Bill and I were told not to imagine we might 'do well' in life as this would only lead to our disappointment.

The only charitable interpretation I can fit over this formulation is they were trying to establish differences between us that would prevent us from competing with one another. Even if it was not their intent, they did effectively block feelings of rivalry or of anything else from growing between us.

Looking back, I do not think my parents were any crueler than parents today who build up an opposing but equally absurd ideology proclaiming their child to be brilliant and prescribing top tier academic performance and a bachelor's degree as the only path to middle class respectability and economic independence. I read (in 2020) a birth announcement from a young father who told, along with the date and birth weight, that the new baby "Will be getting 650 on his SATs and admission to an elite Ivy League university."

Did I find my parents' attitude toward me depressing? Not at all. Not even annoying. I assumed their parenting protocols were normal, and that they had my best interests in mind as parents are supposed to. How could I, or any child, assume otherwise? Our wretched circumstances were probably the perfect set-up for me. No one was looking over my shoulder. Moment to moment, I could make of myself what I wished. Had their attitude ever gotten under my skin, it certainly would not have been as irksome as growing up thinking you failed if you got 610 on your SATs and attended a State College.

"*18 and out*" was the unwavering, overarching design of my childhood and youth. It fit neatly with every other directive and attitude of my parents toward Bill and me. They were cold, not almost bureaucratic, but actually bureaucratic in their parenting practices. In the following accounts, please do not read me as blaming my parents for anything. Except for an unscrupulous luthier in Philadelphia and a plagiarizing colleague who suppressed publication of a scientific finding of mine until he could take credit for it, no one has ever screwed me over in my entire lifetime. Maybe some others have tried, but I did not notice. Even the two who succeeded didn't change my life for the worse. I have zero to blame my parents or anyone for. I thank them for the conditions of my childhood that shaped who I am today, and especially for their emotional detachment. I would not go back and try to redo a single moment.

Proof That I Was An Average Child

Along with "*18 and out*" the other constant in my childhood and sense of self came from my firm belief in my own averageness. When I was 11 my parents got their hands on an old Stanford Binet I.Q. test. We were living in the Cedar Vale Public Housing Project in Seattle's North End. Neither of them had been trained in its administration or scoring protocols. They read the instruction booklet, gave the test to my brothers and me, calculated our I.Q.s, and informed us of our limits.

Until I was four or five, my mother often compared me to the "average child." I was two inches taller than the average boy at my age. I wasn't able to drink from a cup unassisted until a few months later than the average child. I spoke my first complete sentence before the average child. I walked three months later than the average child. Etcetera. Almost any notice of me by other family members and even strangers would elicit such comparisons from her. I came to believe there was an actual Average family—Mr. and Mrs. Average and the Average child. There was a house near my Grandma Fran's where I thought they lived. How had my mother become so intimately familiar with these Averages? I wondered. Because I had never met them. I would have liked to have met this Average child who was so much like me.

The I.Q. test results confirmed my parents' opinion about the differences in our intelligence. It showed that my youngest brother John was a "genius"; Bill, the middle child, was "dumb"; and I was, well, you guessed it, "about average." They told me I had scored above 100 but "well within the first standard deviation above the mean." I had no idea of what a "standard deviation" was, but I loved the phrase and mentally banked it as I always did with other bits of intriguing language that I did not initially comprehend.

What I did understand was that their often-stated opinion about my potential had just been validated scientifically. I was now a proven part of the great middle. I understood that anything I might need or want in life would necessarily come from hard work and the kind of survival instincts that every animal possesses. Not from any quickness of mind.

My father told me that the test result confirmed what they had been telling me all along: there would be no reason for me to attend college. He said I would qualify for a semi-skilled profession. He noted my aptitude for drawing and said I might consider attending a trade school and becoming a mechanical draftsman.

Before I write another word, there is something I must clarify. My brother Bill is not dumb. He started a newspaper on the Alaskan frontier serving mainly Native American communities. He was appointed Regent of

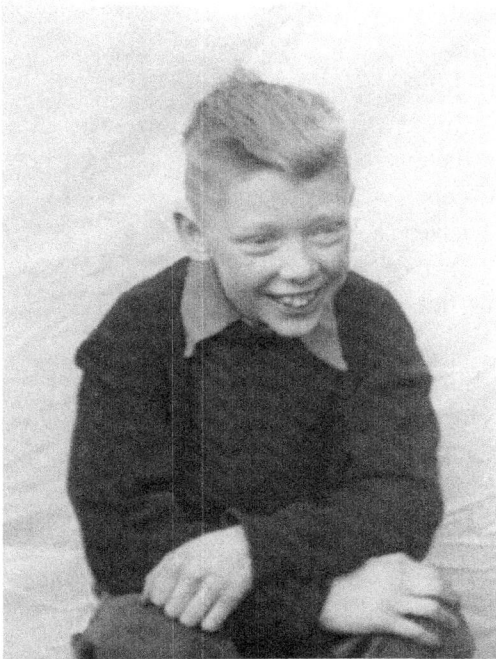

Age six—I was as cheerful and as happy as any other child

the University of Alaska and was founding owner, publisher, and editor of the Island News for over two decades until he sold it for enough to retire on. He is a superb artist and craftsperson. I do not know if my parents rigged the I.Q. test to support their opinion of him, or if they were simply incompetent in its administration. Either way, they foisted their limits onto him--a parenting practice that in subtler form is much more widespread than acknowledged.

My grade-school teachers, all other family members, and parents of friends always treated me as a very bright child. But I accepted my parents' view of me as "average." While I found many of their other opinions faulty, I did not question the results of the Stanford-Binet.

Was it limiting for me to grow up "average"? Hardly. It may have been the greatest gift they could have given me: a distinct outlook. A view of life from the perspective of the masses. Positioned within one "standard deviation" from the very center I never felt I was different from anyone I ever encountered. Certainly not superior to anyone, except, perhaps, those who have nothing to talk about except their inherited wealth. I gave everyone my full respect until they proved to me it was not deserved.

No matter how humble a person's circumstance I could find some basis for connecting. Correlatively, I have never felt attached to or identified with any status I attained as an adult, no matter how honorific.

Bill and me in the Cedar Vale project about the time we received the results of our Stanford Binet I.Q. tests

Every advantage I have enjoyed I trace directly back to that Stanford-Binet test. I never assumed that I would make any kind of serious or important contribution. But I was perfectly positioned to observe the contributions of all others at both ends of the spectrum. Behavior, human and animal, endlessly fascinates me. I immediately perk up when I hear a shift in tone of voice, when I notice a furtive glance, when someone's gaze lingers a millisecond too short or too long, when and why excuses are needed. As a great French poet once observed, "It is not given to everyone to take a bath in the multitude." Notice the contradiction here that sets a fun, ethical and self-sustaining dialectic in motion. What Baudelaire understood was there can be something really special and wonderful about being average.

I did not simply accept my parents' view, I actively sought to validate it. It didn't take me long to discover it was true, everyone I met, even the smallest child, knew things I did not. My main fascination in life and professionally has been to learn about these small and large bits of theoretical and practical knowledge carried around in the heads and expressed in everyday practices by those around me. Each new encounter still today can reinforce my self-view as a lesser light. Certainly I'm inferior to the ten-year-old girl who knows how to throw a curve ball, a fast ball and a change-up.

Moreover, I assumed that if I knew something, you must know it too. Since I am average, why wouldn't you know everything I know and more?

It took me years to realize that every human being knows something different. It is this, our collective repository of limitless knowledge, that makes us human and gives us our advantage as a species. It also guarantees that we are all in a certain sense "average." There is no inter-human mean average. Rankings along a single dimension like I.Q., or years of education, or net worth, assures that what is important about any given individual gets left out. She has a below average I.Q. but one of the most beautiful singing voices ever heard. He has a high net worth, but he's one of the most brutally nasty pieces-of-work that ever walked on its hind legs. Valuing someone by their position in one of these rankings makes about as much sense as valuing them based on how they placed in a hotdog eating contest. It assures that what is important, what is essential about each of us, our potential unique contribution to humanity, gets left out of consideration. Every human is different. How do we access that? What we have before and between us are billions of different intra-human means. All we need to unlock our collective brilliance is to share with others the special things we know at the center of our being.

This memoir is my miniscule contribution to that sharing. My only regret is that I am not holding your story in my hand, comparing notes as I write.

My Fascination With The Written Word

When I was very young the thing adults could do and I could not, the adult thing I most wanted to do, was read. Reading or hearing stories is a passport to other times and places, to the scene of others' lives. When an adult read to me the effect was magical.

Early in my third year, someone read me the story of James Watt and the invention of the steam engine. The main point went over my head. That the industrial revolution had reshaped human life was a bit too abstract. I had a vague image of greatness and invention. The part of the story that got to me was probably apocryphal—the young Watt gazing at his mother's teakettle on the fire. I had watched the steam from kettles many times and I identified with that part. My admiration for the young James was boundless. And I was also angry and upset with myself. Why hadn't I seen the great and wondrous possibility in steam? Millions had observed the same phenomenon and yet he saw something that none of us had seen.

From that moment I began looking at everything in a new way. What other insights are hiding in the everyday objects and occurrences we see everywhere around us? This question continues to drive my curiosity even now. Might there be some unrecognized wisdom in the smallest gesture, in the most banal event? Until someone read me the story of Watt, the steam coming out of my mother's kettle was just meaningless vapor.

Along with my appreciation for Watt's insight came an intuitive grasp of a connection that shaped my thinking for the rest of my life: I am half-blind to what I see unless I can link it to a story. And vice versa.

Whenever I saw an adult reading to themselves, I demanded that they read it aloud to me. Most of my relatives indulged me. I didn't care if it was an automobile repair manual or the Bible. I especially liked richly illustrated anatomy books—all the stuff going on under the skin. If I didn't understand, I didn't care. I liked the passages I didn't understand because I knew that partial understanding gives way to better understanding. The feeling of acquiring better understanding was one of the best feelings I could have. It still is. There were amazing lives and entire new worlds that print unlocks and I didn't want to depend on adults for access.

I learned to read in the following way. I grabbed every discarded newspaper I could find and bothering every adult I encountered, I pointed at individual words in the headlines and demanded, "What does it say?" My mother occasionally indulged me but only rarely and for one word at a time. My grandparents and uncles happily entered my game, giving me pointers about the sounds of letters, and permitting me to pester them through entire headlines. Before very long, I could read anything.

Knowing how to read did not happen after I learned the sounds of all the letters and their variations; after I knew every spelling rule and its many exceptions; after I discovered the function of every punctuation and diacritical mark; after I memorized thousands of combinations of letters and their associated syllables. No. If that was the way we learned to read, no one would be literate. Here is what I learned about learning to read the way I did. I learned to read in an instant long before I know the sound of every letter combination. It happened when the first few letters and sounds I was taught by adults magically combined into syllables before my eyes, and the syllables became a word. That was the instant when linear phonetic notation revealed just enough of its deep secret to me that I was suddenly able to teach myself the rest. When that happened, about age four, my family became helpful guides and collaborators, and the rest is history.

One might be tempted to call this a "theory" of reading acquisition, except it is a straight-forward account of my actual process, not a speculative conceptual model. It does however provide a theoretical foreshadowing of the contours of other crucial events of my childhood and youth. My childhood experiences are unique. But the ways a child's observations connect first to partial understanding, and these random fragmented understandings become whole, and meaning becomes life, is foundational to everyone's stories. This unstoppable dialectic is reproduced in every childhood. It may be the only thing we have in common.

Starting to come to grips with the printed page. Age two on the floor of my paternal grandparents living room in Olympia, Washington.

3
Ages Zero to Five—My Father
Goes to War

MY MOTHER AND FATHER MET at Ellensburg State Teachers College in Eastern Washington. In late Spring, 1939, they married and dropped out at the end of her first, and his second, year. My mother had emigrated from Oklahoma to Washington with her family two years before. They had been blue-collar workers in the oilfields until oil became almost worthless. In their entire lifetimes, I never heard either my mother or my father utter a single word about why they were attracted to each other. Possibly my father seemed "quite a catch" to my mother. All her life, she was ashamed of her family background and tried to minimize it. My father no doubt appeared as Prince Charming in her eyes until she became fully acquainted with his character. He was Boston-bred, a good student and a good athlete. His father, E.E. MacCannell was a retired Army colonel and Washington State Parks Head Architect. My father's background ticked all the boxes that she aspired to.

After ten years of the Great Depression, everything was out-of-reach for my newlywed parents. New store-bought clothes, a car, a cut of beef, a telephone, a restaurant meal, daily newspaper delivery, an apartment of their own, were unaffordable luxury items. No one even considered that I might be born in a hospital. I arrived on my paternal grandparents' dining table after what my mother described to me more than once as a "long and difficult labor." She occasionally added somewhat luridly, "You tore up my insides."

They named me Earle Dean. I was the first-born grandchild on both sides of my family. My mother told me that had I been born a girl they would have named me Earladeen. You can't get any more Okie than that.

For the first years of my life, my father had a number of jobs but was usually unemployed. Two years of college and his often-stated claim to have a genius I.Q. did not count for much in the way of job opportunities for my father in the early 1940s. He was a butcher's apprentice, a lifeguard, and a photographer's assistant among other things. Until I was one and a half years old, we lived either with, or in rentals nearby, my paternal grandparents in Olympia, Washington. I recently found out that my mother's brother, my 15-year-old Uncle Eddie, came to live with my parents when I was a few months old. It was probably an excuse for my grandparents to send rent money. I believe Eddie completed a school year under my parents' roof. This may explain why we eventually bonded so closely.

When I was almost two, my parents tried to build a house for us on dubious land called the Nisqualli Mud Flats near Olympia, but they failed. The Nisqualli Flats was Indian tribal land, all but abandoned at the time by the Nisqualli tribe. Squatting in a shack you built yourself on Indian land was their housing solution. They got as far as the framing and quit. The episode eerily figures-in-little the taking of Indian Territory for white settlement to form the state of Oklahoma. Except my parents did not have to drive any Nisqualli off their land to build there. I don't know what caused them to abandon their ill-conceived project.

E.H. MacCannell builds a house.
This is as far as he got.

My sitter Flossie (on right) with her twin sisters and me in 1941

When we lived in Olympia, my parents hired a pretty blond teenaged girl named Flossie to baby sit me. I had not formed a coherent idea of "love" at that age, but I knew that Flossie enjoyed my company and cared more for my feelings than my mother did. Flossie often brought her younger twin sisters to play with me when she sat. She watched over the three of us like a mother bear.

At the age when most children experience and express "separation anxiety" and wail when a parent leaves, I looked forward to my mother's departures and the arrival of Flossie. My mother noticed and probably never forgave me for it. My earliest memory of my father was from this time. He was slapping me on the face and the sides and top of my head. Not hard enough to hurt. Just enough to knock my head around, sting a little and annoy. They were sneaky slaps. He pretended not to look at me, then 'whap' out of nowhere. He feinted from one side and slapped from the other. He kept saying, "Hit me back. Hit me back." I had no interest in hitting him back and refused to lift a hand. As soon as I determined that he was not going to stop, I let out a shriek that summoned my mother. She witnessed one or two of his hits and said, "Stop it Earle, you're hurting him." My father replied that he was not hurting me, which was true. Then he added, "It's for his own good, he has to learn to defend himself." I was not clever or nice enough to finish his thought with, "Because I won't always be around to defend him." I took him to mean, "Because I will never defend him." That ultimately proved to be his true meaning and probably the reason I remember every detail of the slapping incident. It established the fundamental terms of our father/son relationship: "You're on your own, kid. Don't come to me with any of your needs, wants or desires. The way I help you is to hit you in the face."

The only store-bought toy I remember having as a toddler was a hard rubber Disney figure of Pluto Pup that I carried around by the tail in my teeth when I was still crawling. After a move it disappeared for months and I mourned its loss, asking about its disappearance several times. Almost a year later, my mother finally found it in a box she had not unpacked. She presented it to me with an air of triumph and joy. "I found your Pluto." She jumped up and down clapping. She held it out to me, then pulled it back in a teasing fashion, "Aren't you glad?" she demanded before handing it over.

I studied the toy for a moment and was shocked by its appearance. Without knowing it, in the months of Pluto's absence, I had undergone a complete change in consciousness and perspective. It seemed like a mere passage of time during which nothing important happened. My perception of Pluto's appearance on his return suggested otherwise. My toy was much smaller than I remembered. Initially it did not occur to me that it was the same size as before and that it was I who had grown larger, not Pluto shrinking. I threw him on the floor. How did Pluto Pup get so small I wondered? And before I had thought he was a beautiful doggie. Now, he looked ugly and insignificant down at my feet. Before casting him aside, in the moment I held him, I noticed he was sticky to the touch with lint and dust adhering to his long sausage body. I saw where I had gripped it in my teeth and found its chewed and mangled tail disgusting. It was generally disgusting. I remembered loving my Pluto and was alarmed that my perceptions could change so totally, so abruptly. Total change can happen without your realizing it. Pluto's return caused me to know this—I had changed completely, not him. Without a second glance, I went back to what I was doing. My mother was offended. "I'm sorry," she said huffily. "I thought you'd be happy I found it for you."

My other store-bought toy was a small red Radio Flyer wagon a friend of the family bought me when I was three. My parents gave it back to the store for a refund before I had a chance to play with it. There were still plenty of things to play with. Grandma MacCannell let me play in her cupboards with her pots and pans. I loved making nests for myself in there. There was always something.

My Brother Bill is Born

In early October 1942, a week after the German army broke the perimeter defenses and entered Stalingrad, my brother, William Robert ("Billie Bob" in Okie speak), was born. He was six weeks premature, weighing 4.5 pounds. He had to stay behind in intensive care for two weeks after my mother came home. Bill was born into my world. I don't think our parents ever made the adjustment that he wasn't already my age—i.e., two and a half—at birth. They expected him to be able to do just about everything I was able to do and decided he was stupid because he could not. He was frustrated in his valiant efforts to keep up and understandably hostile toward me. My parents continuously commented about how "slow" he was. When we were alone and he was not trying and failing to keep up, we had a lot of giggling good times together.

For Five Months When I Was Four Years Old, We Were Well-Off

On about my third birthday, my father landed a good job in the Civil Service as district supervisor in a Federal Government office that distributed War Ration Coupons. I believe my Grandfather MacCannell, who was well connected in the state Capitol pulled some strings to get his son the job. The per-person monthly amounts of sugar, butter, milk, and bacon were

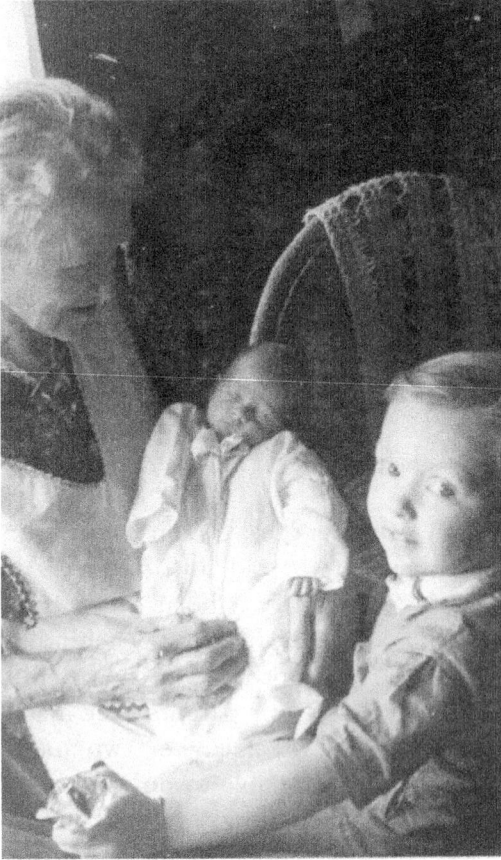

Bill's first visit with our Great Grand-mother Emily Amelia MacCannell. Bill is one month old, I am two years and Emily is 84.

Her arthritic hands did not keep her from kneading our bread when I began spending summers with her five years later.

I am holding the cut crystal doorknob she kept as a toy for her young visitors. It made prisms—a great toy.

limited and controlled by the Federal government, as was gasoline. Every family had a coupon book with tear-off stamps corresponding to the amount of each commodity they were allowed to purchase that month. Sugar became precious. Tires were completely unavailable to civilians unless you were a minister or a doctor. My father reviewed eligibility applications, proof of numbers of dependents, etc., and approved the distribution of coupons. Because of his position, we qualified for Government subsidized housing and moved into American Lake Gardens on the Fort Lewis Army Base. A year later, we were well-off enough to move to a rented two-story house on a lake with a covered veranda that wrapped around two sides and our own beach, dock and boathouse. My father bought a lightly used 1940 Cadillac sedan. It had a sky-blue body and midnight blue fenders with side-mounted spares. Inside was soft, dark blue leather.

E.H. MacCannell with Bill and me on the front porch of our housing unit at American Lake Gardens.

He bought my mother a puppy she named Sabu.

The Moodys Arrive From Oklahoma And My World Grows Larger

Bill started to walk alone, i.e. without holding an adult's hand, and I turned four at the big lake house where we lived from April to October 1944. While I would not know the terms until years later, I got my first lessons in ethnology and comparative linguistics there. My maternal Grandma Fran's younger sister, my Great Aunt Glenna and her husband Frank Moody left Oklahoma with their seven children and Frank's mother and migrated to Washington State. We had the biggest house in the extended family so the first place they landed was with us. Frank Moody, according to everyone who mentioned him when he wasn't around, was a "full-blooded Cherokee Indian." All her life, my mother harbored a racist hatred of Indians that she often expressed openly. But she loved her Uncle Frank while making no effort to minimize his "Indian-ness." Go figure. The logic of prejudice has always eluded me.

Uncle Frank immediately set to fishing off our dock which he did pretty much full-time for the month of their visit. I was told, "Indians hunt and fish. That's what they do." He smoked cigars and wasn't bothered by biting insects including the mosquitoes. "Indian blood" my mother said. He "chummed the water" with breadcrumbs to attract the fish to him. I watched my uncle Eddie fish but had never seen anyone "chumming the water" before.

A middle Moody child, Buddy, was about my age—just a bit older. We bonded somewhat and hung out together on our large lot that had rock gardens, mature fir and pine trees and the dock and beach. The members of the Oklahoma branch of my

H. F. MacCannell holding Sabu in the rock garden at the beach house.

Side view looking down toward the boat house and the lake.

family that arrived earlier in my mother's migration did not have strong regional accents. They were originally from Illinois and Kansas, and the Okie twang never fully sank in. My mother, especially, had gotten rid of all residual Okie intonations covering them with her affected version of an upper crust accent. The speech of the ten Moody arrivals was clipped and twangy to the point of being almost completely unintelligible to me. I could tell it was a variety of the language I spoke. By repeated demands for clarification I was able to make Buddy make himself understood to me. In the course of this exercise I discovered that in Buddy's Okie English, Fir, Four, Fur, Fire, For, Fair, Fare, and Far were all pronounced exactly the same. Something like the way I pronounced Fur, but with the "ur" sound deeper in the throat, the way it might be burlesqued by someone trying to pretend to be ignorant. When we got cold one evening playing outside, Buddy told me we should "build a fur." I suspect I was probably as in-

The Moody family in our living room at the lake house. Bottom row from left: Buddy, Aunt Glenna, Glenna Sue, Frank Sr., Grandma Moody, Barbara. Top row from left: Margaret, Cleo, Dean, Frank Jr.

comprehensible to him as he was to me, but he didn't pester me for any clarifications.

The drama of having ten extra people in the house over a period of three, almost four, weeks, people who were said to be relatives of mine but with a strange way of speaking, made a large impression on me. On the occasion of the Moody visit there was a seemingly minor incident that had huge implications for the way I saw the world. Another of those transformative moments. It caused me to know what compassion is and to realize that some adults are capable of it.

The older Moody boys, Frank Jr. and Dean, who were in their mid-teens, had formed a work party to go up to the main road and re-set our mailbox that was loose on its post in its foundation. Frank Sr. and Glenna had volunteered their sons' services saying they were perfectly capable of doing the job well and it was the least they could do to partially repay my parents for their hospitality. The older boys said Buddy and I could come along to watch them work and learn. I was honored and excited to have been invited to join them. Unfortunately, that morning I put on a pair of bibbed coveralls that had a front button missing from one of its suspenders. It had been missing for quite some time, but the coveralls stayed up with only one suspender buttoned and the other trailing along behind. As I eagerly followed the older boys to the door my mother called out to me, "Deanie, come back here. We can't have you going around looking like a ragamuffin."

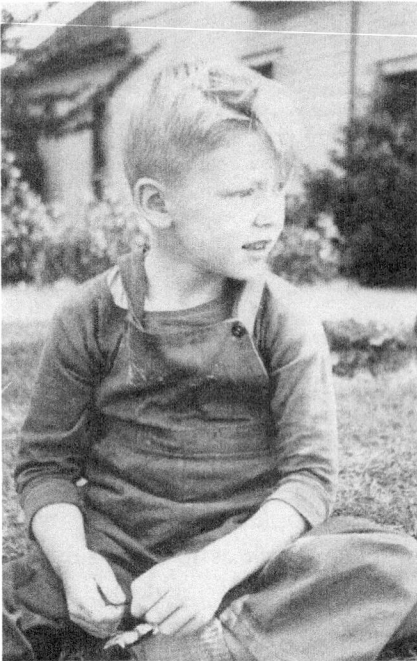

Photo of me in the yard taken shortly before the arrival of the Moodys. I am wearing the overalls with the missing button. My mother has tucked the strap in for the photo.

The older boys hesitated for a moment but when my mother told me to fetch her sewing kit, they shrugged and continued on their way. I was disappointed but I knew that I must not whine, disobey or register any complaint. It galled me that my mother should insist on sewing the button on at just that moment. I had been running around all summer with it off. I interpreted it as a hypocritical display of maternal responsibility for the benefit of her favorite aunt. I made a very conscious effort to back her up by not to showing my disappointment.

My great Aunt Glenna was having none of it. She could see through my mother and also through my brave face. She immediately intervened, "Helen Frances, the button can wait. Don't you see he wants to go with the big boys?" Then, "Boys, boys, wait. Little Dean is coming with you." In that moment, I formed a bond of affection with Aunt Glenna, a bond that never weakened. The incident is fixed in my mind because up to that point I had no idea that an adult could sense a child's feelings and support them, or even care. Flossie could. But I thought that was because she was still a kid herself. That morning I found out that a mother could be something more, or other, than just the random adult who gave birth to you.

Frank Moody, my Native American great uncle by marriage, got a job clearing spun glass and asbestos from an old factory building and died of a lung infection a few months after they arrived in the Pacific Northwest leaving Glenna a widow with seven minor children. She managed quite well because no one in her immediate and larger circles had anything but the strongest feelings of love and affection for her.

My Father Grifts Me Out Of A Government Bond

My life-long sense of my father as a con man, willing to cheat even his own children, was indelibly set during a financial transaction I involuntarily entered into with him when we moved to the lake house. For my third birthday, my Great Grandmother Emily gave me a mature $100 government bond entrusted in the care of my parents. The gift did not register with me because in 1944 I didn't know what a "bond" was, nor did I have any idea of the meaning or value of $100. ($1,600 in 2020) Until my father brought it up, I was unaware that I possessed such an asset.

The day we moved into the lake house he sat me down and with an air of importance he told me that I would now have "a room of my own." I thought, 'OK. I guess.' He further explained that the reason I got this wonderful "room of my own" was because I had "bought it with my own money." He cashed the bond and used the money for the move. He apparently felt a need to concoct this story about my having "bought a room of my own." Even at four years old I knew exactly what he was up to including his motive for doing it. He could have simply taken the bond without telling me, I would never have known. Nor would I have this unpleasant memory of my father trying to justify expropriating my great grandmother's gift. Instead of quietly taking the money, he laid on this bullshit (even to a four-year-old) story that seared the moment into my memory forever. He "explained" how great it was that I could be so handsomely rewarded at such a young age for starting to take responsibility for paying my own way in life.

To this day, I wish he had said, "I needed the money, so I took it." Or, better still, said nothing at all.

At that age, the idea of "a room of my own" was alien to me. Happily bunking with my brother Bill in the American Lake projects, I had not formed any desire for a "room of my own." But my father's pitch did cause me to wonder, 'Is it normal to expect children to buy rooms in their parents' houses?' What was the logic behind this? My brother, who could not pay, would automatically get a room of his own when I, who could pay, got mine. I didn't want or need a room of my own and I was pretty sure Bill didn't want one either. What I clearly understood was that some serious money that once was mine was now gone for something I did not want, that this was my father's doing, and he obviously felt guilt that required some kind of cover story. This incident cemented in me a negative idea of my father's character that stuck with me and was never dislodged through both our lifetimes. I might have forgotten the "room of my own" incident if my father had not, in almost every other word and deed, continuously validated my negative opinion of him until the day he died, and even after.

My Father Loses His Job and We Move Out of the Big House

My father lost his ration coupon distribution job not long after the visit from the Moodys. No one explained to me his abrupt departure from his semi-protected government position. He may have been bringing home more than his salary. He probably should not have bought that Cadillac. Or at least not driven it to work. Or perhaps everything was on the up and up and he was just over-extended. He might have simply burned through whatever cushion my great grandmother's bond provided. Whatever happened, he got a lower paying position as photography instructor in the local community college, and we moved to a tiny house in nearby Parkland, Washington.

It was in the Parkland house that I was able to put everything together and begin reading on my own. There was one children's book in the house that my mother read to us—titled "*The Poky Little Puppy*." But I grew tired of it and especially the insipid moral lesson it contained. There was much more out there, and I wanted access to it. As I have already explained, my mother was the least enthusiastic of my relatives when it came to my wanting to learn to read. She explained her reticence "was for my own good." She told me that when I got to grade school I would soon enough learn to read and it was not her place to do the school's work. She said if her method was different from my grade schoolteacher's it could "mess me up." This is deeply ironic in retrospect. Decades later, long after I turned 18, my mother became widely recognized and acclaimed as master teacher of reading, a reading consultant to a major publishing house and eventually a professor of reading education.

In the beginning, I read newspapers and the articles in several Esquire magazines I found lying about. I remember a particularly gripping account in *Esquire* written by a deep-sea diver who was trapped under water during a violent storm. They could not bring him up because he would get the bends. The diver got seasick from being thrown about on the ocean floor and he vomited inside his diving helmet. How can a five-year-old forget something like that?

I could read aloud without hesitation. Even if I had never heard one of the words I encountered and could only partially surmise its meaning from its context, I could pronounce it correctly almost every time. The adults around me remarked about how expressive my reading was and I was often asked to give reading performances to visitors. My Grandma Fran would say, "Listen to this boy read. It's like the author is here telling us the story. Like there is no book between us."

The first real book I read on my own, pulled off my parent's shelf, was Erich Maria Remarque's *All Quiet on the Western Front*. At that time, they only had about ten books and I have no idea why *All Quiet* was among them. It was before first grade, and I don't remember the vocabulary giving me any difficulty. I have not read it since but can still recall the war scenes in detail. The hospital scenes were particularly vivid and meaningful. Before I was six, I would have first-hand familiarity with wartime military hospital settings. The next book I read was an English translation of *Les Misérables*. I borrowed it from my maternal

Grandfather, Ross Meskimen on his recommendation. It fixed a definite concept of injustice in my mind forever.

U.S. Army Private First-Class E. H. MacCannell

The war had been raging for several years and both my parents were palpably frightened that my father would be called to duty. I overheard them discussing it in hushed tones, "What will we do if . . ." At age 26, with two dependent children and a semi-protected job as an instructor in a community college, my father was low priority for the draft. Until. In the fall of 1944, before the end of the war, before the end of his first semester as a college instructor, he was fired. My mother was furious. They argued. I did not understand why he was fired, but she made it quite clear that whatever happened to cause him to lose his job was his fault.

Private First-Class E. H. MacCannell during basic training at Fort Hood in Texas, December 1944. He is happier in this photo than I had ever seen him.

Within a week he received his draft notice: "Greetings, You are hereby ordered to report for induction . . ." It gave him a week to show up for basic training at Fort Hood. My mother clung to him in our front doorway and cried for an entire day before he could break free of her grasp and hop a troop train to Texas.

After basic training, he came home in January 1945 and moved us back into American Lake Gardens. Our unit at 3 Fir Place was in the "Enlisted Men's Dependents' Housing" section. He was initially assigned to a photo lab at Fort Lewis but that posting only lasted about two months before he was deployed to Europe where he arrived within a week or two of the German surrender.

The war story he told for the rest of his life was that he was initially "deployed as an infantry foot soldier to Sicily toward the end of the war." He humble-bragged explaining that by the time he got there, except for minor, rear-guard German resistance, Italy had already been mainly secured by U.S. and Allied forces. He vividly described walking from Sicily to Rome carrying his rifle and other gear. He singlehandedly captured a demoralized squad of German soldiers without having to fire a shot. He just pointed his weapon at them and told them to drop theirs and fall in line. In his telling of it, this was one of the final acts of the "Greatest Generation" that we hear so much about today. By his account, he met little resistance as he trudged north, especially from the Italian girls and women who delighted in showing him their gratitude "in every possible way."

As a child, I do not recall when it was, exactly, that I realized my father lived at the center of an alternate reality of his own construction. My earliest suspicions were from about this time. Confirmation of some of his most egregious lies would come later as he tried to insert himself into history without taking the trouble to line up the dates correctly. The last squads of American infantry fought their way from Sicily to Rome in May of 1944, about the time he was flimflamming me out of my gift bond, not in May of 1945. He arrived in Europe in time to participate in an allied victory parade through Paris and some sightseeing at the bombed-out ruins of Berlin. Then he was re-posted back to Fort Lewis having been "away at war" for about four months. He did bring back a trunk full of Nazi souvenirs.

My Father Volunteers to Fight the Cold War

Celebrating his "return from the War," he borrowed Grandpa Ross's Model A Ford sedan, took us camping and got my mother pregnant with my brother John. Then in the Fall of 1945, before the end of his mandatory two years of duty, he re-enlisted for a second tour. Because he was now a volunteer and not a draftee, his second tour would mean four additional years of service fighting Communism in post-war Europe.

As a child, I was made painfully aware of one of his reasons for re-enlistment—to have "affairs" with German and Italian women and girls unencumbered by a wife and children hanging around inconveniently. He made no serious effort to hide any of this from my mother. He sent her photographs of his girlfriends and some of the love letters they wrote him in broken English. And she made no attempt to hide any of it from her children. This should not be taken to suggest that she approved. She fumed as she shared her unhappiness with Bill and me. We did not know exactly what an "affair" was. Just that it was something my father did with another woman and my mother didn't like it. Officially he was there to assist the US effort to stop the spread of communism in post-war Europe.

Later in life, he was super sensitive about his decision to re-enlist. When I was asked in the 1990s to write an intellectual autobiography, he read the pre-publication manuscript. I glossed his re-enlistment as follows, ". . . after the war ended, for some reason my father volunteered to stay in Europe . . ." When he read that he became enraged and demanded that I change it before publication. He screamed at me, "I did not volunteer. I had no choice in the matter. I was ordered to go." Fine. Except, again, it wasn't true. After he was drafted, he had been in active duty long enough to qualify for the G.I. Bill. There was no need for him to volunteer for another four years of service. He could have served another six months and been ready to start our post-war lives. Instead, he dropped us off in an Army housing project and disappeared for the next three- and one-half years. Home leave for an enlisted man in Europe was out of the question. My mother's definition of that period of our lives was we were doing nothing. We were on hold. As far as she was concerned, our entire lives consisted in nothing more than waiting for him to come back.

I did not miss my father and was not waiting for the day of his return. I started school at American Lake Gardens and be-

German Nazi swag my father brought back from "the War."

came close with other members of my extended families. I was no longer a toddler. I was a kid.

My connections to my grandparents, uncles and aunts, were becoming my own—not just an extension of their relation to my mother and father. My circle of meaningful relations widened.

E.H. MacCannell in Frankfurt with his twelve-year-old girl-friend Heidi in 1947.

This is one of the pictures he sent home.

4

The Important Adults in My Childhood

I WAS LUCKY TO HAVE SO MANY DIFFERENT VOICES in the family around me who shaped me as much or even more than my parents.

My Great Grandmother Emily Amelia MacCannell (née Hughes)

Emily Amelia MacCannell in 1944

During my childhood the most important adult in my life was my Great Grandmother MacCannell. Beginning in 1947 I spent summers with her in Tumwater, Washington. The day after school got out, I would leave Fort Lewis (and later Stewart Heights in Kirkland) by Greyhound and return the day before school started in the fall. This was the set-up of my first several years of primary school. My father was gone. I was with my teachers during the school day. I was with my mother after school and on weekends, and with my Great Grandmother day and night, every day, all summer long. But her influence was not just a matter of the generous amount of time we were able to spend together.

Emily Amelia made a habit of saying I was her favorite among her grandchildren and great grandchildren, a stance that provoked other members of my father's family. When she was told she should not play favorites, she snapped that she didn't care—that they knew as well as she did that I was "special." When you are a kid, it helps to have an adult family member dependably in your corner. Having the most magical member of my family at my back was a blessing. Being able to spend more time with her than with any other adult was beyond a blessing.

Emily Amelia grew up on Prince Edward Island in Canada, the daughter of a railroad executive. She emigrated to Boston in the 1880s and to the Pacific Northwest in the 1890s. I never knew my Great Grandfather William MacCannell. He was hit by a car and killed in the early 1920s. My artist/engineer/architect grandfather, E.E. MacCannell was her only child.

Emily Amelia was seven years old when Lincoln was assassinated, and she described in vivid detail her horror and sadness on hearing the news. She was the first Registered Nurse to practice west of the Mississippi River, often working in places where the nearest doctor was more than another county away by horse. She came to the West Coast after the transcontinental railroad was completed but before the end of Indian raiding. The Panama Canal had not been dug and there were only two alternate routes from East to West—around the tip of South America on a sailing ship, or across the Isthmus of Panama on foot. The trip across the Isthmus meant being carried on the back of a native. "I could never cause another human being to carry me on his back," she told me. So she came around Tierra Del Fuego. I got my first serious lessons in history and geography from her, only it was not History and Geography, it was firsthand human experience of vast amounts of space and time. Much of what I thought of as the distant past had occurred in her lifetime.

Her small house in Tumwater was a stone's throw from the Olympia brewery. In the 1920s, shortly after her husband died, she sold the house at a deep discount to a woman who lived next door with the provision that she would have life-time tenancy. There were no worries about property taxes or rent. She was in her 70s when the deal was made so the neighbor, a farmer named

Mrs. Briggs, did not think she had long to wait. My great grand-mother was certain that Briggs had cheated her on the sale—that the discount she took for the tenancy was too large. She told me she was determined to outlive Mrs. Briggs, "It's the only way I can get my money back." She did not outlive her neighbor, but she did live for another 30 plus years. Mrs. Briggs often stood in her field glaring over the fence at me during my summer visits. Social security and savings from the house sale provided us with enough healthy and nutritious food to eat.

Emily with two-year-old Dean on her front porch

We burned wood in her stove, not coal. I chopped enough in the summer to get her through the winter. Her house was small, but it was not like a project unit. It was a detached home with its own yards and garden, a separate dining room and matching furniture and china. There were comforters on the beds, not War Surplus army blankets. She had little income, but it was enough for a fresh orange for me every day.

Emily Amelia did all our cooking on a wood burning stove. During those peaceful summers with her, I ate well beyond my mother's meager fare. My mother served a bowl of boiled mush for breakfast my entire life with her. At my great grandmother's, I got orange juice, toast, tea and a boiled egg, sometimes bacon. We made wonderful soups, berry jam, and cottage cheese from scratch, and baked our own bread, cookies and apple pies. Everything was laid out properly on white linen table clothes, engraved silver napkin rings, etc. She showed me how to set the silverware and told me story after story of sociable meals she remembered. I worried about my brothers back home, knowing their split of

my portion did not come close to bringing them up to my summer nutrition standard. Every year, for the first few days after I
returned from Tumwater, I experienced severe culture shock in
my own home. While I sat finishing each bite before taking the
next one, my brothers looked like pigs at a trough gulping and
snorting their way through every meal as fast as they could shovel the food into their mouths.

For the entire time I knew my great grandmother, her sight
was severely limited by cataracts. Cataract removal surgery was
done in the 1940s. But she was ineligible because her doctors
thought her heart would not survive general anesthesia. She
could discern gross shapes. But she could not read or tell a fork
from a spoon without touching them. So long as she was in her
own home, no one could tell she was blind. She could cook, wash
dishes, sweep the floors, make the beds without giving away that
she could not see what she was doing. She knew where everything
was—every book, utensil, napkin, bag of flour, box of salt, everything. I had to learn to put things away in their exact location.
If she took a soup spoon away from the part of the drawer the
teaspoons were supposed to be in it was like I was intentionally
trying to make her look foolish. I only made that mistake once.

Emily Amelia was thin, passionate, sharp witted, and sharp
tongued. I often wonder how I might have survived without her
intervention. Certainly much worse off than I am—probably not
even alive today.

One morning at breakfast she spoke.

"I had the most wonderful dream last night."

"Yes?"

"I had just died, and it was my funeral . . ."

I was seven years old, and I have a very clear picture of
what I was not doing at that moment. I was not slouching in
my chair. If I had slouched in my chair, she would have already
mentioned it and I would have straightened up. If I was buttering a slice of toast, it was not held in one hand while I buttered
with the other. Following her strict protocols, I would have held
it flat against my plate while buttering it. If I was holding a fork,
it would not have been gripped in my fist with my elbow stick-

ing out. It was between my thumb and forefingers like a pencil and my elbow was pressed firmly against my side. I would not have been hovering with my next bite a few inches in front of my mouth while chewing the previous one. When it came to my manners and comportment, Emily Amelia MacCannell was adamant about correcting all these delicts I initially brought with me and myriad more.

When I responded to her, my eyes would not have been downcast. I would have been looking at her directly as I spoke.

Our conversation about her death dream took place near the beginning of the second of the four childhood summers I was able to spend with her. She was already in her 90s and more mentally alert than any other adult I knew. Our first summer together, in a matter of several hectic weeks, she almost completed her project of civilizing me. Without ever suggesting that my earlier ways of doing things were wrong, she impressed upon me that there was a sensible and correct way to sit, eat, walk, talk, dress, bathe, set the table, chop the wood, i.e., a correct way to do every everyday thing that I would ever do. She explained in detail how her recommended procedures reduced effort and confusion, improved health, and the household economy, and increased mental alertness and mutual understanding. If we did not have tea at breakfast she gave me a cup of hot water. "Drink a cup of hot water every day and eat a piece of burnt toast once a week. It will keep you healthy. You will live longer." Any money that entered the house, change from a grocery delivery, etc., went straight to the kitchen sink. The coins and bills were washed in hot soapy water and the bills hung to dry on a little string across the window above the sink. "That's how almost all harmful germs travel," she said. "On money."

Every lesson was delivered with stories and examples. I loved learning from her that there could be an underlying logic to, and connections between, everything we do in life, and I enthusiastically embraced her regimes not because she demanded them, but because they felt right. My unalloyed positive memories of her are embedded in my grammar, yea, in my very posture.

When she told me she dreamed she had died, I know I said "Yes," and not "Yah." The summer before, correcting an unwanted verbal tick I had brought into her home, she told me, "When you say 'jah,' you risk being mistaken for a German Nazi." In the summer of 1947, that was not a mistake that any American boy would want to make.

She went on about her dream. "Yes, I had died and had been dressed nicely for my funeral. I was really dead and in my coffin and I couldn't move, but I could see and hear everything that was going on. Everyone I ever knew and loved was there at my funeral, even those who had passed before me. You were there, sitting in the front row. And I was so happy to see you and my friends and loved ones all present and remembering the things we had done in life and our wonderful times together. They all looked so nice in their Sunday Best and had such nice things to say about me. Of course, that's the way people are supposed to act at funerals. But it was still a wonderful occasion and a beautiful dream."

Emily with Bill and me in 1947, the year she dreamed her death.

My great grandmother sensed how close I had grown to her, how important a place in my heart she had naturally come to occupy, and knew she needed to prepare me for her death in the not-too-distant future. She might have made up her dream, though I doubt it. She wanted to let me know that as far as she was concerned her death would be a happy occasion and that I should share in her happiness. As she told me about the dream, I immediately saw through to her intent which only made me love her more. We had three more precious summers together before she began to decline. I was 16 and she was 98 when she died nine years after her dream. I drove her other six great grandchildren from the funeral ceremony to the cemetery. I don't remember crying. Probably because I was sad in every fiber of my being and also filled with happiness for each precious moment we had been able to spend together and for what she had so generously contributed to my upbringing.

She favored me but she certainly did not spoil me. It was the opposite. She corrected every one of my, even minor, flaws in grammar, diction, pronunciation, posture, hygiene, dress, and etiquette firmly and on the spot. And woe be unto me if I should ever make the same mistake twice. The thought never entered my mind that her discipline was based on anything other than pure love.

Maternal Grandparents: Frances Prestine Meskimen (née Mathews) and Charles Roscoe ("Ross") Meskimen

My mother's parents were important in my life in quite different ways. On countless occasions, I spent weekends and many other days visiting in their modest homes in Tacoma. Fran and Ross lived in separate houses they owned, easy walking distance between them. She said, "He is just too mean to live around." But they never divorced, had "date nights" together, and were devoted to each other to the end.

Our lives were seamlessly woven together as my grandmother continuously and intently watched over her daughter, everything my mother did. She was enormously proud of my mother's eventual academic and professional achievements, but a bit wary of her parenting skills and her ability to provide for our needs when we were young. She was at our house, or I was at her house at least once a week through most of my childhood except during the summers with my great grandmother. Anything extra we had, an extra used toy, an extra warm coat, an extra jar of blackberry preserves, was brought by Grandma Fran on one of her visits. She was completely "no nonsense" and kindly to a fault. Almost every item of clothing my brothers and I wore during our early childhood was sourced by her scouring church rummage sales.

Frances Meskimen wrote a lively memoir (unpublished) titled *Now That I'm Eighty* covering the arc of her remarkable life. She was born in 1899 ("I'm always one year older than the century") and grew up on a small farm in Kansas. Her family did not own the farm. They were sharecroppers. As the oldest of seven children she took on a number of jobs including housecleaning, cooking, raising chickens, helping with the harvest and broom making which was her parents' farm-related cottage industry. She did the laundry, made the beds every day, put up preserves to get through the winter and looked after her younger siblings. She complains bitterly in her memoir. Not about the work. Her beef was that her parents used her as a hired hand and never paid her anything.

Mathews "Open Air Café," Oil Valley Kansas, 1919.

When she was in her early teens a nearby river flooded the farm and carried away all their crops just before harvest.

LEFT: *Ross Meskimen.*
RIGHT: *Frances Mathews.*

*These photos were taken about the
time of their marriage in 1920*

They abandoned the farm, loaded their meager belongings into
a horse-drawn wagon, rented two rooms in someone's house
near a town and opened a café in a clapboard shack. Fran cooked
and waited tables in the restaurant still without pay. When she
threatened to quit and hit the road her parents agreed to begin
paying her a dollar a day.

Ross Meskimen came into the café one day. He was
known to be a highly intelligent and skilled boilermaker and
also a mean bastard. He must have been powerfully attracted
to Frances who never took any lip from anyone, including him.
And she to him as well which is understandable since she had
been poor all her life and he could command pretty much any

fee he asked to repair complicated and expensive machines that no one else could fix. She was 21 and he was 34 when they got married and immediately lit out for Oklahoma. My mother was born in late March of 1921. They announced her birth to their families back in Kansas as having occurred on May 21, 1921, two months after her actual birth, nine months after the marriage. That may be the reason my mother always thought she was ahead of her time.

My Grandma Fran did heavy men's work all her life. She asked Ross to teach her his craft and trade. The story she tells is her hatred of housework drove her into the boiler shop. My grandfather's business was strong in the oil fields of Oklahoma in the early 1920s. She approached him with a question and a proposition. If she could learn the basics of boiler making and blacksmithing would she be able to increase profit in his shop enough to pay for a housekeeper to cook and clean and look after the children? My grandfather's answer was an emphatic yes. She could earn enough as a welder's helper to pay for two housekeepers. Within weeks she was the best welder in the shop after Ross. When her apprenticeship with Ross in the Roxana Boiler Works was complete, she became a Journeyman Boilermaker.

Fran received 15 minutes of fame when, in the 1930 United States Census of Occupations, the nationwide breakdown by sex in the category "boilermaker" had only one entry in

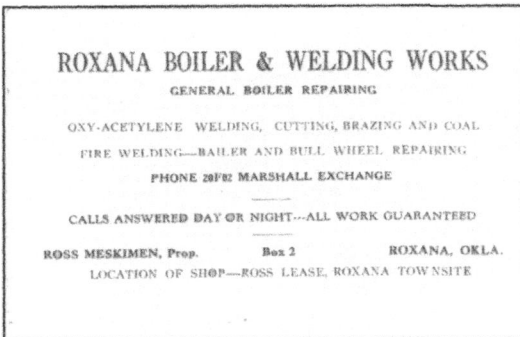

ROXANA BOILER & WELDING WORKS
GENERAL BOILER REPAIRING

OXY-ACETYLENE WELDING, CUTTING, BRAZING AND COAL
FIRE WELDING—BAILER AND BULL WHEEL REPAIRING
PHONE 20F82 MARSHALL EXCHANGE

CALLS ANSWERED DAY OR NIGHT...ALL WORK GUARANTEED

ROSS MESKIMEN, Prop.   Box 2   ROXANA, OKLA.
LOCATION OF SHOP—ROSS LEASE, ROXANA TOWNSITE

*"Roxana Boiler and Welding Works"
business card*

the "female" column. There is a 15-minute film about her in the Warner *Stranger Than Fiction* series that played in movie houses in the 1940s, between features with the cartoons and newsreels, on the "double bills." I have some headline clippings, "The Only

Woman Boilermaker in the U.S.A."

Because of Ross's skills and reputation, the Depression did not begin to affect the Meskimen household for several years. They started to feel it economically in 1936 when the oil fields themselves and oilfield work began to dry up. Ross took the test for "construction engineer" on the Grand Coulee Dam and got the second highest score in the nation. This meant moving the family to Washington State. They owned two working vehicles but had no money for gasoline to make the trip. One of Ross's jobs for the refineries was clearing the traps of dirty gas every night. He got permission to save the gas instead of releasing it onto the ground. He strained it through a chamois; calculated how much would be needed for the two vehicles to make the trip; and built a 400-gallon tank to pull behind his Model AA Ford truck. That is how they got from Oklahoma to Eastern Washington in 1937.

Fran comes to see Bill and me directly from her shift in the shipyards, 1943. I am studying her Boilermaker's Union button which I now possess.

Frances Meskimen was also a published poet and wrote music and lyrics for a country and western song. My son Daniel recently found her song copyright for "Can't Two-Time Me" in the national archives. She was the first woman welder hired at the Bremerton Shipyards in World War II. She did not have to be taught to weld and "burn" (cut steel to pattern specifications). She already knew.

Late in life, long after she retired from the yards, she taught herself to be an accomplished ceramicist. When I was 12 staying with her on spring break, we had a great time experimenting with glazes and native clay. But we never got around to washing dishes. On the third or fourth day she came to me with a serious expression. "We have a problem. We're either going to have to do the dishes or make a new set."

I knew the right answer: "Let's make a new set."

"YES!" and she fired up her kiln. It was on that occasion that she cautiously shared with me her philosophy of life. "Human beings weren't made to do work that just has to be done again the next day." She could build and take apart bridges and repair steam locomotives, but she could never work in an office. Her house was a mess, but everything else she touched had to be done just right.

My mother never forgave her mother for

Frances Meskimen (left) and her assistant, Hazel. It was common practice in WW II for the women welders and cutters to have formal portraits made of themselves and their assistants in their work clothes

doing men's work. She was deeply ashamed of her boilermaker mother—the way she dressed, the way she talked, the way she proudly wielded heavy tools. I cannot count the times I heard my mother snap at her, "You can't go around in public looking like that!" Do not get the impression that my grandmother ever dressed shabbily. My mother was objecting to things like her wearing women's slacks, a floral print blouse ("tasteless," "gaudy," my mother would say) or a sweater that was too bright a color. In my mother's view, any woman seen wearing other than muted, pastel shades was marked as lower class, loose, or an ethnic minority. Probably all three. My mother, Helen Frances, or "little Fran" as she was called by her aunts, tried to be as dainty and feminine as her mother was work-boot tough; as flighty and neurotic as her mother was steady; as helpless as her mother was omni-competent.

Frances Meskimen gave me her 270-page manuscript memoir before she died. She said, "Maybe you can get the damn thing published." I have not. Yet. There is a vivid passage describing how Ross repaired a boiler that had been brought in hot. It had blown a seam in the middle of a time sensitive job and the owner had shoveled out the fire and brought it directly to the Meskimen shop. Ross climbed inside, hammered the metal back into compliance, inserted new gasket material and re-riveted the seams while parts of the box around him were still glowing orange. When he finished the job and squirmed out of the oxygen-starved interior of the boiler box through its tiny access hatch, on contact with the outside air, his clothing burst into flames. The onlookers doused the fire and took the box directly back to the job site. They knew the repair was sound and the boiler could be put directly back to work without testing. That's how tough and competent Ross was known to be, and the reason my mother's family did not experience the full weight of the Depression until the late 1930s. He could always earn "good money" because there was no one else around who could do the things that he could do.

The last time I visited my Grandma Fran in the 1980s she told me take care because there would very likely be another Great Depression in my lifetime. "Don't let anyone try to fool you," she said. "Depressions are not historic accidents. The wealthy create them. With a pencil and paper if they have to. So they can buy up everything of any value for a nickel on the dollar."

Fran was left-handed as am I, so it fell to her to teach me how to use right-handed tools and other things requiring a different kind of manual dexterity. She taught me to write cursive after my third-grade teacher more or less gave up on the project.

Frances Meskimen, "The wealthy create depressions with a pencil."

Grandma Fran was adamant about quality and precision in workmanship. One of my earliest memories was sitting on the floor scribbling with a crayon in a coloring book. She loomed over me and let me know just how wrong it was for me to be coloring outside the lines. She didn't yell or express any anger. But there was a firmness and resolve in her tone that let me know that as her grandchild, I colored within the lines. I was, and am, grateful for this and her other firm directives. After her mother corrected my coloring, my mother noticed and told me I did not have to stay within the lines, that it was "more creative" if I scribbled. I weighed their different advice and stayed within the lines after that.

Ross Meskimen was born in 1884 in Illinois, the third of four children of Benjamin Brice Meskimen and Henrietta Rosalva Meskimen (née Smith). When he was 12 his family moved to Kansas. His older brother Arthur died at age nine and his little sister Mary Margaret when she was three. Ross never stopped grieving for her loss. In 1901 his mother and father and their two remaining children, Ross and his older brother Omar moved, again by ox cart, looking for homestead opportunities in Indian Territory. His father died en route. At age 17 Ross became the sole support of his mother and his older brother, beginning a life of relentless hard work. His first task was to make a grave marker for his father. They could not afford a "store-bought" headstone. Ross bent welding rods into letters and numbers for the inscription, built forms, and embedded the bent rods in the cast cement on top of the marker. In 1972, my mother located the rural graveyard and photographed the home-made monument still standing proud. If a single object could symbolize Ross's sadness, strength, creativity, and unwillingness to give even an inch to poverty, this would be it.

Ross took correspondence courses in engineering at night and worked long days as a welder and blacksmith. When he was in his twenties he already had a multi-state reputation as the go-to person for impossible machinery repair tasks. He also had a multi-state reputation as the toughest and meanest son-of-a-bitch standing.

I do not know the source of his attitude. Maybe it was necessary to become working class top dog in Kansas and Oklahoma at the beginning of the last century. Maybe it was because he grieved all his life for the loss of his little sister, Mary Margaret. Whatever it was, even when I knew him, he had a snarling at-

Ross with boiler showing access hatch

48

Ross Meskimen (on right) with his older brother Arthur and younger sister Mary Margaret

titude and intended to intimidate with almost every breath he took. He could be terrifying. I was terrified of him until I decided not to be.

When my brothers, cousins and I were left in his care overnight he would put us to bed, turn out the lights, and return after about five minutes. "If anyone here is pretending to be asleep, there will be hell to pay." Of course we were all pretending to be asleep and scared witless that he would find us out. He would lean in close and whisper, "I can tell you're awake, don't try to fool me." This only caused us to ramp up our sleep act skills. We couldn't begin to imagine the hideous fate that awaited us should he discern that we were awake. In this way, he succeeded in totally shutting down negotiations about night lights, leaving the door open a crack, a last drink of water, a bed-time story, and all cousin-to-cousin giggling tomfoolery. He put us to bed. We "went to sleep." That was that. He was effective like this, utilizing fear, not force in his control of all day-to-day routines.

Ross was strong as an ox and never hesitated to point out any flaw he perceived in other people's character, to their faces. He took special delight in "getting their goat" as he put it. He especially never spared those who were close to him. When he succeeded in reducing someone to a sniveling pile of raw emotions he always added insult to injury— "You shouldn't let someone get your goat like that."

*Hand crafted tombstone made by 17-year-old Ross Meskimen for his father.
Below: Close-up,*

Twice I observed an adult male target of his needling become completely unhinged and fly into a violent rage, physically attacking him. In neither case did Ross fight back or even make any attempt to defend himself. Instead he compounded their fury by roaring with laughter as their impotent blows bounced off his pig-iron tough head and chest.

From an early age, I got on well with Ross. The character flaws he pinpointed in others were mostly real and his needling, if unwelcome, was usually well-founded. It was his way of trying to get the people around him to shape up. My mother thought her father was cruel. I thought of him more as a stern and uncompromising judge and teacher, albeit one with far from genteel methods; one whose methods were so harsh as to be doomed in advance to failure.

When I was five years old my father was on a short home leave from the military. We did not own a car. He borrowed a Model A Ford sedan from Ross to take us (my mother, Bill and me) on a camping trip. We had the inevitable flat tire. When my father tried to remove the lug nuts to change the tire they were frozen on. We were miles off any paved road and even more miles

Ross Meskimen in the 1950s, the way he looked when I knew him

from a telephone or other assistance. My father tried everything—pounding on the wrench with a boulder; lashing a tree limb to the wrench for more leverage; dribbling oil from the dipstick onto the bolt threads; getting my mother to pull the leveraged wrench with him. We all knew that Ross had driven the lug nuts on with his steam hammer just to produce this difficulty and drama. He had precisely targeted my father's bragging about his mental brilliance and physical strength. Most men, according to my father are either smart weaklings, or muscled morons. Not him. He was both smart and strong. The nuts were Ross's test of his actual strength and ingenuity. My father passed the test. After half a day of groaning, sweating and head scratching, he eventually succeeded. And according to a calculation I made sometime just before or after he succeeded in pounding the nuts off the car, he succeeded in something else. It was on this trip that he impregnated my mother with my youngest brother, John.

When we came back to civilization and returned the Model A to Ross, I wandered alone down to his shop as I often did and our conversation went like this:

60 plus year old Ross: "Good trip?"

Five-year-old Dean: "Yeah. It was okay."

Ross: "Did your dad get a flat?"

Dean: "Yes."

       [long pause]

Ross: "Your dad changed the tire, or a garage?"

Ross's Model A Ford with the stuck lug nuts. This is one of the first photographs I took a year after the camping incident with the used Argus Argoflex 75 camera I was given for my sixth birthday.

Dean: "No he did it. We were out in the woods."

[*longer pause*]

Ross: "Did he have any trouble changing the tire?"

Dean: "No."

Ross: "No trouble getting it off the car?"

Dean: "No. He just took it off."

At this point my grandfather looked at me directly for a long while. I could tell that he could tell I was lying but that was not exactly the look I was getting. It was a mixture of admiration and frustration. His dissatisfaction was not because I lied but because I withheld telling him about my father's trials and eventual success. Admiration because he knew I was giving him a dose of his own medicine, that I was emulating him. I was, in my five-year-old way, trying to "get his goat." No one had coached me to keep quiet about my father's difficulty changing the tire. In fact, when we got back up to the house both my mother and father really laid into Ross about the lug nuts. He didn't confirm or deny their accusations. "Sometimes they're just hard to remove," he said. Throughout the harangue, he kept lowering his chin and looking over at me with one raised eyebrow and an ironic half-smile.

Ross did not snitch on me for having lied to him, nor did he call me out about it later in private. He now knew I had lied, but he understood my intent which was to let him know that I had figured him out and wanted to deny him any sadistic pleasure he might have derived from my father's frustrations. After that incident he treated me with respect, almost as an equal, and the character lessons he had for me were conversational not confrontational.

Ross leaned left, well into socialist territory. Not 1960s Bernie Sanders hippie type socialism, but a hard core, ironworks, Lenin type of socialism. When I was four and five years old, He took me with him often to the Boilermaker's Union Hall in Tacoma where he would drink coffee, play checkers, and trade stories with the younger men hanging around waiting for a job call. He was an acclaimed master boilermaker, possibly one of the toughest who ever lived. He paid his membership dues in the Boiler Makers' Union all his life even in retirement until he died. It wasn't until I was an adult that I realized how odd this was. Ross was a boss, not a worker. For most of his life he owned his own shop and hired union workers. He had no reason to be in the union himself. I now think he took me with him to the union hall to make certain that I witnessed his extra-ordinary solidarity with the other men who cut, riveted and welded the steel that holds our infrastructure together. I only hope that he did not know it would take more than a half-century for his lessons fully to sink in.

As much as Ross delighted in expressing his disdain for humanity in general, he exempted my parents from his withering critiques—at least in my presence. He did not exempt his own sons, daughters-in-law, and his grandson Jimmy. He was relentlessly awful to his son, my Uncle Ed. I cannot forgive him for that.

The idea of someone "who never stood a chance in life" was a salient concept on both sides of my family. My Grandma Alice MacCannell once opined in my earshot that my brothers "Didn't stand a chance in life because they were raised by Dean [me] and he isn't a good mother or father." Ross once told me, "Your cousin Jimmy never stood a chance in life. When someone who has little piggy eyes positioned right next to his nose [he's speaking now of his own son, Elwood] marries someone who has little piggy eyes positioned right next to her nose [his daughter-in-law, Neva], their child will be born with little piggy eyes right next to his nose [my cousin Jimmy] and he will be unable to deal with what life throws at him, for sure."

The peculiar thing about Ross's declaration and appraisal was that, of the three, only Neva might be regarded as having the physiognomy described. I think that, more than an effort to strike an accurate blow, it was his way of warning me about taking care who I married.

In the lead-up to Christmas, 1944, Ross began building a toy train in his shop. It was an engine, coal car, flat car and caboose, welded heavy gauge sheet steel. The engine was big enough for me to straddle and move by kicking my feet. Its front wheels (the proper term I knew at the time was "front truck") could be steered by turning the funnel-shaped smokestack. I pestered him persistently about who he was building it for. His answer was always the same, "It's for a nice little boy." I thought it was my cousin Jimmy although no one would have ever described James Meskimen as a "nice little boy." The thought that it might be for me never entered my mind until I saw it under the tree on Christmas morning. It was the finest gift I ever received as a child, but it unaccountably disappeared a month or two after I received it. It may have been simply too big for our cramped project housing unit. If my parents sold it, I hope they got a good price. Today on *Antiques Roadshow*, it would draw a huge appraisal in the American folk-art category.

Ross seemed invincible to me. This was not true, of course. But when you are a child, it is good to have someone in your corner who you think is invincible. It helped that he also had guns. Two matched Colt 44 caliber revolvers. On my sixth birthday he asked me if I wanted to be a cowboy when I grew up? And I said, "Sure." Every little boy in the 1940s wanted to be a cowboy when he grew up. Then Ross said, "Do you want to be a one-gun cowboy or a two-gun cowboy?" Of course I answered, "Two-gun." "Okay," he said, "let me show you what it's like to be a two-gun cowboy." He got his guns and an ammunition belt with a bullet in every loop. He let me put on his tailored vest with real pearl buttons and his Stetson hat. With the holsters empty he wrapped his gun belt around me twice and buckled it. I could already feel its considerable weight just from the bullets.

Then he dropped the guns into the holsters. My knees almost buckled. I think they might have actually buckled. Carrying all that weight, I knew I could not walk without stumbling. I put on a game face for my mother to photograph me, but I resolved to myself that I would never be a 'two-gun cowboy' or, for that matter, an any gun cowboy.

"Do you want to be a one-gun cowboy or a two-gun cowboy?"

I believe that was his intent.

None of my relatives in my immediate or extended families were cuddly or given to open expressions of love or even general praise. They were mainly neutral and reserved in their interactions with one another and with me. Even without any overt expressions of affection, I was able to discern that some of them loved me a great deal, some of them just enough, and some of them not at all. This proved to be more than sufficient emotional support to give me the self-confidence necessary to get me through my first 18 years.

Earle Edgerly Mac-Cannell with my Grandmother Alice c. 1940

Earle Edgerly MacCannell—my paternal grandfather

They were as different as any two men could possibly be, but I regarded both my grandfathers as strong, competent, and courageous. They owned guns, but not in the way the people we hear about today own guns. It was not a thing with them. Grandma Fran devoted a chapter to Ross's guns in her manuscript memoir. She explained, almost apologetically, that they had to be ready to be their own law in Oklahoma in the 1920s. The sheriff visited their town only once in the time they lived there—to murder one of his enemies. She was glad they never needed to use their guns to protect themselves.

Earle Edgerly MacCannell had a U.S. Army officer's automatic pistol with walnut grips. The MacCannell gun was kept in a walnut burl wall sconce mounted in his dining room at about seven feet above the floor. My grandfather carved the sconce to serve as the gun's quick-release holster hidden in plain sight. If you did not know it was there, you would never notice that the middle decorative element of the sconce was the handle of his gun. If someone asked him to raise his arms, he could brush against the sconce and the pistol would pop into his hand. I never knew where Ross kept his Colts.

Neither of them ever spoke about their guns. There was no palaver about "protection" or "security." Nothing about "gun rights." Their silence was one of the reasons I respected them. Had they regaled me with blah blah blah about keeping us safe, I could not have thought of them as courageous and strong. I would have regarded them as paranoid and weak. They both thought that firing their guns for fun, or for "target practice," would be a foolish waste of time and ammunition.

E. E. MacCannell, was an M.I.T educated architect and engineer whose first career was in the United States Cavalry where he rose to the rank of Colonel. He had to leave the Army after losing his right eye. His horse broke a leg fleeing a forest fire. Following army regulation, he shot the animal in the brain and began to remove the saddle, halter and other gear. As he performed this task, the horse had a violent post-death spasm and kicked my grandfather in the face, crushing his cheekbone and knocking his eye out.

His disability forced his retirement from the military, and he settled in Monterey, California where he made his living as an artist, painting local scenes and selling his paintings to tourists. For several years, he continued to live in California apart from his wife and children, a pattern my father repeated with us when he volunteered to stay on in Europe after the war. During his absence, his wife, my Grandmother Alice (Dyer) MacCannell and her children, my Uncles Charles and Robert, Aunt Genie and my father lived in upper-middle class comfort in the multi-generational Dyer family compound in Randolph Mass.

My grandfather put his family back together again in 1929. He moved to Massachusetts long enough to build a camper type structure on the back of a new Dodge light truck chassis he bought with proceeds from his paintings. It had beds, a stove, sink and other amenities and was arguably one of the first RVs. He christened it, *"The Land Yacht Illahee."* His aim was to use it

E.E. MacCannell at the wheel of the "Land Yacht Illahee" he built, 1929

to move his family, wife, and four children, across the USA to Olympia Washington to be near his mother.

It was the end of the "Roaring 20s" and as he was a skilled engineer and architect he assumed he would easily find work. When they reached Ohio, the Stock Market crashed. The crash took down the Boston bank where he had stashed all his savings to be drawn upon as they made their way to the West Coast. Stranded penniless in Middle America they continued by following the transcontinental rail line, stopping at each refueling station and offering to work. The railroad hired him and my father's older brother, Charles, to shovel coal for the steam locomotives in use at the time. The pay they received for shoveling coal was a cent and a half per ton. Sixteen tons per day was the benchmark standard shoveling rate for a strong adult male. The 25 to 35 cents my grandfather and Charles could earn in a day was enough for two gallons of gasoline and a basket of vegetables. Just enough to get to the next train refueling station. They also picked potatoes and harvested wheat and eventually made it to Olympia.

While my grandfather looked for work, Alice and the children ended up living with my great grandmother in her small house for almost a year. (The same place I lived with her later.) It must have been a tense time as my great grandmother hated her daughter-in-law with a passion for having "trapped" her son "into marriage," curtailing his "promise and potential." She spoke to me about this often, neglecting any mention of it taking two to tango. She called it a "shotgun marriage," and told me my Grandma Alice had "dragged him down to her level."

After months of searching, E.E. MacCannell was appointed lead architect for Washington State Parks with a nice office in the capitol building. The current system of Parks and Waysides in Washington was built out by my grandfather in the 1930s. His masterpiece was the park and Indian Museum at Vantage where the Snake and Columbia Rivers converge. He designed everything—the buildings, gardens, the display cases, the displays themselves, and he painted the murals.

When I was still a toddler, he took me with him in his state car to make park site surveys on public lands. He taught me how to tell the difference between virgin, old growth forest and second growth forest, and enjoyed testing my discernment when we entered new wooded areas. He would point to the old growth and say, "this is the original forest. It's been here forever. It will never be cut." It never was cut under his stewardship. I wish the same could be said for those who followed and am glad he is no longer around to see what actually played out.

After he retired from the Park Service, E.E. MacCannell painted a few more canvases, but mainly he devoted himself to creating an entire HO scale world in his garage. In HO scale, a large steam locomotive is about eight inches long. He carved mountains out of plaster and covered them with forests made of small twigs and bits of sponge. The snow was soap powder. Everything was meticulously painted. It was as real as a photograph of an actual landscape. The lakes and rivers were made of clear plastic, carved and sanded if there were currents. The trains disappeared into tunnels only to re-emerge elsewhere in the diorama. He carved every house and building in the towns to scale and painted them perfectly. I.e., in the poorer sections of the villages, he painted the paint to look like it was peeling. There were lumber camps with working sawmills, inter-urban rail, street cars, freight lines, and an operational railroad round-house. He built all the rolling stock from scratch using specialized tools like a jewelry lathe that I could hold in the palm of my hand. He named his miniature world, "Hillport."

In Hillport when the sky (on a rheostat) darkened at crepuscule, the streetlamps and lights in the homes and apartments would flicker on revealing miniature families silhouetted in the windows, sitting at their eve-

ning meals, arguing, greeting the man of the house coming home from work. I could look at it for hours and still find previously unnoticed details he had conceived and created. Contemplating the massive "Hillport" diorama, I realized there would never be any need for me to "grow up." All I had to do to be man, a good man, a competent man, is to become an ever more knowledgeable, patient, skilled, exacting, and imaginative, child.

E.E. MacCannell was the closest thing we had to Google in the 1940s. There was never any arcane reference or complex procedure that he couldn't explain off the top of his head. He took a call one day when I was visiting him in his office. A whale had beached itself at a State Park adjacent to a small town. The mayor was on the line, at wits' end. They had tried everything they could to move the dead whale back into the water, but no tractor in town could budge it. The stench was so overpowering that the people were having trouble breathing in their homes. It was on park land. Could my grandfather do anything?

"Do you have seagulls?" he asked.

"Plenty," was the answer.

"Then you don't have a problem, just feed it to the gulls."

"They're picking at it but making no progress."

"Of course," my grandfather answered. "Go to the hardware store and get a couple of sticks of dynamite. Dig under the whale and blow him to smithereens. The gulls will carry away all the bits in a few hours."

Problem solved plus a spectacle the entire town could enjoy.

When I was five or six, on the radio I heard a song called the *"Gandy Dancer's Ball."* The lyrics included, "They dance on the ceiling, they dance on the wall at the gandy dancer's ball." Of course, after hearing that, I had to know what a gandy dancer was. I asked everyone and no one knew.

Until the next time I got together with Grandpa Mac: "A gandy dancer is the worker who holds the spike in position for the man with the sledgehammer to drive it into the railroad tie. They must be fast to move and with excellent reflexes or their hands and wrists get hit by the sledge. If they jump back too soon, the spike falls over before it is struck. If they jump back too late, their hand gets smashed. Most Gandy Dancers are Negroes. And, yeah, they could probably dance on the ceilings and walls." You want to satisfy a six-year-old's curiosity. Have an answer like that on the tip of your tongue.

One of his assistants told me about a problem he solved when the State acquired an old pulp mill. His crews were in the process of demolishing it to turn the area into a park. The buildings had been torn down, but a 100-foot brick smokestack remained. The problem was how to knock down the stack without risking it falling on the workers and especially on an adjacent fragile footbridge across a river. My grandfather wanted to preserve the bridge which was easily in range of the top of the stack if it fell wrong. The solution required causing the stack to fall on an exact predetermined line. But the workers could not attach cables and use tractors to pull it down with any accuracy and without risking pulling it down on themselves.

My grandfather told the crews to find an oak and bring him a half dozen logs about five feet long and eight to twelve inches in diameter. When he had a few logs, he ordered two of the biggest guys to begin knocking the bricks out of the base of the stack with sledgehammers. When they had made a hole the right size he shaped one of the oak logs and had it pounded into place where the bricks had been. They proceeded like that, halfway around the stack on the side where it was supposed to fall. Knock out bricks, wedge an oak log in their place. And repeat. When almost half the base was oak, E.E. MacC told the men to build a huge fire in the stack and on the outside next to the oak supports. The updraft from the fire inside the stack sucked the fire outside through the oak supports like a whirlwind. It took about two hours before there were signs of distress. Then everything happened all at once. There were several loud pops like gun shots and a ripping sound as the entire stack fell with the loudest crash anyone had ever heard in their entire lives. It stayed in one piece until it hit the ground. The top end exploded into individual bricks. The bottom end broke into two half rounds. A huge cloud of black soot and dust covered everything. It fell exactly on the line my grandfather had marked off on the ground. Problem solved and a spectacle for the entire crew to enjoy.

The sound of the crash was a horrendous "CRACK." If I ever need to smile all I have to do is close my eyes and imagine that stack coming down in slow motion. Then, wait for it. Yes. The loudest CRACK anyone ever heard.

About the time my grandfather's Hillport diorama was completed to the point of only needing maintenance and minor remodels and revisions, an out-of-control car careening down the alley at high speed, rammed through the wall of the garage. The accident totally destroyed Hillport and its surrounding countryside. The driver of the car was not hurt. The plaster hills and supportive framework of Hillport fell to bits progressively, probably saving the driver's life in the days before crumple zones and mandatory seatbelts. Was it a disaster?

No. Once again the dialectic providentially prevailed and the disaster turned into its opposite. My grandfather, a lifelong chain smoker who was always in poor health, immediately set about building a new and bigger and better Hillport. The destruction of the original Hillport may well have added ten years to his life.

E. E. MacCannell rebuilding the town of Hillport on his H.O. model railroad, 1957

It will not have escaped my reader how very little I needed his son as a "father figure." Between E. E. MacCannell and Ross Meskimen I had a clear sense that in my family a dedicated, strong, competent, honest adult male could succeed at anything on earth from fine oil painting to toppling 100-foot towers to locomotive repair. A world of possibility was always before me.

E. E. Maccannell's Wife, My Grandma Alice
Maccannell (Née Dyer)

Grandma Mac was a Born-Again Christian. Even if she "had" to get married, I'm sure she was forgiven. Just not by her mother-in-law. She played the organ in her church every Sunday and when her grandchildren spent the weekend with her, she would gather us around and tell us how wonderful it was that we would be able to attend church with her. My grandfather rarely joined her at church, though every year she successfully volunteered him to design and build elaborate crèches with life sized figures for the Christmas display. On Saturday nights, he polished everyone's shoes, the adults' and the childrens', so we would look our "Sunday Best."

Sunday morning Grandma Mac would order taxis to take us, an enormous investment it seemed to me as a child. When we were scrubbed, dressed and ready to go, and a taxi was on its way, my grandfather would hold up the newspaper and say: "If anyone doesn't feel like going to church, you can stay home with me and I'll read the Sunday funnies to you." My grandmother would exert some moral pressure and get a few followers, but I always chose the funnies. His stratagem caused me to grasp at a very young age the crucial connection between humor and effective subversion.

My reading of *All Quiet on the Western Front* had made me into a confirmed pacifist, determined that I would never go to war even if called. I would be a conscientious objector or a draft dodger. I confided my pacifism to both my grandmothers. My Christian Grandmother MacCannell enthusiastically supported my position and told me to stick to it— "War is wrong. War is evil." Grandma Fran, on the other hand, told me I was wrong. She said, "We defeated those Nazi sons of bitches but before long they will be at it again, and when they start it's on you to get a gun and kill the bastards." Still, today, I weigh both their positions about equally.

Maternal Uncles—Charles Elwood ("Doc") And
Edwin Ross ("Eddie") Meskimen

My mother's younger brothers were crucially important in my life from infancy until I was on my own. I saw one or both of them almost weekly. They both cared for me in ways my father never did. They gave me many important gifts both material and spiritual. First among these were their vivid stories of their childhood and youth, never omitting the troubles they had gotten into, and the "stupid stuff" they tried. The only story of his childhood that my father ever told was about how he accidentally shot and killed a neighbor's cat with his bow and arrow. He seemed to think it was funny.

Eddie kept me supplied with reams of 8.5" by 11" unlined newsprint all through my childhood. I never ran out. When I was about to run out, he would magically appear with another ream and sometimes a coloring book or two. Later, it was a comic book or two. I doubt that a day went by from age three forward that I didn't produce at least one drawing, usually many--something that I could not have done were it not for his thoughtful intervention. It is impossible to overstate the value of his concern that I never run out of drawing paper. As a child, once I got a pencil in my hand, my power was unlimited. Anything on earth and beyond was within my grasp. I drew king's castles, haunted houses, super villains, space/time transporters, damsels in distress, imaginary poisonous flowers. None of this would have been possible except for Eddie figuring out my need for paper. And I would not be who I am today without this singular, thoughtful gift.

Eddie also gave me an old *Boy Scout Manual* that I still own. We both knew that I was too poor to join the Boy Scouts of America. My parents could not afford the dues and certainly not a uniform. But he got me interested in the merit badges and told me that he would assist me and I could teach myself the merit badge skills and test myself against the standards in the manual. I especially enjoyed completing all the requirements for "Knot Tying" and "First Aid." I recently heard from his daughter, Janie, that when he was a boy, Eddie had been an active Boy Scout, rising to the top grade of Eagle if there had been an Eagle designation in his day. He never mentioned this to me. Probably because he felt bad knowing that I would never be able to afford membership.

Eddie twice tried to instill values in me via direct hortatory. When I mentioned to him that my first serious girlfriend
was from a wealthy family, he immediately snapped, "A man is
never supposed to live off a woman." Much earlier, apropos of
nothing in particular, he sat me down and very earnestly told me
that I should "Never steal food from a farmer's field." Why? Perhaps it was from the depression. If the farmers couldn't get their
product to market, everyone would starve. His words stand out

Elwood ("Doc") Meskimen, age 19

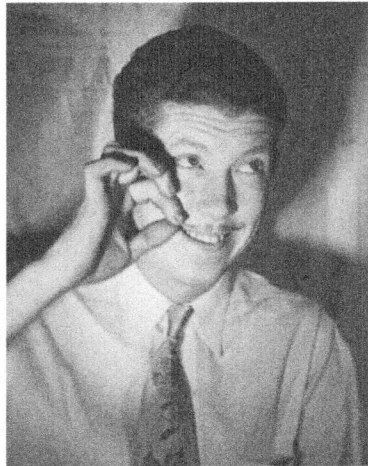

*LEFT: Eddie with his nephews and niece in 1946—Dean and Bill and Jimmy
and Barbara (his brother Doc's children): RIGHT: Eddie always had sly word
or a joke ready-to-hand and enjoyed keeping us on our toes and in stitches when
we were kids. Here he entertains with a painted-on moustache.*

among the very few direct moral lessons imparted to me during my childhood and youth. Every other moral lesson I had to learn by example from observing others' behavior and its outcomes. The negative examples were just as important as the positive. Probably more important.

Eddie was quite sickly all his life and eventually treated himself with alcohol. When I was very young, he earnestly explained to me that if you get so sick you can't walk it is crucially necessary to wrap yourself tight in blankets and wedge yourself in a standing position in the corner of a room. He explained that if "people like us" were ever found lying down and unable to get up on our own we would be taken to a hospital, and if we ever ended up in hospital, we would most likely not come out alive. The story seemed crazy to me, even at the time, but in retrospect there may have been some truth in it. If a medical facility had no extra resources, its "treatment" of the indigent might well have consisted in stashing them in out-of-the-way beds and forgetting about them until after the end. Eddie believed that. More than once I found him shaking, sweating profusely, wrapped in blankets and wedged upright in a corner of my grandmother's house. As a child, I was occasionally tasked with spooning gruel into his mouth while he shivered violently.

Not a day without a drawing

In 1970, Eddie went for a walk in a park near his home in Seattle and bent down to feed a squirrel a peanut. He fell over dead. He was 45 years old. That was the oddly detailed story of Eddie's death that both my mother and my Grandma Fran told me. I recently learned from my cousin Janie that none of it is true. He was found dead lying on his front porch by his wife returning from work. The zoo, the squirrel, the peanut—all that was made up stuff. By whom, and why, Janie and I will never know.

Eddie's older brother Elwood (always called "Doc") made me a professional grade artist's easel for my 10th birthday. It was from gestures like these that I knew Eddie and Doc were watching over me more closely, and understood my interests, and cared about me in ways that neither of my parents did.

Every two to three weeks in the summers, Eddie borrowed his mother's car and drove from Tacoma to Tumwater to visit me when I was at my great grandmother's. He would pull up with a ream of paper and some Boy's Life magazines. My great grandmother always asked him to stay for a meal. She favored him because she could see he loved me the way she did. She never let anyone smoke in her house or on her porch. She called it a filthy and unhealthy habit. She made an exception for Eddie. "He's such a sweet boy, I'll overlook it. But only in his case."

Elwood was nicknamed "Doc" because he could fix anything, mostly broken machinery, but also including medical interventions from purges to setting bones to digging bullets out of flesh wounds. During his lifetime Doc was a problem solver of last resort for industries from Alaska to Mexico. When a high speed ten-foot circular saw blade broke free of its shaft and sliced through an entire mill, they called Doc from two states away to put it back on the shaft and repair the damage it had done to the other equipment. When a giant earthmover working above the tree line threw its tread, they helicoptered Doc in to put it back together.

Eddie could do the work of his parents and brother. He went into the shipyards as a welder with his mother during the war. But he did not continue in that line. He spent most of his life as a driver—ambulance, taxi, short haul truck.

My friend Susan Schwartzenberg, one of the artists who made the National Rosie the Riveter Memorial in Richmond California, solicited this photo from me after hearing some of my family stories. She caused this image of Eddie, Fran, and me to be etched in steel on the Memorial. Even though undeserved, I am proud to be on the "Rosie the Riveter" memorial. Legacy is a weird, complicated, and often accidental thing.

Fran with her son Eddie and me before they left for work in the Bremerton Shipyard, 1943. I am doing my best to emulate working class tough guy posture.

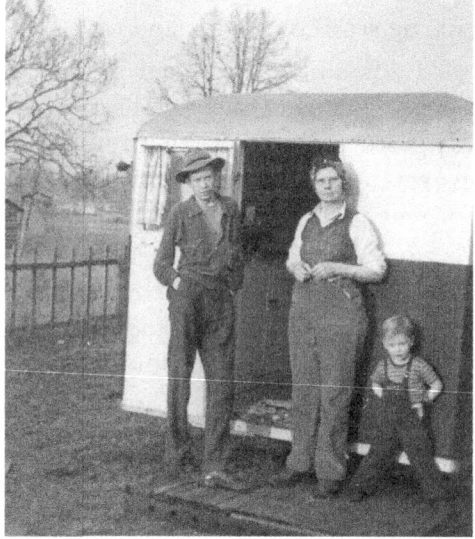

The main lesson I learned from my maternal grandparents and uncles was that a job is something you do, not something you have. They regarded the regularly employed as quasi-failures—as not being quite good enough to make a decent living from the reputation gained for their skills, know-how, and work ethic. Before there was an internet, they had multi-state reputations. Their passionate goal in life was to be untethered from any boss except for the duration of a specific task, ideally half a day or less, sometimes as long as a week if needed: set the overturned cement mixer back on its wheels, collect your fee and move on; true and weld the 10-foot sawmill blade back on its shaft, collect your fee and move on.

My Father—Earle Hector MacCannell

No matter how poor we were, my father always regarded himself as superior in every way to everyone in his purview. It made no difference that his working-class in-laws were better off than us, he was their social superior. Both he and my mother termed our dirt-poor economic situation as "only temporary." In a very real sense, I grew up in a completely different socio-economic class from my parents. I lived in abject, sub-proletarian poverty while, in their minds, they were upper-middle class professionals suffering a temporary setback. Their "setback" lasted from before I was born until I was in middle school.

My father never left the house wearing a shirt without a collar. He spoke well, cultivating an outsized vocabulary sprin-

Earle Hector and Helen Frances ("Fran") MacCannell c. 1940

kling his everyday speech with words like "specific gravity," "percent incline," "Möbius strip," "propinquity," "standard deviation," and various other middle-brow technical terms. He controlled conversations by repeating and verbally underscoring words and phrases he had reason to believe the person he was talking to did not know—domination by inflection and vocabulary. He was a master at it. He was a strong student of mathematics up to quite high levels. He was athletic, winning high school competitions in track and field, gymnastics, archery and swimming. He pursued quirky competencies as an adult, e.g., teaching himself to type on the Dvorak keyboard and routinely exceeding 180 error-free words per minute in measured time trials. I have already said that he was a braggart and a habitual liar. He exaggerated all his accomplishments, even those that were worthy of admiration without exaggeration. He was mainly interested in the notice of strangers. He would spend hours preening and fawning over someone he just met, but he exhibited no interest in, or care about, what his children were up to. He certainly did not care about what we thought of him. When he knew that we knew he was lying to someone, he expected us to keep our mouths shut and back him up with our silence. And we did.

He was also a serial philanderer. He tried to have sex with almost every woman and girl he ever met. His need for affirmation was bottomless. As nearly as I can tell, there was no category of human female that fell definitively outside his seduction catchment area. Not his students. Not his co-workers. Not his teen-aged son's girlfriends. Not morbidly vulnerable neurotics. Not his sisters-in-law, daughters-in-law, or nieces. Certainly not his neighbors' wives. I do not know his success rate—he never discussed it with me—but I do know he was often successful and he was often turned down. Beginning in my early teens I got a steady stream of complaints about him from girls and women I knew who had to rebuff his advances. From my infancy forward, there were very few, very short, periods when there was not "another woman" in our lives. The true reason he volunteered to stay on in Europe after the War was less to stop Communism, and more to cavort freely with recently "liberated" and apparently grateful German and Italian women and girls. My mother made no effort to cover for him. Quite the opposite. From when I was a young child, she used me as a sounding board for her usually half-hearted but detailed complaints about his infidelities. She may have been trying to let me know that that's what it takes to be a real man.

Scores of 1940s glamour and "pin-up" type shots of my father's other women are scattered through the family photo albums alongside similar pictures of my mother. The girlfriends are all clearly labeled in my mother's hand—their names and the places where the photos were taken. She sometimes supplied an adjective like "Pretty" Penny.

One of his girlfriends from the early days of their marriage whose picture appears frequently in the albums was named Lu-Verne. She came to visit my mother years later when my father wasn't home. I was ten at the time. The affair was long over. Mother and LuVerne talked quietly for several hours. We were still living in the projects and the room where they sat together on a lumpy old couch was messy and shabby. LuVerne's hair was done, she was noticeably "made up" even to a ten year old boy, and dressed in a "classy" outfit, professionally manicured nails, and expensive matching purse and high heels. She seemed to me to be very far out of context. They kept their voices low so I could not tell what they talked about. When she left, I asked my mother, "Who was that woman?" She drew herself up and haughtily replied, "'That woman' was very nearly your mother." Her answer puzzled me. I knew if some other woman had been my mother, I wouldn't be me. So what difference would it make? I did not pursue the matter.

That was probably my mother's aim.

My Mother, Helen Frances MacCannell, Née Meskimen

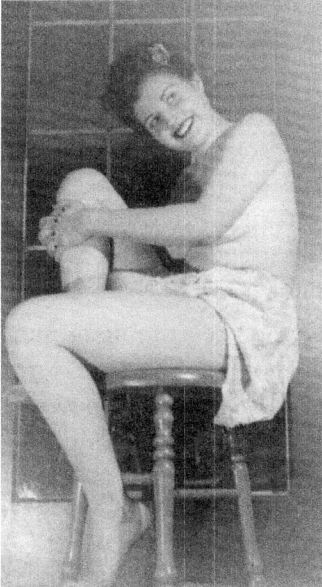

Top: LuVerne—She "was very nearly your mother"
Left: "Pretty Penny"; Right: My mother.
All photos by E. H. MacCannell found in our 1943 family album

When my mother died in 2017, Juliet and I proposed a piece for the group show "Day of the Dead" by San Francisco artists. We made an altar honoring our mothers, two women as different as any two women could possibly be. Sadly we had lost

Juliet's mother 40 years before. But our fond memories of her are as fresh as this morning's coffee. My mother-in-law, Patricia Flower, had been my closest and best friend in life. For our *Day of the Dead* piece, we were able to highlight her unique and superlative character.

After the fashion of a standard obituary, my part of the altar for my mother emphasized her many laudable accomplishments. I told of how two years after my father re-started college in 1949, she went back to school part-time and finished her bachelor's degree in 1957. I told of her getting a Ph.D. in Education when she was 50, and her faculty appointments after that, her brilliant crafts and sewing skills, and her brave teen-age trek with her family out of Oklahoma.

I said nothing of her personality, or my relationship to her, nor did I mention *18 and out*. Here, I will fill in some of the blanks.

As soon as we could speak, my brothers and I were told that the proper term of address for our mother and father were "Mother" and "Father." We were admonished against any overly familiar usages like "ma," "mama," "mom" "mommy." Or "dad," "daddy," "pa," or "papa." These variants were said to be "disrespectful" and permitted only by "stupid," usually ethnic minority parents "who let their children run roughshod over them." As an adult, I noticed that my brother John was permitted to call our mother "Mom" and he often slid into that usage. Bill and I never wavered from Mother, even in adulthood.

Mother was always personally neat and presentable in public but she was a terrible housekeeper in private. She would not clean or put away anything for weeks at a time. Then she would spend a day or two stuffing things out of sight and cleaning furiously but not deeply. She called it "picking up." Mess. Mess. Mess. Pick up. And repeat. The house before the "pick up" always looked like a bomb hit it.

She made herself clothing that allowed her to look better off than we were. At first, she used an old treadle Singer sewing machine given to her by my Great Grandmother Emily. She had a large vocabulary and good grammar with no class markers except her accent and diction was East Coast pretentious when she was trying to impress which was often. I have already told that in the course of her lifetime, she developed a number of admirable craft skills any one of which she might have turned into a successful vocation. She was an amateur botanist with dazzling plant identification skills, rock-hound, tailor, silversmith, and bead worker. She even once taught herself lace making and she was good at it.

She was also more full of herself than anyone need be. She thought she was a Leonardo type genius whose brilliance would only be fully recognized after she was gone. The problem was she only created one worthwhile work of intellect while she was alive. Her Ph.D. disserta-

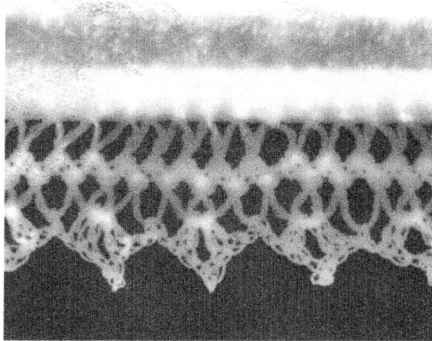

Contact print of lace made by H. F. MacCannell in the 1940s

tion measuring the impact of teachers' behavior on student reading acquisition is actually well-made and path-breaking. But she published nothing from it.

She possibly believed herself to be such a genius she should not be bothered with small stuff like publishing articles, painting pictures, writing prose or poetry, or experimenting.

My mother was unalterably certain that she was never wrong about anything. That's how I learned about gender equality at an early age. Her ego was at least as inflated, fragile and about to explode as any man I ever knew. No matter how low we sank socio-economically, she was always better than everyone else. Her only acknowledged superiors were royalty.

My son, Jason, recently observed, "As a teen-ager, she walked most of the way from dust-bowl Oklahoma to Washington State at the height of the Depression, and she still thought that the most important thing that ever happened in her life was the marriage of Charles and Diana." She took any non-royal display of affluence, skill or joy, as an insult directed at her personally. There was a period in the early 1950s when she had a thing about red convertibles. We had not been able to afford even a used car for over a decade, but when a red convertible passed by, she would hiss, "Just who do they think they are?" She would lose it, or as we said back then, "fly off the handle," if anyone suggested to her a way of doing anything that was different from the way she did it. "How dare you?" she would say.

When I was about eight, I happened to remark that my great grandmother was an excellent cook. I did not make or imply any comparison, but my mother's face immediately darkened and contorted with rage, and she shrieked, "I'm a much better cook than she is, dammit." Everyone, including especially her children, quickly learned to choose their words carefully in her presence. That's how she was able to live in a bubble, believing everyone around her regarded her as highly as she regarded herself.

In the course of my lifetime I have been privileged to know more than my share of people who actually were almost always right about anything they observed. But my mother wasn't among them. Those who get things right are the first to say that we should not listen to them; that we should form our own opinions. My mother, on the other hand, insisted that we agree with her on everything. Any sign of disagreement, even a facial expression, would be met with another "How dare you!" Or, "Don't you dare contradict me!"

I thought I was the kind of son who kept his head down to maintain the peace. But I now realize there is something wrong with this picture. If I was nothing but subservient to my mother's self-importance, she would have fawned over me as she fawned over anyone who flattered her inflated self-image. But she never liked me.

Did she detect that my silence was hiding judgment? That my seeming agreement and acquiescence was only superficial? Did she suspect I saw through her? Probably.

5

My Language, Politics, Poverty and Sports

"Okie" Then And Now

I do not think there is anything ultimately determinative about place-based identities. But they can affect the way a person is perceived. My mother's family and my mother were Okies. So I am half-Okie. This may have had some kind of half-assed impact on who I am.

A politically correct reader might question my use of a slur to describe this part of my heritage and my forebears. My mother and maternal grandparents and uncles were a part of the diaspora in the 1930s that produced the pejorative label "Okies." Trekking out of Oklahoma with whatever meager belongings they could carry to look for a better life, Okies were disliked by insecure locals the same way that "migrants" are met with prejudice today, and for the same reason—they would work hard and long for next to nothing. "Okie" meant someone from Oklahoma and was intended to suggest one who was simple minded, ignorant, gullible. That this old label is negative does not concern me. I am concerned that someone who is paying attention to the current politics of "deep red Oklahoma" might mistakenly assume my Okie relatives held similar attitudes to Oklahomans today. They did not.

As I use the term, I insist on its original meaning as it was explained to me by my Okie relatives. Okie is someone from Oklahoma. It should not be applied to anyone who stayed behind in Oklahoma. Merle Haggard ironized some of these issues in "I'm just an Okie from Muskogee." The singer claims to be both "from Muskogee" and to be living there still, "waving Old Glory down at the Courthouse." Haggard knows that to be a true Okie, he would have to be in some other state picking fruit, working construction, or writing a song. Certainly not waving flags down at the Muskogee courthouse.

From an early age, I was taught by my Okie relatives that if someone calls you stupid, just smile and own it. If they believe you are stupid, it makes it that much easier for you to outsmart them. There is no greater advantage in any negotiation than for the other parties to think you are dumber than they are. It is especially easy to better one who regards himself a genius deal maker. You can get everything you want simply by convincing them they are taking advantage of your naivete. My Grandma Fran used to say, with a smile, "The only thing stupider than a dumb Okie is a dumb Arkie." My maternal uncles loved telling Okie jokes. E.g., A Texan walking north hits the Red River that separates Texas and Oklahoma. He wants to cross but there is no bridge, no boat, and no passable shallows. The current is too fast to swim. He spies a man on the Oklahoma bank and shouts. "Hey, can you tell me how to get to the other side?" The Okie answers, "Why do you want to know? You're already there."

My maternal relatives were a part of the same generation of Okies that produced Jim Thorpe, Will Rogers and Woody Guthrie. Will Rogers said, "Never miss a good chance to shut up," and "Everybody's ignorant—just on different subjects." There is no one comparable coming out of Oklahoma today. If there was you can bet that, like Merle Haggard, they already left.

The Okie Way With Language

Except for my mother, my maternal relatives out of Oklahoma had colorful ways of speaking. It is important for contemporary readers to know that working class and middle-class children in the 1940s could easily reach adulthood without hearing any profanity. Swearing in public or even among intimates was strictly tabooed. There was zero cursing in popular culture—the movies, on radio. In my entire life I heard my father say "damn" and "bastard" once each and my blood ran cold on both occasions. Except for two or three "dammits" I never heard profanity from my mother. At the end of *Gone with the Wind*, when Rhett Butler says, "Frankly Scarlett, I don't give a damn," the audiences couldn't believe their ears and gasped. In public discourse, not even "damn" was allowed. Period. If you heard someone curse, it was regarded as a clear sign that they were going to hell and furthermore that they did not care. My maternal relatives' casual use of profanity set them apart as an almost distinct tribe or even species. I was told never to mention it to anyone that my maternal grandparents and uncles cursed a blue streak. Of course, I knew I should never curse, but I also knew that I had descended from a tribe of the surely damned.

I also learned that their cursing was nuanced, and I needed to pay close attention to it as a matter of safety. While I was driving on my learner's permit, Grandma Fran often volunteered to be my required licensed passenger. I already knew how to drive off-road where there were no other vehicles or pedestrians present. And I also already knew that Fran had some choice words for her fellow drivers on the road. Driving in traffic for the first time, I was unnerved by the co-presence of other moving vehicles and pedestrians. Even though I could handle the car, the whole idea of "right of way," and other vehicles posing danger, was new and alien to me

This is how I learned to pay close attention to nuanced cursing. With my Grandma Fran in the passenger seat, on several occasions I came close to hitting other cars. Her way of warning me that I was about to violate someone's right of way was to yell, "Hit the bastard!" She didn't say "Look out for that guy!" or "Hey!" and point to the danger. She yelled, "Hit the bastard!" She made no effort to hide her glee. Like she thought it would be a barrel of fun if I actually did hit the bastard; if I got into a fender-bender that was my fault. Like she would enjoy having something to hold over me, to razz me about from that moment forward. Her glee made her ironical warnings 100 percent effective. I am certain that was her true aim. Here is the nuanced part. One time when she noticed someone about to violate my right of way, she yelled, "HIT that stupid bastard." Her tone was entirely different, like she meant it this time; like the other guy deserved to be hit; that a fender bender with him in the wrong would be a perfect administration of on-the-spot justice. The "stupid" made all the difference. I knew I was both in the right and in danger. Again, her warning was completely effective. I swerved out of his way in time. This may have been the moment I learned that taking the trouble to understand language, really understand it, could be a matter of life and death. Even cursing. Especially cursing.

All the Meskimens had very creative ways of cursing, and they had an interesting ethic of cursing. As a child my mother told me simply never to say anything I had heard my grandmother or grandfather say. Of course, such a blanket imperative was impossible to obey, but it did cover the fact that almost their every utterance contained at least one or two profanities. Never "fuck." Not once did I hear any of them say "fuck."

Neither my grandmother nor my grandfather ever told me not to curse. But they strongly warned me against cursing inanimate objects. If a tool or an article of clothing went missing or otherwise thwarted me, it was not to blame, and I should never presume to hold it responsible by cursing it. "You don't curse lifeless things." "You only curse beings with consciousness." "If you hit your thumb with the hammer, it's your fault not the hammer's," Ross said. Throughout my life, I have found this imperative almost impossible to obey. But every time a goddam, fucking wrench slips off its nut, I feel a twinge of guilt. Especially when Juliet who picked up where Ross left off reminds me of his dictum—I shouldn't curse inanimate objects.

I learned from my maternal relatives that simple vernacular English could be worked into something poetic, often beautiful. Their thoughtfully figured speech had greater heft and more power than words that just come tumbling out. If someone spoke without having anything worthwhile to say it was called "running at the mouth." "Stop running at the mouth!" was an admonition that rang in my ears in early childhood. I figured out that "running at the mouth" was one of the biggest affronts to the Okie order of things. It taught me, in effect, that words are precious; to speak only when something needed to be spoken about; and if I wanted to make and secure a point, I should use figured language.

Here is an example of Okie lexical frugality and creativity in action. When my Uncle Doc was asked for his opinion he would always pause to consider the matter. If he regarded the topic to be something too precious for his serious regard, or a class or two above him, he would decline to answer. "Sorry, I ain't no connoisseur," he would demur. It was a put-down, meaning 'Don't get above yourself' suggesting that he regarded the subject as something that people like us should not be bothering with.

For example, "What do you think is the best aftershave?"

"I ain't no connoisseur."

Here is the finely figured part. If you listened closely, you would hear him momentarily lapse into a slight Okie drawl allowing him, very purposefully, very wickedly, to pronounce connoisseur as "corner sewer." "I ain't no corner sewer." His implication was clear: "'You, friend, a man who wears a scent, could end up smelling like a corner sewer."

Linguists have a term for what my Uncle Doc did with "connoisseur." They call it an *oronym* and sometimes an *eggcorn*. It refers to a misuse of language that results in a meaning that is plausible but not the same as would result from proper usage. The only problem with the linguist's concept is they claim that every oronym is the result of the speaker's ignorance. In Doc's case, this couldn't be further from the truth. "Corner sewer" was always deployed as a sly triple move—first his lapse into an Okie accent that he didn't ordinarily have; then to mispronounce "connoisseur" in such a way as to land a strong insult; then to slip out of any blame for the insult by hiding behind his pretense of ignorance. Apparently, linguists cannot imagine someone so smart pretending to be ignorant in order strategically to deploy an oronym that is not a mistake but is, rather, a carefully crafted speech act.

In classical rhetoric Doc's "corner sewer" would be called a *metaplasm*, a misuse of language that may appear to be an error but has been purposefully introduced to amplify a poetic meaning. On this matter, Aristotle, as he often was, is a bit smarter than current linguistic theory.

Among my Okie relatives, I understood from the get-go that "old" as an adjective to describe a friend or family member was a strong term of endearment with no actual age connotation. "Old Aunt Nadine" simply meant the speaker loved her. When I was five, I might ask my mother, "Where is old Bill?" She would know that in the moment I was feeling especially well disposed toward my three-year-old brother. This probably came over from the British Isles. In English TV dramas I occasionally hear a husband calling his not yet middle-aged wife "old girl."

My mother's admonition never to say anything I'd heard her parents say caused me to be especially attuned to the forbidden words I only heard from them. I quickly figured out that "bastard, "shit," and "son of a bitch" were listed words. I was not entirely certain about "crap."

Until I was six, I thought that "pope" was the filthiest word in the English language. Ross's hatred of organized religion was so strong that I often heard him growl, "That goddam, rotten son-of-a-bitch, rat bastard Pope." Or some equivalent string of curses ending in "Pope." Coming at the end as it always did, I thought "pope" was just another adjective, the worst of them all. Until one morning I heard a radio announcer say, "Today, the Pope in Rome . . ." I was shocked to the core of my being and ran to my mother who was not registering any appropriate horror.

"Did you hear what he said?"

She had been listening to the same broadcast. "No." She was alarmed by my agitation.

"He said the most horrible thing, the worst thing anyone can say, ON THE RADIO."

"What did he say."

"Oh, I can't tell you. It was so bad."

"Go ahead and tell me."

"I can't. You'll wash my mouth out with soap."

"No. It's okay. Just this once you can say it and I won't punish you."

"He said . . ." (I whispered in her ear so my brother wouldn't hear.) "He said *'pope.'*"

My mother got a very strange expression on her face like I had suddenly somehow become mentally unhinged.

"What makes you think 'Pope' is a bad word?"

I wouldn't rat out my grandfather so I answered, "It just sounds bad." Still looking at me strangely, she proceeded to tell me about the Pope, the Vatican, the Catholic Church, etc. "It's okay to say 'Pope.'

"It's just I heard Grandpa say it."

"Your grandfather doesn't like him, that's all."

Sometimes what you learn comes at you from a very oblique angle.

Grandma Fran could curse like a sailor. It was not habitual with her. It was only for special emphasis. Like, "Hit the stupid bastard!"

When I was 12 or 13 she confided in me. "There is something I want you to know."

"Yes?"

"All my life I have worked with men. Not just any men. Some of the toughest, meanest men who have ever walked the earth."

"I know, Grandma."

"Here's the thing. Not one of those men. No matter how rough. Ever. Ever used a foul word in my presence."

I spontaneously blurted out, "How would you know, Grandma?"

She gave me a look and said, "That'll be enough out of you, sprout." "Sprout" was her way of keeping kids in their place if they got above themselves. "Whippersnapper" was her put-down of teen-age exuberance that might lead to trouble.

Some of their aphorisms were, so far as I know, completely unique. My far-left leaning, boilermaker Grandpa Ross's favorite saying was "Mother Jones is safe to say." The reference was not to the magazine which did not exist at the time. It was the magazine's namesake, Mary Harris Jones, the firebrand activist from the turn of the 20th century who was known as the "most dangerous woman in America" for her effectiveness at organizing mineworkers. "Mother Jones is safe to say" meant there were no metaphorical bosses or Pinkertons around to punish us for our views. As a small child, I knew nothing about labor organizing when Ross would turn to me in a conspiratorial way and say these words. But I knew what he meant and that "Mother Jones is safe to say" was an incantation that would protect us even if we spoke our minds freely.

Uncle Eddie had a plethora of poetic "sayings" that I never heard come out of the mouth of any other human being. If someone ran fast to avoid trouble, or just ran fast, or sped away in a car, Eddie would say, "He took off like a striped-ass ape." Very high speed on foot, in a vehicle, or any quick response time, Eddie expressed as, "Faster than a streak of blue shit." I learned sexual slang long before I knew what any of it meant from a certain look he would give me. I often caught and played with a type of pillbug that curls defensively into a tight ball if you shake them in your hand. They are sometimes called "roly-polys." I called them "ball bugs." When I told Eddie about them he gave me the look and slowly repeated, "Ball bugs, aye." There was just the tiniest flicker of expression and inflection that told me that "ball bugs" might mean something different from the insect I was telling him about and that the "something different" was probably of an adult, sexual nature. I carried the phrase around in my head for several years before learning that "balls" was slang for testicles. Now I understood his facial expression—testicle bugs, hmmm. The same with "a piece of tail." We were walking near my house one day and I pointed out to him where a kite had become tangled in the electrical wires. "There used to be a kite up there. Now there's nothing left but a piece of tail." He gave me the look. "Nothing but a piece of tail, aye." I carried that one around in my head for a few more years than "ball bugs."

The Okie way with language flows seamlessly into the Okie way of life and work ethic. I do not remember Doc or my Grandpa Ross ever having a regular job. They simply waited for someone to call with a one-off task that no one else could do. They could fix blown boilers that everyone else had declared beyond repair. They trued and welded high-speed shafts that had been condemned. They designed and poured concrete cesspools for mountain cabins on impossible terrain. They were never rich, but they were also never poor. The Meskimens did all their business

with cash including purchase and sale of real estate. If they sold
something that the buyer could not afford to pay full price up
front, they acted as their own bank, taking payment in install-
ments. They drew up their own contracts without the advice of
lawyers. When someone failed to pay, they repossessed their
property without the assistance of the sheriff. To my knowledge,
no one ever tried to resist a Meskimen repossession. In one of my
last conversations with Doc's son, my cousin Jimmy told me, "I'll
never be broke. Everyone knows I have the best cesspool forms
on the West Coast."

While I have spent most of my life as a white-collar professional, I have always approached its components— research to
conduct, reports to write, lectures to prepare, interviews, publishing deadlines to meet— with the Meskimen blue-collar attitude; as tasks to be done well; better than others could do them;
to be over and done with; then to move on. I have always regarded writing as a form of manual labor, and I have never had any
difficulty obtaining quality professional appointments and top
tier publishing venues for my work. In my own way, I possessed
the best cesspool forms on the West Coast.

My Politics

My politics were probably formed before I was toilet
trained. My grandparents and uncles were unalterably democrats. Ross claimed to be a Communist, but probably just to piss
people off. Even my Lincoln-loving great grandmother shifted
from Republican to FDR Democrat during the Depression and
the War.

Here is my Grandma Fran's poem for the 1944 presidential
election:

PURE POLITICS

While Franklin D. R. is concerned with the war,

And whipping the pants off the Axis

Tom Dewey came through with some hooey for you

About the reduction of taxes.

That taxes are high we will not deny.

But we eat without chasing down rabbits.
The G.O.P. way of more work for less pay
Is a voter's idea of bad habits.

Let the elephant rave about taxes we'll save
Other promises too, we remember.
Of the office they seek
Let 'em read 'em and weep
When ballots are cast in November.

                              —Frances Meskimen

Except for my mother, my father and my brother John and his wife, I do not know that I have ever been close to any Republicans. I get along well with those of different political persuasions so long as they are not belligerently aggressive and do not imagine their political beliefs to be the core of their being. It has always eluded me why someone who has never held office, who would never run for office, could think that their political beliefs might somehow be of general interest. I enjoy hearing thoughts and observations about work, books, hobbies, pets, childhood, friends, travels, children, etc. Griping about taxes and remarks about the size of government rarely interest me. Unless you do something real with them like run for office, or organize labor, or a community. Or write a poem. Or a song.

Or if they are symptomatic of other psychological issues. For example, my mother probably should not be counted as "Republican" because she voted with whatever boyfriend or husband she had at the time. It just happened that they were all Republicans. She did not really have any political leanings of her own except for a very idiosyncratic form of racism. She hated American Indians. No other minority. Just Indians. I don't believe she ever used the word "Indian" without the adjectives "big" and "stupid."

Observing my mother, I inductively determined at an early age that prejudice is directed at people you feel you have wronged in some way. Today, my childhood thoughts on this matter still have some traction. I would sloganize it as 'Racial hatred is repressed guilt.' At least that is the way it played out in my mother's case. She was not directly or personally responsible for the mistreatment of Indians. But she was very much aware that the place of her childhood, the red Oklahoma dirt she loved so much she kept a precious jar of it for the rest of her life, was "hers" only because the Indians had been forcibly sent there and then as forcibly removed. She identified with the white version of the history of Oklahoma and unconsciously assumed a share of the burden of guilt for the atrocious treatment of the Indians. Her way of dealing with her guilt was to place the blame for their ill-treatment squarely on the Indians themselves—if forced to face it, she would have to say, 'We shafted them, but they were savages and had it coming. They would have squandered any advantage we might have given them anyway.' She liked to tell the story of a "Big, stupid, oil-rich Indian who drove his Cadillac until it ran out of gas then went into town and bought new one." Etcetera. In her telling, it was not an apocryphal story but something that actually happened. In one variant, the Indian "Shot the Cadillac for running out of gas." In another variant, the car was a LaSalle, a short-lived General Motors near-luxury brand positioned between Buick and Cadillac.

Our Poverty

Until I could purchase my own clothing, if I needed shoes or a winter coat, it was sourced from Church rummage sales, the Goodwill, or we made it ourselves. Our adjective for any luxury item was "store-bought." From infancy until I was a teenager and could pay my own way, I ate two restaurant meals. Bill and I were so skinny our Grandpa Ross in true Okie fashion took to calling us "the little refugees" which never failed to get a rise out of my mother. One summer I went shoeless. My mother reasoned that I would not grow out of them so quickly if she waited until just before school began to buy them.

In the United States there is a dominant meme that associates poverty with moral weakness. Since I was born poor, I have some difficulty accepting the idea that it was because I was lazy or had bad habits. Nor can my family situation be attributed to any stereotypical moral weakness on my parents' part. They did not smoke, drink, gamble, use drugs, or spend money on unneeded consumer goods. I am not certain that anyone's poverty is caused by moral failing. If there is a correlation, it is just as likely the causal arrow points in the other direction. The only "moral" difference between rich and poor is the rich can afford to smoke, drink, gamble, use drugs and wallow in unneeded consumer goods.

We had nothing for almost my entire childhood. My parents dreamed of a better life and eventually worked hard to achieve it. But they had also been teenagers during the Great Depression. When I was born, they had known nothing but scarcity and hardship. Well into the 1950s, they proudly dealt with our impoverishment that was not, after all, materially different from their childhood and youth. For me, the Great Depression ended around 1952 when I started to earn my own living.

My mother did have a thing for cheap perfume and costume jewelry. As I have already mentioned, the only other "luxury" they spent money on was the paper, film, chemicals, and equipment for their photography hobby. In retrospect I am not certain that I would have clawed the photo processing money back to put more food on the table. The costume jewelry? Yes.

Our poverty was caused first by my father's voluntary service to stay behind with the U.S. occupational forces in immediate post-war Europe. He moved us into base housing at Fort Lewis, Washington on a meager monthly enlisted man's family allotment where we eked by for the next three and a half years. Then, after the military, it was my parents' pursuit of bachelors and post-graduate degrees that kept us poor. If we were cold, sick and hungry it was for two worthy causes. At least that was the way it was repeatedly explained to my brothers and me. We were not really poor, at least not like the other poor people around us who, we were told, would remain poor forever because they were not trying to "better" themselves. We were making "temporary" sacrifices, first for the "greater good" of our nation, and then for our own future prosperity.

The only problem with that construction is that for my brothers and me "temporary sacrifice" was our entire lives from birth into our mid-teen years. It is easily predictable that my family would implode precisely coincident with our escape from poverty and entry into the middle class.

My mother had strict rules to conserve our health and resources. No wading in nearby creeks or lakes if the outside temperature was below 70 degrees. No eating between meals. No playing outdoors after a rain until the water stopped dripping off the eaves. Et cetera. When we did not have warm enough coats in the winter, she would wrap us in newspaper insulation before we got dressed to go outside. She was firm, sensible, and her stated intentions were good. But she was not always honest with us.

Throughout our childhood she told my brothers and me that she had studied the minimum daily nutritional requirement for children our ages and weights. She further explained that she undertook a close analysis of the cheapest way to get us to the minimum— the cheapest source of protein, the cheapest carbohydrate, etc. to make the minimums. So, during my childhood I was told that even though I felt hungry, I wasn't actually hungry. Not technically, according to nutritional science.

"The little refugees" Bill and me on our back porch at American Lake Gardens, 1946

Later I discovered it was true that she studied the minimum requirements for children. But she arrived at precisely the opposite conclusion than the one she told us—i.e., in fact, we were starving and she knew it and dismissed it. Among my father's effects after he died, I found a term paper he wrote in 1950 for an undergraduate sociology course. His title suggests he had already absorbed the norms of sociological discourse: "Level of Subsistence and some Adjustments, Modifications, and Developments Required to Maintain The Family in its Customary Institutional Form Under Conditions of Extremely Reduced Income." It is 48 pages long and it describes in minute detail how exactly, over the course of a year (1949-50), we spent every penny of the G.I. Bill student living allowance ($120.00 per month for a family of five) and how we scrounged to make up the gap between that and "subsistence." He listed the cost of every can of beans, every dime bus fare, every used item of clothing. Nothing was left out. There was a little residual income at the end of each month. Probably condoms.

Anyone reading his title could be forgiven for forming the opinion that 1949/50 was an anomalous year and that our income was usually much higher. Far from being "extremely reduced," the conditions he describes was pretty much all I had ever known.

An Okie reading the paper would have told him to stop running at the mouth and easily surmised that he was describing our life, not a period of temporary belt-tightening. At the end of the "Introduction," he asked my mother, "the Wife," to provide a "Statement of the Wife Concerning Adjustments in the Period of Reduced Income." Here is what my mother wrote about our "so called" minimum nutritional requirements:

> I proceeded on the thesis that appetizing food, varied in the manner of preparation, would suffice if served in a quantity to turn out well-filled children, even if it lacked many of the so-called minimum requirements. Our food allowance was such that the minimum protein requirement was never satisfied, and through the winter months the green and leafy fresh vegetables were non-existent. Compensation had to be made by adding more of less expensive more filling foods.

Apparently, she also felt that "compensation had to be made" by trying to fill us with reassuring words about how we were not really starving. But her words never reached our stomachs.

My brothers and I felt hungry all the time.

Crucial Gifts My Parents Gave Me

As parents, they were missing a few parts. My mother told me point-blank when I was seven years old that my father would have no interest in his children until we were teenagers and could learn about the kinds of "adult" things he would teach us. It did not seem to occur to either of them that boys begin learning how (and how not) to be men from birth. You cannot ignore your child for their entire life until their teen years and then suddenly become their pal, confidant, and mentor.

But they were far from 100 percent awful. While I learned most from their negative example, they did provide several crucial spiritual and material gifts that I want to acknowledge.

My Supportive Extended Family: The most important gift my parents gave me was accidental. My reader will already know it was the larger cast of characters attached to them in my extended family who filled in where they were lacking.

Humility: The second thing I give my parents very high marks for is how successful they were at teaching me humility. I grew up knowing that starting with them, everyone was as good as or better than me. It was not, "They might think they're better." It was simply, "They're better." A fact of life with zero resentment. Given my upbringing, it would have been impossible for me to imagine anything resembling privilege, arrogance, entitlement. Maybe not John. But Bill and I were consigned to some kind of limbo between the dregs of humanity and the Übermenschen like my mother, father and John. We could never be as great as they were, but, with luck, we might not get sucked into the sub-proletariat.

Self-reliance: My parents did not stint on training me to become self-sufficient and self-reliant. My father imparted this to me mainly by neglect. From my personal standpoint, I am quite certain that had my father stayed with us from 1945-49; had he shown any sustained interest in me; had I ever thought for even a moment that he spoke the truth; that is to say if he had ever tried to be a "father" to me in any conventional sense, it could well have crippled me ethically and emotionally for the rest of my life. Those who believed his lies apparently did care for him. I never did. Sitting dry-eyed at his funeral

I was surrounded by scores of mourners I had never met who were sobbing so hard they shook the benches. Fabulists find their followers. Did they know something I did not? If I could peel away all his lies, would there have been something resembling a worthy human being in there? Possibly, but I'll never know. My mother did not believe half his lies and I think she did love him for at least half of their marriage.

Nevertheless, he made some positive interventions as I was growing up. When I was nine, he taught me how (and permitted me) to use his Speedball pen set and India inks to outline my pencil drawings and fill them in with watercolors. When I was 11, he showed me how to make strong glue joints when building balsa model planes. In balance, however, it was his neglect that was truly benign. He may have known this—that I would be better off feral than having been raised by him.

My mother provided positive, detailed instruction on how to deal with practical, day-to-day matters. When I was six she taught me how to use public transportation. By the time I was seven, I could ride Greyhound buses unaccompanied between Tacoma, Fort Lewis, and Olympia. This was to visit grandparents or my Great Aunt Glenna and for music lessons. These trips involved multiple transfers to local lines. The first few times I did it by myself I was not certain I was getting everything right. Every stop and transfer required hyper-vigilance—my eyes darting around for familiar landmarks and bus numbers—and occasional requests for information and confirmation from strangers. But I never messed up. By the time I was seven I could make these trips with my younger brothers in tow and without my mother. The sight of young children riding the Greyhounds alone in the 1940s caused notice on the part of the drivers and other passengers, but never alarm. Sometimes a friendly stranger would ask me where I was going and if I knew how to get there? When I told them the correct stops and transfer lines, they were relieved and made no further inquiries or they switched subjects, often asking about other things I knew how to do. I remember giving a nice woman seat-mate step-by-step instructions on how to make

Leaving with Bill and John to visit our Aunt Glenna in 1947. Were they afraid I might not know the way? Bill looks a little apprehensive. No need. I was fully competent to handle the transfers.

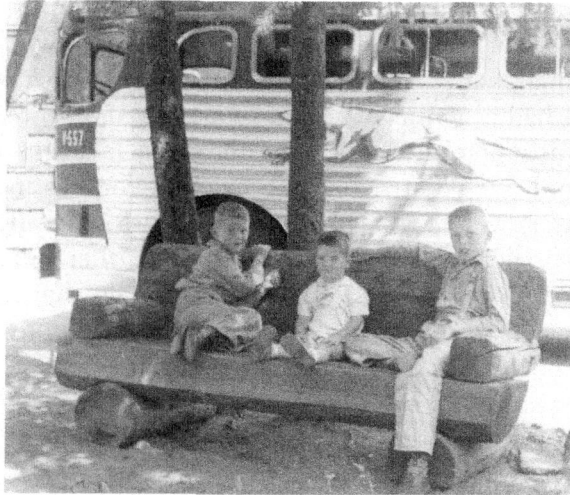

a proper cup of tea including warming the pot before putting in the tea water.

There were also material gifts that must not go unacknowledged. In spite of their self-absorption, on several occasions they voluntarily provided some quite wonderful things that made a big difference in my young life. I hope my brothers can make a similar perhaps overlapping list. Here's mine: a *World Book Encyclopedia,* a German student microscope, a violin, Zaidenberg's *Anyone Can Paint,* a speedball lettering pen, and a Spanish/English—English/Spanish dictionary. I think that's it.

The *World Book Encyclopedia*

Soon after we moved back into American Lake Gardens and my father returned to Europe, a travelling encyclopedia salesman came through the project offering the *World Book* on installment. If she did not order the luxury binding and the custom shelving to hold it, the monthly payments were small enough my mother felt she could afford them. In the depths of our poverty, she contracted to purchase the full set. When the 18 heavy volumes arrived, as promised by its title, it really did open up the world to me. It was printed on heavy, shiny stock with rich full color illustrations. The articles on every subject were simple and clear and not at all condescending and I enjoyed reading every one. I did not use it to look things up. I treated each volume as a book to be read straight through from entry to entry in alphabetical order. I continuously learned about many things I had never heard of and I never tired of re-reading the articles I most enjoyed. "Dog" was one of my favorites, as was "Art." I had only seen mutts, and the images of Poodles and Wire-haired Terriers were a revelation to me. My way of using the World Books carried me from pillar to post and hither and yon in a deliciously random fashion. I remain profoundly thankful my mother decided to bring this resource into our home. It was my TV; my movies; my video games; my summer camp; it was my more than satisfactory substitute for every childhood diversion anyone ever came up with.

I will unwrap each of the rest of their crucial gifts in its proper moment.

The Most Unexpected Gift: Violin Study

Soon after John was born, I began my study of violin. Supporting my instruction was the most improbable and elaborate childhood gift my parents gave me.

My Great Grandmother Emily Amelia owned a quality 18th Century French violin. She told me I could have it but only if I learned to play it. I do not know how she came to possess such a fine instrument. No one in her immediate family was musical. And I will never know why my parents decided to throw their support behind my violin study. But they did. They went out of their way to make sure I could embark on this improbable quest. Word at the time was that children should not be introduced to this formidable instrument until age twelve at least. I was six. The Suzuki Method had not yet come to the United States. My mother found and convinced a violin teacher in Tacoma to take me on and she further convinced him to give me lessons at the only rate we could afford, free of charge. His name was Mr. Kerr. I never knew his first name. When Kerr determined that my great grandmother's full-sized violin was too big for me to play, my mother wrote my father in Europe who promptly purchased and mailed me a good quality half-sized German instrument. He told me he paid two packs of American cigarettes for it on the black market. Since he never told the truth about anything, I cannot be sure of what it actually cost. Maybe it was two packs of cigarettes.

Given their otherwise dim view of my potential, I do not know why they went to this level of effort on my behalf to undertake what most considered to be the impossible. Did my great grandmother lobby them heavily? Did they harbor some notion that I might be more capable than they thought? Perhaps. They had not yet administered the I.Q. test that confirmed my mediocrity. Did they think there might be some monetary value in the instrument that I could garner for them by learning to play and receiving it from my great grandmother? Whatever their motive, they supported my violin study.

Mr. Kerr made it crystal clear that his free lessons would end abruptly if I did not practice diligently. I had to show up for my half-hour session each week having mastered the exercises he gave me the week before. Anything less than perfection would result in a demand for payment, which would be tantamount to immediate termination of instruction.

Kerr openly admired my valuable French violin and did not hide his preference for playing it over his own instrument. Even after I got the smaller one he asked me to bring my full-sized violin to my lessons. Carrying both cases, I rode three buses, one of them inter-city, between American Lake Gardens and Kerr's walk-up studio in downtown Tacoma. Since every transfer stop served multiple bus lines, and I had my choices of more than one bus route, initially I was never fully certain I was getting on the right bus. My mother wrote me a note I could give to a stranger in case I got lost. It began, "My name is Deanie and I live at 3 Fir Place, American Lake Gardens. I can find my own way home if you put me on bus number . . ." Etc. I strategically ripped the top of the note to tear the hated "*ie*" off of "*Deanie*." But I kept the rest of the note just to be safe. I never had to use it.

My mother's support stopped with the logistics of securing lessons and a smaller instrument. She had zero tolerance for the sound of my first efforts. She made me practice outside in the yard. I would tack my music to the coal bin and play away to the consternation and occasional amusement of our neighbors. On rainy days I practiced in the boys' bedroom with the door shut.

About those shoestrings: When my shoestrings broke, the replacements that adults bought me were usually the wrong length. Too long. I found from experience that if I cut them down to size, the frayed end wouldn't go through the eyelets. So I spent much of my childhood like this—with a few extra twists of the laces around my ankles before the tie. In the picture (above) at the Greyhound stop my shoes are laced the same way.

The first difficulty Kerr and I encountered was not a matter of my size or age. It was my left-handedness. He briefly considered turning the bridge around and reversing the order of the strings so I could bow with my dominant arm. But we quickly rejected that idea since it would have rendered it impossible for me to play in a group or an orchestra without risking injury to the player to my right. Moreover, it would have looked ridiculous, like we were sword fighting. Visual appearances in

Playing my half-sized German violin in 1947. The positioning of my fingers, both hands and wrists is correct.

an orchestra are important. The violin scores have discreet little commas telling us when to breathe so our inhalations will be synchronized with those playing the wind instruments. Certainly a bow moving opposite to all the other bows would never be tolerated. Kerr reckoned my fingering would be "strong."

I studied with Kerr until my father returned from Europe and moved us from American Lake Gardens to Stewart Heights. Kerr included me in his public recitals. I always drew a big laugh from the audience when I walked onto the stage last. His other students who had begun when they were twelve were mostly in their advanced teens. I was half their size.

The first scale Kerr taught me was G major. He called it the "scale of F sharp" which was more helpfully descriptive than "G major" as all the F notes were sharp and nothing much more is going on. He had a brutal but effective way of teaching. After about four months of scales and simple songs in G major, he placed a new sheet of music on my stand and told me to play it. I got about three notes into the first measure when he grabbed my hand and forcefully shoved my fingers into different positions on the strings. I asked him why he would do such a thing? My fingers were correctly placed. "That was before. This is now," he said. Then he pointed to the single flat notation after the clef and told me somewhat scornfully that I had failed to notice the "change of key." At that point I didn't even know there was such a thing as a "different key." I thought all music was scored and played in G major. He kept thumping on the F major notation and pulling and pushing my fingers into unfamiliar positions until I began to coax the correct notes from the instrument. I would have preferred if he had sat me down in advance and talked some music theory with me. But I never forgot that lesson.

In a year, I grew into my great grandmother's violin. It was still a little large, but I could handle it. The grain in its ebony fingerboard was so fine it was invisible to the naked eye. The violin was so old and had been played so much that the ebony was visibly worn into shallow buckets under certain finger positions. The worn spots were in my first key, G major. I thought perhaps it had been played only by students whose teachers had never grabbed their fingers and taught them the other keys. Today I suspect it had gone through much of the 19th century as a country fiddle.

After graduate school, in 1970, I took my 200-year-old instrument to a violin maker by the name of Primavera in Philadelphia to re-glue it. I did not ask him to, but he also removed the ancient fingerboard and replaced it with a very grainy new one, sans indentations of course. He explained that fingerboards have to be perfectly smooth and flat as he rushed me out the door of his shop. He clearly did not want me to ask him for the parts he had removed. He also "traded" my old bow for a new one he made, and my 18th century carved wooden case for a modern one. "Your instrument is too valuable to be carried in a fragile 200-year-old case." One of the only things I ever lose sleep over is recalling the way Primavera screwed me over. When I think about the loss of my antique bow, fingerboard, and case I get such a jolt of adrenaline I cannot go back to sleep.

At Stewart Heights there was no music in the school and paid lessons were out of the question, so I practiced on my own. I was able to stay limber but made little progress. I never found a book on "How to Play the Violin." The following years in a succession of Seattle public schools there were music teachers. None of them knew or understood the violin, but they could criticize my tonality, phrasing, and meter and encourage me to figure out improvements on my own. They gave me access to a wide variety of sheet music and I made some progress. In Laurelhurst School, there was a girl in one of the other sixth grade classes who had reached a skill level exactly the same as mine. I never knew her story, or how she started her study well before age twelve. Neither of us was twelve yet. I don't remember her name probably because she was not in my class. Our public school music "lessons" consisted of playing Mozart pieces scored for two violins for 45 minutes twice a week in the teacher's break room. Our timing was precise, and we were note perfect together. The teachers on break sat in stunned silence with beatific expressions on their faces.

When I turned 12, I tried out for the Seattle Children's Summer Orchestra Program. It was led by the conductor of the Seattle Symphony Orchestra assisted by several of his professional players. Almost everyone else was a high school junior or senior and had four or five years of serious (store bought) instruction under their belts. The violinists were almost all better than I was, but I still played myself up to a second chair. When we got to the final piece that we would be rehearsing for a public concert at the end of summer, there were several sections that required the second violins to shift to the second fingering position. I had never been taught the second position. I could reach the first C on the E-string by extending my pinkie. But that was it. The score called for more, so I had to drop out of the orchestra before the final concert.

Here is my most slow-motion epiphany. From the first scales I played for Kerr, I knew that I would have no future in music. Oddly my understanding came from a part of my training that I mastered easily and immediately. I learned to read music as fast as Kerr could teach me. He remarked about it. He told me about the different notations for rests of different duration once and never had to tell me again. I enjoyed copying songs and exercises on blank, five-line music paper. I didn't have to buy any sheet music or books until I could afford them from my own earnings babysitting, mowing lawns, etc. I could fill in the treble clef, scale code, meter, measures, notes, rests and repeats as fast as I could think.

But here is the rub. I only copied. I never wrote notes of my own. This was uncharacteristic for me. Whenever I picked up a pencil to do anything else, to draw or to write, I always made up something new. When I was in third grade, I wrote love poems to an imaginary girl with lines like "Your beauty my poor Scottish heart it doth break." Yes, "doth," in third grade. In fourth grade I obsessively drew architectural floor plans for haunted mansions with secret rooms and passages for the ghosts. But the secret room of music was never within my grasp. All I could do was copy what others had written. Even though I kept at it for seven years I was aware the whole time that it ended before it began. I learned a great deal, but it was entirely mechanistic. There was no creativity in it. Everything I learned playing the violin would eventually have to be applied elsewhere.

When I walked away from my last rehearsal for the Seattle Children's Symphony Orchestra, I was sad, but that was that. I did not pick up the instrument again for 20 years. My attention turned from tuning the violin to tuning cars.

Would I take back the thousands of hours I practiced the violin to use for some other purpose or project? Never. Not even a minute of it. As I write this, I am fighting the temptation to pull my great grandmother's beautiful instrument from the closet three feet away from the desk where I am sitting. Perhaps just to touch it and remember her— "You may have it if you learn to play it." It is humbling. Even if I knew from day one that I would never be a superb violinist. Especially if I knew that. I learned to treat my instrument with ultimate respect; I learned that even if you will never be a virtuoso, diligent practice leads to improvement; I learned my proper place on the spectrum of violinists. No serious effort ever actually goes to waste.

One of my greatest pleasures today is listening to a Beethoven concerto or string quartet, following along with the violin score in front of me, seeing and hearing notes that I could never play. How does anyone play a quadruple stop on the violin? It's technically impossible. Yet there it is. Beethoven knew how to play the violin, that is to say he knew better than to score a quadruple stop, and still he scored it. And the performer I am hearing got his bow across all four strings almost simultaneously. It is a kind of wondrous magic to see and to hear that. Marks and traces remain of everything that has gone before, especially a struggle that you ultimately lose. I am privileged to be positioned both completely inside the music and completely outside of it at the same time.

Twenty years later, my sons started to play the violin at ages six and three. In the meantime Mr. Suzuki had come up with "tukka, tukka, tuk, tuk" and "popcorn and ice cream." I enjoyed going back through the basics with them and especially observing the new humane teaching methods. Daniel and Jason grew out of Suzuki in about a year and we found them a more advanced teacher in the next city. They quickly progressed to my level. And we played Mozart trios together. When they grew out of the more advanced teacher, we found we would have to commute 70 miles to San Francisco (a 149-mile roundtrip) for further instruction. So we all quit. Me, for the second time.

When I began to study violin Eddie had a field day. As soon as I was told the proper name of all the parts of the instrument, the scroll, the bridge, etc., I shared them with him. "And these are the f-holes" I told him. That moment is burned into my memory because I caught him uncharacteristically suppressing the look he was about to give me. "F-hole" must be really bad, I thought. He was not similarly guarded about the names of the strings. When I was first learning to tune the instrument, I often over-tightened the strings before I backed off and got the correct note. The E and A strings are quite fragile and easy to break. The D string is a bit stronger. The G string is thick, wire wrapped and very strong. Soon after the second time I broke the E and A strings I also snapped the D string. When I told Eddie of my tuning misadventures he said with a big smile, "So what you are telling me is you are down to your G string."

My History in Sports

Mickey Mantle was so poor as a child he had to get up early in the morning to collect roadkill for his mother to cook. American boys in my situation dream of escaping their poverty through achievement in sports. I didn't. As a child neither my father nor anyone else ever hinted that I should do sports. This is at least partially on me. As a lefty I am initially awkward at almost every physical skill I attempt to learn. My father and my uncles may have noted this and simply given up on me in advance. Consequently, I had little awareness of the existence of sports in general and zero awareness of professional sports. There was no TV in my house until I was in my mid-teens. Doc Meskimen trained as a boxer. But he never considered it as a career. It was to give him an advantage in barroom brawls and workplace labor actions. None of my maternal male relatives stopped working long enough to play any kind of game. Their main form of entertainment during "down" times was telling dirty jokes. Eddie made up some one-liners that were classics: "Did you hear about that plastic surgeon who hung himself?"

I did not take my father's word that he was a competitive swimmer and diver, runner, archer, and gymnast. I never took his word for anything. But there is evidence of his sports prowess in his high school yearbooks. He never suggested that I try to do any sport. I suspect he thought I was too scrawny, weak, and uncoordinated to bother with. He never put a ball of any size or shape in my hands, much less suggest that we toss or kick one around together. I couldn't be more grateful to him for this. Had he encouraged me to attempt some sport, I likely would have failed at it, or been just "average." I am certain that the marks and traces of any sport I might have tried and failed would not bring me the kind of satisfaction, or be transferable to other pursuits, as studying the violin.

About the time I was in fourth or fifth grade I noticed my classmates playing baseball after school but I never joined them. In junior high school when it became a required component of gym classes, I taught myself the rules of baseball by reading a book. But I was lousy at it. Watching other kids playing, I thought the pitcher was trying to hit the swinging bat with the ball. Out in left field, it did not occur to me that the ball might come my way and that I should know what to do with it before getting my hands on it. When it did come my way, I would look around and start to analyze the situation to figure out where to throw it. What I always saw was my teammates jumping up and down and screaming at me while someone scored off my hesitation. By the time I understood that I should anticipate the play, I was known to be so wretched that no one would play with me. Which was fine.

In about sixth grade I began to enjoy soccer and basketball but not seriously, just for fun. In my mid-teens I threw myself quite hard into two sports that kids don't usually prepare for— mountaineering and auto racing. Possibly because kids don't usually prepare for them and and probably because they are about neutralizing danger.

As a result of this peculiar early childhood relation to sports, I have never felt competitive with anyone. And I have never been able to formulate a life goal that involved "winning," or "success." My single abiding goal has always been to find challenge and pleasure in doing the task at hand and to enjoy it to its fullest. From my maternal uncles, I learned that even filthy, odious jobs can be the bases of pride, co-worker camaraderie, and funny, sometimes hilarious, stories to tell.

Whatever the task, I have always tried to do my best, never measuring my performance against someone else's. I now know that this is a cliché of aphoristic sports advice: "It's not whether you win or lose, it's how you play the game," and all that. This was not some maxim imposed from without, it is the way I am wired.

In my late teens, when I took up mountaineering and auto racing, for me it was all process, not the competition. There are two modal personality types on most racetracks. Senseless hotheads who often trust their fate to luck. And those who regard their craft as a complex set of skills that require constant attention and honing. More like professional golfers than human cannonballs. My heroes and mentors were exclusively the golfer type. My sporting desires, even the ones I seriously pursued, never involved fantasies of winning or summiting at any cost.

That concludes the larger themes of my childhood and youth. I will now get back to the business of growing up.

6

Years Six to Nine— American Lake South Projects

AFTER HIS "RETURN FROM THE WAR" in the winter of 1945-46 and his re-enlistment, my father was sent to Illinois and New York for several months of special training for his role in U.S. occupied, post-war Europe.

My mother honestly told us that she had little maternal feeling for Bill and me and she tried to provide an explanation that fit the times we were living in. She said that mothers who become overly attached to their male children are stupid. "They will just grow up, go to war and get killed. What's the sense of becoming emotionally invested in that?" Her logic was faulty. Somehow, "You will just go to war and get killed" did not fit with her, "If you can't support yourself at age 18, you can always join the military." Really? Even at the time, I thought that the true motive for her flat affect toward us must lay elsewhere. My father and all five of my uncles had gone to war, and all six of them returned without a scratch or bruise. A normal mother would at least hope that her male child might make it through a war unharmed. Why the fantasy about my certain death in war combined with her casual advice that I should join the military? I found it appalling even at age six.

My brother John is Born
While my father was away getting his special training, John Scott MacCannell entered this world on February 28, 1946. Five days later, Winston Churchill delivered his "Iron Curtain is descending across Europe" speech. It was a bleak time. The United States government was busy evacuating the people from around Bikini atoll in preparation for the first peacetime test of a sec-

ond generation of nuclear bombs. My Grandma Fran was away visiting her sister, Echo, in Detroit. While my mother was in the hospital, Bill and I had to stay with Ross. There was no one else around to look after us. Ross took his child-minding duties very seriously. He kept a pot of cow brains boiling on the stove to feed us. And to keep us busy he had us sweep the carpet in the living room on our hands and knees using whisk brooms and dust pans. When we finished sweeping the entire carpet, he made us go back to the beginning and start over again. We drank brain soup and swept the carpet for three days until my mother showed up in a taxi with our new baby brother.

My parents framed John's birth as something miraculous for the entire family. Even before he was born my mother regaled Bill and me with accounts of what a wonderful human being she was carrying in her womb. This baby, she told us, would be the one who would realize the promise of our family. This baby would be worth the drudgery of raising a child. "I'll be breast feeding this one. He'll be worth it. She pointedly added, "Unlike the two of you." And she did breastfeed him.

Since I was always on the lookout for something to be happy about, I got on board with the

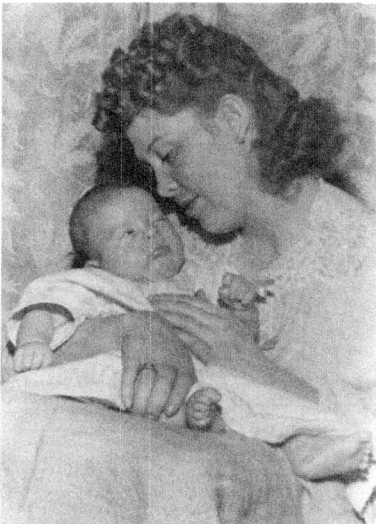

Mother and child—John Scott MacCannell, b. February 1946

John breastfeeding

idea of having a miraculous brother. This is fabulous, I thought. I have a magical baby brother. I'll teach him everything I know right away and then step back and take my place among his multitude of admirers. I'm not kidding. My mother's enthusiasm was completely infectious. She promoted his every gurgle as "way above average." Her only disappointment was that he was a boy child. She wanted her brilliant baby to be a girl that she could make into a clone of herself. She actually pretended he was a girl and presented him as a girl when they were around strangers. She was delighted when her ruse worked and he "passed." This lasted for about 18-20 months. Then she shifted gears and genders and began raising him as a boy to become a "real man."

My parents were not wrong about John. He is very smart. As soon as he could talk, he could count beyond 100 and quickly mastered simple arithmetic. From when he was two years old, I could amuse and astound strangers by inviting them to ask him to calculate simple sums and subtraction like "What is 27 minus 9." When he gave the correct answer, they would accuse me of having coached him. So I

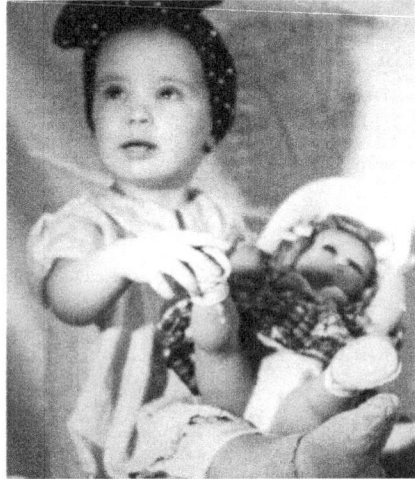

Until John was almost two years old my mother dressed him as a girl and presented him as a girl when they went out in public together. She made many girl outfits for him and gave him dolls to play with.

would invite them to make up their own problems. More often than not, he could supply the correct answer in a flash.

John was also physically agile as an infant and, unlike me, completely trusting of our mother. He liked to be tossed around and cuddled. His every developmental milestone came early was something more my mother could crow about.

He walked, talked, drank from a cup unassisted, etc., "way before the average child." Bill and I were right in there with her cheering him on. The drama of his arrival and his manifest precocity actually did bring us some relief from our squalid day-to-day existence. And in fairness to my mother and father, I must also report that their open favoring of John did not result in him receiving larger food portions or better clothing than Bill or me. Except for the baby girl outfits, materially, we were treated equally. I thank them for that.

I do not think John was ever included in "*18 and out.*" Certainly not as he entered his teens. I have correspondence between my divorced mother and father when John was in high school discussing which university to send him to and how to share the costs of his education. In one letter my father strongly advocates for them to share the expenses of giving him a car for when he was "away at college." All plans that were unthinkable for Bill or me.

John demonstrated his precocity by managing to do "*18 and out*" in style. When he was 17, he got my parents' permission to emancipate himself from them, drop out of high school, and join the United States Air Force with the US government acting in loco parentis. I suspect he knew the government would do a better job than our parents of finishing his upbringing. John repaid the Air Force by serving as ground support in Vietnam and sticking it out below officer grade until his retirement. The U.S. Military was lucky to get 30 years of loyal service in enlisted men's ranks from someone as brilliant as John.

Bill fulfilled his "*18 and out*" destiny by going into the Air Force at age 18 without requiring parental release. But he did not make a career of it. Before completing his four-year tour of duty, he was honorably discharged for having an "attitude problem."

Shortly after my sixteenth birthday, I extracted myself from my parental household, but staying true to my pacifist side I avoided military service. All three of us dutifully managed "*18 and out*" on or before our eighteenth birthdays without further burdening our parents; to his credit, even John who did not need to. From our mid-teens, I don't think any of us wanted to be around my parents for even another day.

Mrs. Weatherby's first grade class at American Lake South School on the Fort Lewis Army Base, 1946-47. I'm the serious one on the left end of the middle row.

My Wonderful Military Base Grade School

In late summer of 1946, my father returned to Europe and my mother informed me about "*18 and out*." In the fall, I began first grade at American Lake South grade school at Fort Lewis. My first-grade teacher, Mrs. Weatherby, was a gem. She saw immediately that I arrived with a complete grasp of the reading skills she would be teaching over the course of the year. Every morning after explaining what we would be learning that day and carefully determining that I already knew it, she would lift me by my armpits onto a high shelf at the back of the room where I sat while she taught the rest of the class. My shelf was strewn with story books and some non-fiction. I was particularly drawn to *The Legend of Coal* which caused me to work out by inference what a "legend" was. Only later did I realize that the shelf I perched on was my grade school's "library." Mrs. Weatherby kindly let me read quietly to myself while she taught the other students the sounds of the letters and how to put them together. I did not encounter a teacher who hated me until fourth grade.

Our "Hunger Games"

In my father's one letter to me in the three plus years he was away he says the Italian children "Have no clothes and are always hungry." I could relate to that. While he was passing out American tax dollars to quell communism in immediate postwar Italy, our entire household income back in American Lake Gardens was from "allotment checks." I do not know the amount of the allotment checks but it must have been paltry. My mother had no expensive habits and except for the *World Book Encyclopedia*, no revolving credit bills to pay, but there was never enough food. Breakfast, seven days a week, was a bowl of oatmeal mush with two tablespoons of sugar and a dollop of canned condensed milk on top. Lunch was Campbell's soup served with two saltine crackers. The soup was almost always tomato, made with water, not milk. One can divided among the three, and eventually, when John was old enough, the four of us. She made casseroles for dinner. The only recipe I recall was macaroni with an undiluted can of Campbell's cream of mushroom soup plopped over the top and heated in the oven. The rare bologna sandwich on Wonder Bread with salad dressing was highly regarded by my brother Bill and me as a gourmet treat. She would occasionally "splurge" on a jar of peanut butter. "Salad Dressing" was always called "mayonnaise" by my mother. I did not know the difference until I was a teenager and made some embarrassing shopping mistakes when I began dating girls who did (know the difference). In the winter she made us "ice cream" by putting a cap-full of vanilla extract and some food coloring in sugar water and pouring it over a bowl of snow. We didn't get this treat often as snow in

H. F. MacCannell in 1947. She made it to 185 pounds before starting to lose the weight and get back to the size she was before my father left for Europe. Her timing was perfect.

She weighed 135 pounds, almost her weight on his departure, when he came home in the spring of 1949.

winter was rare in Western Washington. Even if we might have afforded it, real ice cream was out of the question because an ice box never got cold enough to keep it frozen.

While our child's portions were meager, within a few months after my father's departure, my mother gained 50 pounds. I have been told that there is a Swedish word, "snorping," meaning the practice of some housewives to indulge themselves generously from the family larder between meals when no one is watching. I suspect my mother may have been doing some serious snorping after my father left for Europe. It would be surprising under the circumstances if she had not sought some alternate pleasures. We all knew he was having the time of his life. Nervous sneaky eating was probably her only comfort during his absence.

The allotment checks were mailed monthly from Washington, D. C. I knew this because in the winter heavy snows in the Midwest sometimes stopped the mail train and the checks would be a week or two late. During these distant disruptive weather events my mother and the other women in our row house would put all their canned food together and cook collective meals. They listened anxiously to the weather reports from the Midwest and tried to divide and ration the food so it would last until the trains broke through. Once a three-year-old next-door neighbor named George (nicknamed "Hotshot") got into the collective food stash and peeled the paper labels off every can. For several days each meal consisted of opening three or four anonymous cans at random and eating whatever strange combinations came out—like asparagus and peaches in syrup. Hotshot also once helped with the cooking by "salting" a collective stew with a can of powdered soap. The women intervened quickly skimming the soap off the top of the stew. Not eating the slightly soap flavored stew was not an option. We all had diarrhea for a week. Our affliction had a name, the "G. I. scours," something entire divisions of soldiers got when the cooking utensils in the mess hall were insufficiently rinsed after washing.

Everyday Life in the Immediate Post-war Projects

At American Lake, every one of the hundreds of "barracks style" single story, multi-family row houses was identical to every other. Our two-bedroom unit was identical to the four other units in the row house we occupied at 3, Fir Place. Each unit measured 400 square feet comprising two 10'x 10' bedrooms, a bathroom with a toilet, sink and small shower stall, and a kitchen-dining-living area. A cast iron, coal burning stove provided both cooking and heat. Food preparation, eating, and all other activities were in a single room large enough to accommodate the stove, a sink and counter, some shelving, and a table and chairs. I do not remember feeling cramped. It was all the space the four of us needed to do everything we needed to do.

Across the road from our unit was a grassy area, about an acre with a dozen or so cedar, fir, and pine trees. There were no sandboxes or swings, but it was a great play space if you made up fanciful stories about where you were and what you were doing. The project grocery store, laundry, and post office were visible from our front steps and my grade school was only a few hundred yards away. The other children ate lunch in the school cafeteria, but I was able to walk home for lunch. My mother always had a bowl of soup on the table and was delighted that we lived close enough for her to save the 25 cents lunch charge. We made friends with the other women and children in nearby units and visited with our close neighbors every day. It was more like one giant house than a series of separate living units. I was quite content with the entire set-up. The people seemed nice enough. There were interesting woods and ponds to explore nearby. I entered first grade and loved going to school.

My mother never considered taking a job while my father was away. In general, she was opposed to the idea that a married woman should have to work at a job outside the home. Her definition of this period of our lives was we were on hold, waiting for my father to come home. The idea that we might use the time to accomplish anything beyond living hand to mouth, day-to-day never entered her mind.

Coal was a robust industry. It was used in coal-fired power plants as it is today. But mainly almost every household in America was heated with coal. They could not get it out of the ground fast enough. It was then considered to be a modern advance over the alternative—wood that had to be sawed and chopped before it was burnt. With coal, you just threw another lump into the fire. If the lump was too big, you could drop it on the sidewalk and it would break. The 5'x5'x5' coal bin in the yard was ubiquitous, as was the coal scuttle beside the stove. Deliveries to fill the bin were once a week in winter and once a month in summer.

From age four it was my chore to watch the coal scuttle, take it out to the bin before it emptied, refill it, and bring it back to the kitchen. I looked forward to the day when I would be big enough to carry a full scuttle so I wouldn't have to make so many trips. Coal was filthy. Our local county museum had a dead coal miner's diseased "black lung" on display in a large jar of formaldehyde to remind us of the sacrifices the miners made to keep us fed and warm. The "black lung" (it was actually black) was displayed next to a pink "healthy" lung in its own jar of formaldehyde. As a preschooler I wondered if my coal duty might give me black lung.

Refrigeration was via an "ice box" built into the wall next to the kitchen sink. A one cubic foot block of ice was delivered directly into the ice box weekly through a small door in the outside wall of our unit. As he opened the outer door and inserted the ice block, my mother sometimes opened the inner door and chatted with the iceman through the wall.

During my childhood and youth, every project I lived in had identical row houses, with identical living units. Four different housing projects each administered by different agencies but with zero variation in unit size or floor plan and the same patterns of coal and ice delivery. We moved three times between 1949 and 1952, but I did enjoy a strange continuity. The bedrooms, bathrooms, kitchens, back porches, etc., were always the same size and in the same arrangement.

The outer walls of the houses were covered with sand-impregnated tarpaper much like roofing material still in use today. Our house at American Lake was an insipid cocoa brown color. In subsequent projects our houses were beige and faded green tarpaper. It was possible to hear normal volume conversations through both interior and exterior walls. The left end apartments were considered best. At American Lake they were occupied by the wives and children of enlisted men of higher rank—

sergeants, not privates. The left end apartment bedrooms had an outer wall, not a common wall with an adjacent apartment. This was a sensitive matter in WW II military base housing because every apartment was occupied by the same type of household—a married woman and her children, if she had children, temporarily separated from her husband who was fighting in the war. Any use of a bedroom for other than sleeping could not be hidden and was noted and broadcast throughout the entire project.

My father went into the army as a private, so we were in a middle unit. Even though he eventually rose through the ranks to "Tech Sergeant", we stayed in the same middle unit with common walls on both sides.

His return from the European theater after VE Day was for a brief "family leave"--less than a month. He took us on a camping trip—the one in the borrowed Model A with sticking lug nuts. The one where John was conceived. And he informed us that he had volunteered for an extra tour of duty with the U.S. occupation forces in Europe.

For the three and one-half years after his second deployment, I lived in what is now called a "single parent household." My mother constantly reminded us that our family was intact. My father was away on government business and would return in a few years and we would all be happily together again. That is when our life would begin again. Once each year he sent us a box of gifts—Italian coloring books, a toy car, scarves for my mother, figurines. My mother made Bill and me write him thank you notes and occasionally other letters.

While my father was away, my mother received no nighttime visits from the iceman, the coal man, or any other man. Her fidelity, remarkable under any circumstance, was even more so given that she received letters in broken English from several of my father's Italian girlfriends pleading with her to let him go so they could marry him. She remained faithful during his prolonged absence, but an inexorable pressure was building. My father's philandering was taking its psychic toll.

Corporal Punishment in My Household

From 1946-49, my mother was our only disciplinarian. There was almost no sibling fighting in our household and very few verbal disagreements, certainly no tantrums were tolerated. When John had a tantrum, she put him in the yard in his high-chair and told him to scream as loud and as long as he wanted. "Louder," she would yell. "The neighbors three blocks away can't hear you." When Bill threatened to "run away from home" she grabbed him by his collar, dragged him to the porch, put him out and locked the door. When he knocked to come back in, she told him, "Go, run away, get out of here." He sobbed quietly and never left the porch. "That'll teach him," she said before opening the door and letting him back in after about an hour and a half, well after dark. I was a complacent and obedient child. I disagreed with my parents often, perhaps even always, but I held my tongue.

She prided herself in being a liberal about corporal punishment. Anything Bill or I did wrong would immediately be met with a bare-bottom spanking with a razor strop. Every time she hit one of us, she would repeat, "I'll not hurt my hand punishing you for something you did." She told the wrong-doer, "Go get the strop, drop your drawers and bend over." She would deliver one or two strong whacks with the strop to our naked bottoms, occasionally citing Pavlov as the reason it had to be done on the spot, even if in front of guests or neighbors. How was this liberal? She told us that, as a child she and her brothers were disciplined with a riding quirt that left lasting welts even when administered through their clothing. Her method was "modern and humane." I cannot remember ever doing anything that caused me to be beat with the strop. The threat, and the embarrassment of having to fetch it and expose my bare butt was deterrent enough. That was probably the point. While I suspect I may have gotten a few, I do not recall any beatings.

While I don't remember being beaten myself, sadly I vividly remember watching helplessly through several beatings of my brother Bill. For the most part, these were perfunctory, one or two hard whacks, administered as neutral justice. On one occasion, however, something having to do with him making a mess with bubble gum, she beat him harshly and at length causing him a great deal of pain. Then after the beating she proceeded to use cleaning fluid to get the gum off his face. He became almost uncontrollably terrified. It was evident to me that the reason the beating went on for too long followed by the use of a volatile sub-stance on his face, was not the severity of his crime. It was be-cause she was enjoying it. A large measure of any future respect that I might have had for her was lost in that moment when I saw she was getting pleasure from my brother's pitiful cries.

What it Takes to be 'Somebody'

It was probably a good thing that no matter what our ac-tual situation, my mother always thought she "was somebody." From my earliest childhood, I understood that "being a some-body" did not mean you were incapable of needless cruelty; it did not mean you had enough to feed your children; or warm clothes for the winter; or a house or a car or a telephone; or even a mod-icum of human kindness. From my mother's example, I knew that someone with none of these things or qualities could still be a "somebody." Unfortunately, I deduced from closely observing my mother that possession of these qualities and things (kind-ness, etc.) probably disqualified you from being "somebody."

Yet another positive lesson came crawling out of the fis-sures in my parents' character. From that point forward I could not stop myself from thinking that anyone harboring the belief that they "are somebody" must be a world-class asshole.

At that age, indeed throughout my childhood and youth, I had little sense of differences in material well-being. The condi-tions I am describing seem harsh to me now, but at the time it was just life. Hunger was a simple fact of life that was not expe-rienced as deprivation. It was merely an ongoing bellyache that you got used to. I was mainly happy with the world I knew. There were woods nearby that I could explore on my own, wild black-berries to be picked and eaten on the spot in the summers, and a seemingly endless supply of empty wooden apple crates scattered around the neighborhood. These crates were big enough to sit inside and could be used like giant blocks to assemble anything we imagined—full-sized forts, airplanes, race cars. I looked forward all year to Thanksgiving at my paternal grandparents' where I could eat my fill and go back for more.

"Yo Ho Ho, I'm a Big Ape"

Sometimes, I was even exuberant. On one memorable occasion, my mother, working in the kitchen, heard me holler at the top of my lungs, "Yo, ho, ho. I'm a big ape." Immediately followed by a horrendous boom that shook the entire house. Immediately followed by what sounded like a car crash. She rushed to the boys' bedroom where the noises were coming from.

In the bedroom, between the bunk-bed Bill and I shared and John's army cot was a decommissioned ice box. It had come from a previous house and was not needed at American Lake where the iceboxes were built into the wall. We were using it as a chest of drawers for clothing, bedding, etc. I had climbed from my upper bunk onto the top of the ice box and mimed a prowling animal, crouching and growling to entertain my brothers. They rewarded my performance with smiles and giggles, so I decided to take it up a notch.

After shouting "Yo, ho, ho. I'm a big ape," I launched myself with a mighty leap as if to capture fleeing prey mid-air. My plan was to land on John's cot. My error was in failing to note that I was only inches from the ceiling when I launched myself as hard and as far as I could. The force of my leap was so great that my head almost went through the ceiling causing a boom and a shudder that shook the two adjoining units. And instead of a gentle arc down to John's cot, I bounced violently off the ceiling straight down to the cot, hitting it with sufficient force to destroy it. All four legs broke off and the frame and mattress crashed to the floor. I was dazed but unhurt. Probably the cot's collapse let me down easily enough to prevent injury.

As soon as it was evident that none of us were hurt, everyone thought it was pretty funny. Ever after that, a quietly muttered "Yo, ho, ho. I'm a big ape" became a family catchphrase for any plan that had not been well thought through. Sometimes all that was needed was "Yo, ho, ho . . ." to mark something as really stupid.

I Endure a Biblical Scourge of Boils

During our first year in base housing, I became covered in boils. Not all at once, just one or two at a time in overlapping succession without relief for about a year and a half. If I could not "bring the boils to a head" by poking at them with a sharp stick, I was taken to Madigan General Hospital to have them "lanced and drained." I still bear the scars on my hands and legs. The only other marks I have from my impoverished childhood are crooked toes and crooked teeth. My crooked teeth are a genetic, northern European trait. There was never a word about correction. Orthodontia would have been regarded by my parents as something akin to buying a new Rolls Royce. Not even remotely possible and even if possible, certainly not something to spend good money on. My bent over toes resulted from waiting too long between shoe purchases as my feet grew.

The largest hospital in the world at the time, Madigan General at Fort Lewis, not far from American Lake Gardens, had beds for over 7,000 wounded soldiers in an enormous 250 building complex connected by miles of corridors. The good doctors at Madigan treated my infections with sulfa drugs because all penicillin went to the war wounded. My boils were likely caused by malnutrition, but my mother decided that they had been caused by the sulfa drugs the doctors were using to treat them. When a new boil appeared she said, "It's because you are allergic to the sulfa drugs they used to treat the last one." For many years I wrote "sulfa drug allergy" on medical questionnaires even though I was not at all certain that this was true. I now know that I have no allergy to sulfa drugs. With this single exception my mother said there is no such thing as an "allergy." She said anyone claiming to have allergies is just malingering.

Just as my father left to fight the Cold War, the other WW II draftees who were not killed in action came home to American Lake Gardens and moved their wives and children out, taking them away to the baby booming, suburb developing, immediate post-war situations that shaped the second half of the 20th century in the United States. We did not move to the suburbs and start having babies. All the off-spring my parents would have were already born or on the way. When World War II ended, nothing changed for me and my mother and brothers except our project slowly re-filled with "career military," mainly from southern states, and their German war brides.

My mother finessed my father's post-war, extended absence by explaining to me that the "real war" against communism was just beginning.

Poverty in the 1940s

We were not the poorest of the poor. We always had a housing project roof over our heads. The projects of that era accommodated everyone at prices anyone could afford. There were a few homeless, but no "homeless phenomenon." If my family was positioned in today's economy where we were in the 1940s, we would certainly be among the homeless.

There were skid rows in every city where the "bums" would sleep in single room occupancy hotels for 25 cents a night. I knew quite a bit about skid row life from my Grandma Fran's younger brother, my Great Uncle Forrest Mathews.

He was a colorful drunk who showed up on our doorstep several times during my childhood. "I've been in every state in the union, mostly in the state of inebriation," he would bellow. From him I learned that if anyone slept outside it was only because they were too drunk to make it to a flop house room. He took care to prepare me for a life on the road in case his lot ever befell me. From him I learned if I drank a popular heating fuel, "Sterno," to get high, I would go blind unless I first strained it through stale bread. From the color of the fuel, the resulting "safe" drink was called a "Pink Lady." The "hobo jungles" were for people in transit on the road, hitchhiking or riding the rails. They were not permanent residences.

When Forrest wore out his welcome, usually after no more than three or four days, Eddie was told to drive him out of town and drop him off beside the road. I accompanied Eddie on several of these missions and helped him pull our dead-drunk uncle's limp body out of the back seat of the car. We would find a sunny spot with soft grass to put him on to "sleep it off." Then jump back in the car to make our get-away before he stirred.

Uncle Forrest "went cold-turkey without the help of God" when he was in his 50s and married a "rich widow woman" (he pronounced it "widder") and moved into her beautiful home in

Pasadena where, as a teen, I visited him often. After he sobered up, the only lingering effect of his lifelong drunk was he could never sleep for more than an hour or two at a time. He spent his nights delivering coffee and donuts and chatting up the crews who worked through the nights in factories, offices and police and fire stations in the greater Los Angeles area. He spent his days pier fishing.

My Father's Cold War Duties and his

Famous Warning Letter

Earle Hector MacCannell was one of the very first volunteers in the U.S. war against communism. Perhaps he should be recognized as a Cold War hero. The post war Occupation Forces work he did in Rome, Florence, Frankfurt and Livorno required him to wear civilian clothes. He put on his uniform only when travelling outside his administrative district. His job in Italy involved distributing cash payments to men he recruited to beat up people attending Communist Party rallies. When I asked him what he did during the war, he explained it to me this way, "I never tried to harass or shut down the speakers. I instructed the 'anti-communist volunteers' to attack people around the fringes of the rallies, targeting especially those who appeared to be only half-interested in what was being said. Rally attendees quickly realized it might be dangerous to show even small interest, or even just to be standing around nearby, and they would start to drift away. If we had attacked the speakers directly it could have underscored the importance of what they were saying, and the crowd might have turned on us. It was much better if it looked like the audience was just losing interest." The one letter he sent me from Europe describes his mission—though not the "beating up" part.

My mother gave my father's letter to the *Tacoma Tribune*. I suspect this was their intent all along. *The Tribune* editor published the entire letter above the headline on the front page, Monday April 5, 1948. Here is about one fifth of it. The ellipses mark my removal of condescending repetition seemingly intended to make certain I, and every other average person, would understand him. The editor provided the following headline:

Tacoma Tribune front page

"WARNING BEWARE THE COMMUNISTS

Every Adult and Child Should Read this Unusual Letter From an American Soldier in Italy to His Son in Tacoma"

"Dear Deanie:

Italy is very pretty and the weather is almost always nice, but the people are not very happy. [. . .].

If you could see these people you would know what happens to people who can't think.

[. . .] They must decide if they are going to follow Russia as a communist government, or if they will try to govern themselves as we do in America [. . .] .

The children have no clothes and are very hungry.

The communist leaders are telling the Italian people that if they vote for the communists, the government will make everyone work and the money will be taken away from the rich people and given to the poor people.

They do not tell the people that in order to have the government do that, all the people will have to be slaves and do exactly what the government and Mr. Stalin tells them to do.[. . . .]

They were like little children under Mussolini and couldn't do anything unless he told them it was all right.

The children and even the grownups steal whenever they get a chance and stand on the street and beg. [. . .]

The Russian government is making sure that the communist party makes the loudest speeches and biggest signs and many people will vote for the communists because of that. [. . .]

Last Sunday a big crowd of women, more than one thousand of them, came to Rome from all over Italy to demonstrate for "Peace."

They were organized by the communists and made a big parade, singing "Lay That Pistol Down" and carrying pictures of doves and signs that read: "We Want Peace," and "Vote for the Popular Democratic Party."

The popular Democratic Party is the communist party in Italy.

They didn't say how electing the communists would bring "Peace," but a lot of the people say they will vote for the communists in order to have peace, because of the demonstration.

You see, they don't think at all. [. . .]

The Christian Democratic Party has a much better argument.

They say: "We want a government in Italy like the government in America which is sending us food and clothes and money, and which makes people like those who sent us the Friendship Train.

Of course all Americans hope the communists will not win the election.

Watch the newspapers on the 18th of April and see who finally wins this big contest that will have so much to do with how big Russia will be able to grow.

Maybe you will like to show these propaganda papers to the boys and girls in school. I know they would like to know what is going on over here in Italy . . .

Goodbye for now, Deanie. DADDY."

The "propaganda papers" were Communist party leaflets handed out at the demonstration that he included, with "his" translations—I do not think he ever really learned Italian. In one of his rare moments of honesty, he did not sign it "Love, Daddy."

I won't go into detail about how repugnant I found this letter, then and now, beyond noting that I always hated being called "Deanie" even as a very young child. Both my mother and my father insisted on calling me "Deanie." Fortunately it did not stick with my other relatives who must have sensed my objection. His addressing me this way guaranteed that I would reject everything else in the letter. Oh, and the Christian Democrats (my father's side) won that election even though, or perhaps because, they "couldn't think."

For the most part I shrugged off the letter and its publication. A few weeks later, on my eighth birthday, my Grandma Fran gave me a plastic flashlight with rubber gaskets that "would work under water." I never used it under water, but I thought it was so cool that I could if I had to. I was soon back to drawing and finding fun wherever I could. Meager resources and strange parents never limited my ability to find and improvise interesting things to play with, including, once, a dead dog.

Medical Care for "People Like Us"

In the 1940s, for almost everyone I knew, and especially for my maternal relatives, medical care involved simply not acknowledging illness—i.e., riding everything out with home remedies until death. Medical care was DIY. During the course of his life, Ross Meskimen self-amputated one thumb and part or all of two additional fingers, finishing partial amputations that were initiated by getting his hands mangled in machinery. When I asked him about his missing fingers, Ross coolly explained to me that a sharp knife is best if you have one handy, but he had to remove his thumb with an ax. He told me the cutting wasn't painful. The only really painful part was cauterizing the bleeding stumps with a red-hot iron.

Doc and Eddie separately told me slightly different versions of an incident on a camping trip in their teen years. A large red ant had crawled into Eddie's penis, bitten him an inch or so inside the urethra and caused swelling that made it impossible for the ant to back out. Doc used sterilized needles to extract the ant bit-by-bit without causing his brother further injury or infection. This incident was the origin of his nickname, "Doc." They both seemed to think it was important for me to know the procedure should I ever have occasion to need or perform it. So far, such an occasion has not presented itself. Knock wood. Eddie told me that if I was ever shot or stabbed, I should force my thumb into the hole as far as it would go to staunch the bleeding while I went for help.

This general medical situation for "people like us" carried through at least until the 1970s when I could no longer technically count myself as among "people like us." The last conversation I had with Doc's son, my cousin Jimmy, ended abruptly when he said he needed to excuse himself to "take care of something." He had become engrossed in our talk and had forgotten an obligation. He looked ashen. I asked him if everything was OK? He told me that a friend of his had "gotten the diagnosis." He did not have to say it was terminal cancer. He explained that his friend was uninsured and was not going to put his family through the disease. He asked Jimmy to come over that afternoon and find his body after he'd killed himself. He didn't want one of his children to find him "like that." I offered to go with him to the death house. Jimmy refused saying, "You ain't needin' to be seein' that neither."

My mother took these pictures of me with my brothers a day after one of my hospitalizations at Madigan General in 1947. Grandma Fran knitted the caps Bill and I are wearing. She had a contraption for making pompoms.

I had several serious illnesses while my father was away, but I was lucky. As a dependent child of an active service member I could access the services of Madigan General. In spite of my uncle Ed's warnings, my access as a civilian to free military medical care was a life saver. Not just for my scourge of boils. While my father was away, I had my tonsils taken out at Madigan, and also a two-month hospitalization in isolation with scarlet fever.

After my tonsillectomy I spent two days recovering in a 30-bed burn treatment unit filled with Army flier plane crash survivors from the Pacific theater. The men were solicitously concerned about the effect their appearance might have on a six-year-old child. They gathered around to tell me stories and make jokes about their burnt flesh and the ways their broken skulls and limbs were pinned and wired together "like Frankenstein Monsters." Or how they could "play a mean hand" of poker with only one hand. (Which, I observed, was actually quite difficult even if the cards were dealt with their bottom edge hanging slightly over the side of the table. Go ahead and try it. It involves contorting your good arm and torso.)

One man's face, lips and nose, had been burned and ripped off when an explosion blew him out through the side of his bomber. He had a special hood over the head of his bed so he could sleep in the daytime without eyelids. I peeked under and saw him staring fixedly even though he was sound asleep. In the burn ward I learned that some members of "The Greatest Generation" actually were great.

It is probable that Madigan General did not have pediatric dental care. My first visit to a dentist came when I was nine years old. It was for two emergency extractions of teeth that had become decayed beyond repair. After that, had no routine dental care until I could afford to pay for it myself. My two or three trips to a dentist before I became economically self-sufficient were because the pain had become unbearable.

My Early Religious Instruction

During my summers with her, Emily Amelia made sure I had strong biblical instruction. She insisted that we begin at the beginning with Genesis. So off we went through Adam and Eve, Cain and Abel, Moses, Abraham, Sarah, Joshua, Lot, Noah, Samson and Delilah. We read ten or so pages every night before going to bed. We began with her reciting the next passage from memory. I read along silently while she spoke the words. There were long tracts that she had committed to memory, word-for-word. She insisted that I stop and correct her if she deviated from the text. Or she would offer a summary and tell me to take over reading because she had gotten to a stretch she could not recall perfectly. She knew every syllable of King James' Samson, Daniel, David and Joshua. We never made it to Matthew, Mark, Luke, and John. Even though she was a good Christian, she somehow caused my early religious instruction to be entirely Jewish.

Even so, there was more than enough Christianity to go around. Public projects in the 1940s were ground zero for evangelical, street corner preachers. They could always get a good audience of kids who had nothing more entertaining to watch than a semi-shaven guy waving his arms, thrusting the bible at us, and ranting about Jesus for an hour or so. Our mothers were happy not to have to watch us while we were in the thrall of one of these half-crazy dudes. They must have been highly dedicated to their calling as there was no money to be had for their efforts to save our young souls. If they had thirty kids gathered around I doubt they saw more than 25 cents for an hour's worth of hortatory. Most of them who came to preach in the projects were as skinny and ragged as we were. One of them made us memorize

John 3:16, and it stuck with me even though I have never understood the appeal of everlasting life, perhaps because I've never
understood it. At the time I thought it must be for those who are
not satisfied with the life they had.

One of the crazy Evangelicals tried to give me a lesson in
anti-Semitism. He began by asserting that the Jews were the
most evil people on earth. Why? Because Jesus was a Jew. He
was born one of them. But they refused to take him into their
hearts as their Lord and Savior. He went on to tell the project
kids what it would be like for us to be treated the way the Jews
treated Jesus. He said, "Imagine you come home from school one
day and go up to your door and find it locked. And you knock
but nobody comes to open it. So you go out in the yard and look
through the windows and you see your mother and father inside,
and your brothers and sisters. And they are looking out at you
and laughing at you and telling you to 'Go away. You're not one of
us anymore.' How would you feel if that happened to you? Well,
that is exactly what the Jews did to Jesus."

The lesson did not take. At least for me it did not. I recalled
that my parents had already given me notice that on my eighteenth
birthday I'd be locked out. My brothers would still be inside observing my plight pretty much the way the preacher described
it. If they locked me out before I turned 18 I thought, 'I'd just
go live with one of my grandparents or my Uncle Ed.
No problem.'

Or, most probably, I would go live with my great grandmother who never took me beyond the Jewish part of the Bible.
It would have been a better life for me.

Extended Family Involvement in Our Life
While my Father was Away

During the years that my father was in post-war Europe
stemming the tide of communism, Grandma Fran visited us once
or twice every week. She had a broken-down old Oldsmobile car
that she loaded up with the things we needed to "get by." She
supplied our second-hand clothing, used books, soap, and occasional odd-ball objects she picked up at rummage sales. Noting
my interest in the violin, she brought me an out-of-tune zither

or "auto-harp" that I wasn't able to coax even the semblance of a melody out of. She told me it was "okay," she'd only paid a nickel for it anyway.

The route from Fort Lewis to my Grandma Fran's house in Tacoma took us past McCord Army Air Base where we got a good look at the runways through the cyclone fencing. I witnessed the transition from fighters and bombers that had tail wheels to the new kind that had nose wheels. The attitude of the two types of planes, at rest and taking off and landing, was dramatically different. The old style looked like they were dragging their rear ends. The new planes with nose wheels looked confident and proud compared. In 1948, I also saw the first jet aircraft at McCord. They were incredibly loud and so fast. It was one of those moments. I immediately knew that the next half of the 20th century would be as different from the first half as the first half was from the 19th century horse and buggy world of my great grandmother.

My maternal grandparents did not have any extra beds so I slept in the bathtub when we visited. I kept the covers over my head and managed not to be too bothered by nocturnal company who came to use the only toilet in the house. That toilet was an early design with the water tank located up near the ceiling and a pull chain hanging down to operate the flush. It was a loud contraption. Ross called it "The Growler." It wasn't his special name for his toilet. He called all indoor toilets "growlers." Sleeping in the tub, I worried that some adult needing a bath might stumble in and turn the water on without noticing me. Since my habit of mind is always to imagine the worst-case scenario, I was not completely sure I would wake up before I drowned.

It was during these visits that I got to hang out with my Grandpa Ross. In addition to taking me with him to the Boilermaker's Union Hall, he made sure we would walk to town if there was something interesting to see. A man shot two very large cougars just outside the city and they were put on display at a sporting goods store. Of course, we walked downtown to see that. The main way I passed the time at his house was reading his vast collection of *National Geographic* magazines. I think he must have subscribed continuously from Vol. 1 No. 1. Like the *World*

Book Encyclopedia, National Geographic exposed me to people and places beyond imagination and wonder. Of course I wanted to visit every place the magazine featured to see it for myself. I can still remember my favorite articles: "The Stone Money of Yap," "The Whistle Languages of the Congo Jungle," "The Valley of 1000 Smokes," etcetera.

On one of these visits Ross gave me a large and powerful horseshoe magnet off his work bench. "You can have it." "To keep?" I asked. "To keep," he answered. I couldn't believe my luck. I was overjoyed. Kids love magnets. They are our proof that magic is real. I tied it to a piece of twine, attached it to my back belt loop, and dragged it behind me on my peripatetic daily rambles, periodically reeling it in and checking it for whatever ferrous metal objects it picked up as I went. I poured over my collection of nuts, bolts, rusty nails, cotter keys, sparkplugs, can lids, etcetera looking for anything that might prove useful for my next project.

From the example of Ross and my other relatives, I was entering a new phase in my life where I became aware that if I lacked something there was a good chance that I might be able to make it myself. I made myself a bookcase from a wooden apple crate. I built wheeled toys from four can lids, four nails and a block of wood. The random supply of ferrous objects supplied by my towed magnet permitted me to build a series of useless contraptions that looked like they might have some kind of mysterious purpose.

On one of my walks with Ross I asked him what kind of plant eggs grow on. He looked at me with a puzzled expression and asked me what I meant. I told him in all earnestness that I knew apples grow on trees, and blackberries grow on vines, but I had never seen or heard of the plant that eggs grow on. As soon as he knew I was not pulling his leg, he slowly allowed that "Eggs grow on chicken bushes." We both got a giggle out of that. I answered him, "Yes, of course, I knew chickens laid eggs. I just wasn't putting two and two together" at that particular moment. "I'm sorry." He patted me on the head and smiled. Sometimes the best way to learn a lesson is to forget something you know and learn it for a second time. For a moment I forgot that a chicken is an egg's way of making another egg. And that enabled me to learn that my fierce and unforgiving grandfather, my aggressive and character-challenging grandfather, actually had a sweet and gentle place somewhere in his soul. It was small, but there.

It was also on one of these walks that Ross gave me my first lesson in critical theory. We were in downtown Tacoma when the air raid alert sirens were tested, as they were then once a week at noon.

"What's that?" I shouted.

"It's the atomic attack siren test," he answered, or something to that effect. (I remember the word atomic and that he pronounced siren "*sigh-reen.*")

"Why do we need it now that the war is over?" I asked.

"So the people who make sirens will have a market for their product," was his instant reply.

The Cold Warrior Returns

Even though my mother thought we were "on hold," waiting for my father's return, I was delighting in my growing closeness with my larger family. It is probable that because of my father's absence, I benefitted from an extra measure of attention from them. If so, his second deployment to Europe was one of his greatest gifts to me. While he was away, I had a strong sense of gaining valuable competencies—playing the violin, riding the Greyhounds, making my own toys. Getting to know my grandparents, uncles and aunts.

My father's return from Europe had been hyped by my mother as another great moment like the birth of my brother John, a turning point in the history of our family. She told us that our immanent re-unification as a family would bring joy and set us on the path to prosperity. My father would enter the University of Washington on the G.I. Bill. His first field of study was K-12 Education, preparing to obtain a certificate to teach high school. I can only begin to imagine the disaster that would have been.

We had a welcome home party at our house in American Lake Gardens attended by my mother's brothers, Doc and Eddie, and my Grandma Fran. Ross did not come, nor did anyone from my father's side of the family. Everyone at the party acted like it was a happy occasion. They tried to draw me in. I wanted to be happy too. But just beneath the surface, I felt a kind of cold detachment. Not between my parents. They seemed to be delighted to be back in each other's arms again. But my father showed no more interest in Bill and me than we might have received from a stranger we sat next to on a bus. Less interest than I usually received from strangers, actually. We were in the same space together, next to him on the couch. I remember feeling heat from his body and it seemed a little gross to me. That was about it.

A few weeks after his return, school ended and I left to spend the summer with my great grandmother. No one suggested that I might break pattern and stay home that summer to get to know my father better. And I do not recall any conversations or other interactions with him that took place before I left. He made no moves to connect with me. No questions about my likes and dislikes or anything that happened while he was away. No interest in hearing me play the violin. His lack of interest was so rigorous and total that I would have felt awkward telling him anything about my life as it evolved while he was away or asking him about his. School ended and without fanfare I left for Tumwater. Exactly as I had done the previous two years. His coolness did not have any emotional tinges. It did not feel like a failure to connect, or to keep some implied promise to act like a dad, or any kind of betrayal. I did not expect anything different from him. Zero affect between us felt completely natural.

My Arrival at my New Home in the Stewart Heights Project

My family moved out of American Lake Gardens to the massive Stewart Heights Government Housing Project while I was in Tumwater with my great grandmother. Finding my way to my new home at the end of summer meant I had to manage the Greyhound bus from Olympia to Kirkland. The bus passed my old stop at Fort Lewis, stopped briefly in Tacoma, then onto Seattle, the huge city to the north that I had never visited. In the Seattle terminal,

Our unit (1st set of concrete steps with garden hose)—note the coal bins.

I got on a bus that went around Lake Washington to Kirkland where I got off at a newsstand in the middle of the two or three block Kirkland "downtown." From the newsstand I got on a local line to Stewart Heights. All of this had been explained to me in a letter that concluded with instructions on how to thread my way on foot from the last bus stop through the ranks and files of Stewart Heights row houses to my new front door. I was nine. In 1949, nine was almost adulthood. It was a piece of cake.

My thoughts as I walked those last two blocks were full of wonder and anticipation. "So this place that I had never seen or heard of before will be my new home? What's it going to be like living here?" With my father home and in these strange surroundings, clearly a new chapter in my life was beginning.

What can I surmise about my own future observing these strange houses like the ones at American Lake only much longer with more units, and much more decrepit looking. And all the ragged people I saw around me? Who were they? Where did they come from? What would they eventually mean to me? They were much more varied than the military families I was used to.

I was full of hope, but the portents were not good. Shortly after I arrived in my new home, I was informed that Stewart Heights was known as "Stupid Heights on Pregnant Hill."

It is only as I am writing this that it occurs to me as odd that no one came to meet me at the bus. Perhaps it was too hard to coordinate schedules without telephones. But I made it, and a new phase of my life began.

7

Bomb Awareness and Life in the Stewart Heights Projects, 1949

A FEW DAYS after my arrival at Stewart Heights I got up at dawn before my parents and my brothers and drew a portrait of Abraham Lincoln. I used his image on a penny as my model.

My childhood was exactly half over. I was nine years old, half-way to my consequential eighteenth birthday. The 20th century was also a few months away from being half over. The Korean War had just escalated in earnest and a couple of months earlier the Soviet Union detonated its first nuclear bomb. It would be another year before bomb awareness was forced on us via the "duck and cover" drills taught in our grade schools. My classmates and I wondered if we might be blown to bits on our way to school before we could get under our protective desks. I told them not to worry, our desks would not offer any real protection from the awesome power of The Bomb and especially its poisonous radiation. Between the project where I lived and my school there were a number of cyclone fences. Always given to theorizing, I wondered if the radiation from a distant nuclear event might get caught up in and transmitted via the fencing. After forming this idea, even though I knew it was probably baseless, I thought it prudent, in case the bomb should fall, to walk on the opposite side of the street from steel mesh fences.

Korea Loomed Large in my Awareness and Imagination

In the news there was a lot of alarm about "red Chinese gorillas" fighting on the side of North Korea. Every newscaster pronounced guerillas as "gorillas." I had never heard of a guerilla. I closed my eyes and saw bright red apes with machine guns. Because my father had just returned from "the war," before I found out otherwise, Korea seemed a continuation of World War II now with heavily armed, terrifying animal adversaries. I don't know who set me straight, but it clearly did not involve spelling or learning a new term, "guerillas." I thought "gorillas" was just our insulting way of characterizing our new Asian enemies like when my Grandpa Ross called German Nazis "rat bastards." These were gorilla bastards.

When I heard on the radio in 1949 that very few Americans were volunteering to fight communism in Korea, I thought my father might volunteer and go off again. I did not understand his motivation for leaving the army and returning to college. My mother explained that becoming a high school teacher would give him some job security and a way to support the family.

My Father Returns to College to earn a
Secondary School Teaching Credential

Even at age nine I suspected that the real reason was the G.I. Bill made college a free good. I knew my father to be a notorious free-loader. In his entire life, he never reached for the tab in a restaurant and thought he had gotten over on anyone who offered to pay a bill. He bred guppies as a hobby because they are a live birth species and he never had to replace a dead fish by buying a new one. Each pregnancy, he would save a few of the babies from being eaten by the male guppies. So the aquarium was always well-stocked free of charge. I thought he decided to go to college so he would not have to find a job to support us. He bragged that not only did the G.I. Bill pay for tuition, fees and books, it gave him a $120.00 a month stipend as long as he maintained passing grades. Wow. He needn't find a job if we could somehow squeeze by on $120 a month for a family of five. (That's $1,300/month in today's money.) And that is exactly what we did.

Stewart Heights was a sprawling public housing project on a hill behind Kirkland, a few miles from what would much later become the main campus of Microsoft. At that time, every public project in the Pacific Northwest had a distinct reputation. The worst was Shalishan in Tacoma; Stewart Heights in Kirkland was second worst. It was the best we could afford on $120.00 a month.

The Family "Draw a Lincoln" Contest

My Lincoln drawing made an impression on my family at breakfast. They said it looked like I had drawn Lincoln from life, not from a penny. My father studied it closely and declared that we should have a family "Draw a Lincoln" contest. My drawing caused him to want to show off his skills as a portraitist. He was a decent amateur artist, having received instruction and possibly some talent from his father, my grandfather Earle Edgerly Mac-Cannell, who sold scores of paintings during his lifetime and for several years supported himself and his family from his art.

My younger brothers were frustrated to tears by their efforts to produce a likeness of Lincoln. At ages seven and four, they should not have been subjected to a portrait drawing contest. My mother's was almost recognizable as Lincoln but it made him look more like a dissipated homeless person. My father's accurately captured Lincoln's features, but not his spirit. When all of our Lincolns were displayed together, he had to admit that mine was best. To my knowledge, this was the only time in his life that my father ever admitted he had been bested at anything. To hear him tell it (which he did every chance he got) he was the most brilliant student, the bravest soldier, the most accurate shot, the most agile gymnast, fastest typist, deepest diver, etcetera, etcetera, probably who ever lived. But on that fall day in the middle of the 20th century, in the middle of my childhood, he was not the best portraitist.

Even though it was my only Oedipal moment, I took zero pleasure in his self-inflicted humiliation. My drawing was made for the joy of drawing, not as a contest entry, and certainly not as an effort to best my father. His grandmother, my paternal great grandmother, Emily Amelia, remembered when Lincoln was alive and she enjoyed telling me stories about him, especially stories that illuminated his wit and wisdom. Her stories made me realize that all the dead dry leaves of history had once been vibrant and alive for the people living in the moment. Her appreciation of Lincoln connected me to her, and through her to him. My drawing was an image of my feelings of these connections as much as Lincoln's physical profile.

The contest results suggested to me that my generally negative view of my father might not be baseless. Up to that moment, I was never quite certain. He seemed to me to be a talented creep and blowhard. But maybe I was wrong. Still, if he could be bested by a mere nine-year-old, how could he really be the best at everything he ever attempted, as he always claimed? Moreover, it was not some child prodigy who bested him. It was me. An average kid. He did not change his view of me. He said my drawing was a "fluke." A lucky accident. It would never happen again. But the seeds of doubt were sown. Once our Lincoln portraits were displayed in a row, it was possible, just possible, that my view of my father was correct.

Stewart Heights Elementary

Stewart Heights had no surrounding social context. It was out in the woods. I estimate that between three and five thousand other luckless souls lived there at the time we did. Very few of the families owned a car. Kirkland, a mini city with a communist mayor was a 15-minute bus ride away. We had to make do with one another as best we could.

That fall, I entered fourth grade at Stewart Heights Elementary. The wonder and anticipation I felt on entry into a new school, my first school transfer, was overshadowed by a wretched injustice my parents inflicted on my brother Bill. It was as if they were trying to make certain their prejudiced opinion of him settled like a dark cloud over his childhood. He had matriculated first grade at American Lake Elementary with good marks in all subjects. Over a period of several days, they had a prolonged discussion of his "subnormal I.Q." that they did not bother to keep from us children, Bill included. (This was two years before they administered the test that "proved" their negative view of our capabilities.) In the end, they decided to claim he had never gone to first grade. They brashly enrolled him as a beginning student at the new school and made him repeat first grade there. At the time I thought what they did was needless and cruel. Today I think it was worse than cruel. It was actually vicious.

At Stewart Heights Elementary, my teacher, Mrs. Boley, took an immediate dislike to me. It happened so fast, it may have been a case of simple prejudice against redheads. Or the left-handed. She was the only teacher I ever had who tried to make me switch to my right hand and yelled at me for resisting her efforts.

The Halloween Art Contest

The school sponsored a Halloween art contest and gave everyone who wanted to enter a single sheet of over-sized drawing paper. This was a month after my father's "draw a Lincoln portrait" contest. The piece of paper the school gave us was about 14 by 16 inches. It was a fine-grained, heavy rag content piece of snow-white art paper. I had never had such a big, beautiful sheet of paper before and threw myself into the contest with joy and abandon. The grand prize, best in school, was five silver dollars or more than $50 in today's money. The grade winners would receive a dollar each. I made a tableau of elves and fairies living in a corn and pumpkin patch. My pumpkins were carved into apartment houses, and slides and teeter-totters for the children were fashioned from corn stalks and leaves and gardener's hand tools. I outlined my figures with speedball pens and filled them in with watercolors. When the submissions were tacked to the wall in the school auditorium you could see the difference from across the room. Mine was the standout across all the grades.

Mrs. Boley immediately announced to my class that, of course, my entry would be disqualified because I had obviously gotten my father or mother to do the art for me. She supplied motive for my crime, telling the class that my parents would try to cheat because we "needed the money." She went to the principal of the school about the matter. I was called to the principal's office where he informed me of Mrs. Boley's accusation and asked me to state truthfully whether or not it was my work, and if I had help. I told him it was entirely my work and I would gladly sit in his office while he watched and do it again if he would just supply me with another beautiful piece of paper. He believed me without needing a demonstration.

At the assembly, the principal announced my victory with some words about how there was some controversy but he determined to his satisfaction that it was my work. In front of the assembly he called me to the stage and asked me to hold my hand out so he could drop the grand prize plus the class prize, six silver dollars, into my palm. "Clink, clink, clink, clink, clink, clink" reverberated in the auditorium.

My parents insisted that I spend all six dollars on clothing—probably a wise decision—pants, belt, shirt. They let me choose. I bought new grey corduroy pants, a tan belt with cowboy motif tooling, and a beige plaid shirt. Not well coordinated but everything store-bought. Dressing with the best fit from a thrift shop all my life, no one had given me the concept of a well-coordinated outfit.

The Finger-Cutting Gang

The damage done by my teacher's accusation was not erased by the principal finding me "not guilty." On my way home from school the next day I was surrounded in the woods by a gang of fifth and sixth graders who told me I had "robbed them" and they were going to cut off my fingers. "I drew it myself," I protested. They said, "We know. That's why we're going to cut off your fingers. So you can't ever draw again." They produced a folding knife and grabbed my wrist. Had I cheated to win, they would not be threatening to cut off my fingers. In mid-twentieth century, white, sub-proletarian America they would be inviting me to join their gang. Their intent to maim me was their way of acknowledging that I was the artist.

Throughout this encounter, I felt no fear. I could not even begin to imagine that eleven and twelve-year-old boys could muster the stomach or resolve to amputate my fingers. Or even the strength to do it with the kind of dull jack-knife that most twelve-year-old boys carried at the time—that I myself would be carrying in a couple of years. I did not struggle or complain. I just stared at them blankly, unclenched my fist, spread my fingers wide and extended my hand toward the knife. Looking intently at the expression on my face, and seeing my gesture, one of them yelled, "Let's get out of here. He's got something wrong with his head." And they took off running for their lives.

I felt no fear because they had grabbed my right hand. Even if they were seasoned finger choppers I was truly not alarmed by the idea that they might actually go through with it. They got the wrong hand. Even if they had cut some right-hand fingers off, I would still be able to draw. My Grandpa Ross continued to do all his exacting work missing several digits. I was thinking, "Go for it. If it's my lot to go through life disfigured in the way my grandfather is, so be it."

My Days in the Washington State Museum

When I told them of the incident, my parents pulled me out of school for several days. On each of those days, I rode with my father to the University of Washington in a rattle-trap army surplus bus that the ex-G.I. students of Stewart Heights bought to make the hour-long commute around the lake from Kirkland to Seattle. My father made it clear to me that he was not overjoyed about having a skinny nine-year-old kid in tow. He dropped me at the Frosh Pond on our arrival in the morning and told me to meet him back there at 4:30 in the afternoon.

I quickly discovered the Washington State Museum near the center of campus with Erna Gunther's wonderful collection of Northwest Coast Indian artifacts. Gunther, an anthropologist trained by Franz Boas, had done ethnographic fieldwork among the Klallam and was professor of anthropology at the University of Washington. She had assembled and curated the displays of masks, utensils, totem poles, blankets, baskets, etc. from coastal tribes that lived north of the Columbia River, extending to Alaska—Tlingit, Kwakiutl, Salish, Haida, Nootka, Klallam, Bella Coola, Tsimshian. I stood in flat-out awe in front of these magnificent semi-abstract figural paintings and carvings. They did not strike me as things I should copy into my sketchbook. I recognized them as Art with a capital "A," already perfect in itself, not needing any elaboration or perspective that I might try to provide.

Clearly the native artists had not adopted my hands-off stance on these works. Collectively they were like a brilliant ongoing re-invention of distinctive "traditional" forms. One of the displays that impressed me most was an elaborately carved wooden cooking pot and associated ladle. The sign explained that the pot was boiled by dropping red-hot fire-heated stones directly into the stew. I thought that was a marvelously clever use of natural materials. But what impressed me most was the size of it. There was room in the pot to cook me and my brothers with a small cousin thrown in for good measure. And the ladle was the size of a canoe paddle. I wondered how the curator was able to determine that it was a cooking pot and not a small boat. The sign on the wall said it was used in "potlatch feasts." "Potlatch" was one of those words I had to carry around in my head for quite a while until I found out what it meant. Eight years later, by a lucky accident, I would be hugely fortunate to learn about it directly from Professor Gunther herself.

I don't know how much of my situation I explained to them, but the staff of the museum very sweetly adopted me as their temporary charge. I spent several days sketching in the museum, mostly the taxidermy birds. One of the staffers looked over my shoulder and said, " The young Audubon." I had never heard of Audubon, but I could tell from her tone and attitude that I was receiving strong affirmation.

Perhaps because I am unable to forget anything, I have never understood the concept of "letting things blow over." In my entire life, I have never been able to let something "blow over." Apparently, it works for others. When I returned to school after a week Mrs. Boley was no more hostile toward me than before. It was as if nothing had happened. Except the finger choppers avoided me in the halls.

What The Children In Stewart Heights
Did For Fun And Profit

Stewart Heights was surrounded by dense woods that we needed to pass through on our way to school. It was a perilous passage for several reasons. I was fortunate not to have to worry about the biggest risk. Being robbed. Older, larger boys lurked in the woods, knocked you down, and searched you for any money you might be carrying. They quickly learned I never had any. Not even lunch money. My parents made me ask if I could work scraping plates in the cafeteria in exchange for lunch. I got the job. The other people who lived in Stewart Heights were dirt poor, but I was the poorest of the poor. They at least had lunch money. I was not even worth robbing.

One of the Stewart Heights woods robbers was a feral kid who wore nothing but a filthy pair of jockey shorts and lived in the tree canopy. He preyed on the kids who went off the paths to avoid the other robbers. When he spotted someone sneaking through the undergrowth he brachiated across the canopy then dropped straight down in a branch-to-branch controlled fall directly in front of his victim, hit them with a stick, or threatened to, and demanded they turn over their lunch money. He sometimes robbed the robbers. He was a white kid about twelve years old who told me his family left him behind when they moved out of Stewart Heights. He was a strange brown color all over except for the whites and blue irises of his eyes. It was a combination of pine pitch covering his entire body and the earth from the forest floor embedded into the pitch. His jockey shorts were the same dun brown as the rest of him except his eyes. After two or three attempts to get money from me he gave up. But he occasionally dropped down for a chat.

I do not think a single week passed that there were not horrendous episodes of domestic violence in Stewart Heights. I witnessed a man chasing his wife swinging a double-bladed ax at her with all his might. She took off like a striped-ass ape and managed to stay just far enough ahead of him as they disappeared from my sight. The main way we knew about a fight in progress was when one of the unit windows exploded outwards as a flatiron or frying pan came flying toward us. And, of course, the crash of overturning furniture, the screams, and full volume cursing. The children from the violent households would wander over and pretend to play with us for the duration. But they were always listening intently for aural signs that things had gotten better (or worse) and constantly looking over their shoulders.

How to Blow Up a Frog, the Great Marble War, and Other Misadventures

When you are a boy living in a violent project you learn to avoid older boys at all costs. Sometimes even if the violence is not directed at you it can be ugly. One day I was catching frogs at the edge of a pond in the woods when two older Heights boys approached. "Watcha doin'? Blowin' up frogs?"

"Er, no. Just catching them and letting them go."

"You know how to blow up a frog?"

"Er, no."

"Go get me a hollow piece of grass and I'll show you."

I wanted to get away from there fast because it did not sound good. But I knew if I tried to run, they would catch me and beat me up for disobeying. "Hollow grass?"

"Yeah, you know, like a straw."

So I went over to some clumps of grass and found hay straw that was hollow and brought it back to the boy who was probably about sixteen. He took out a sharp switchblade and produced a four-inch length with angular clean cuts on both ends. "Get me a frog and I'll show you how to blow him up."

Again I wanted to run, but after the knife came out, I dared not. I found and caught another frog and handed it over to "Switchblade."

"OK, first you lick the end of the straw then you poke it up its ass." And he proceeded to do exactly that. Then he put the other end of the straw in his mouth and started puffing into it. The frog began to inflate. It flailed in agony as its skin stretched tight, and it became almost spherical about the size of a tennis ball. The boy then withdrew the straw and capped the frog's anus with his thumb. "It'll take two or three minutes for him to go down." Saying this he threw the frog about ten feet out into the pond. The poor frog tried to dive but it could only bob around on its horribly distended belly, its legs and feet spinning wildly out to the side well above the surface of the water. "Now we can use 'im for target practice." He and his pal picked up some rocks from the water's edge and began throwing them at the defenseless frog. "Here." They offered me rocks. "Try to 'splode 'im."

I was on a razor's edge. I was horrified that I might hit the frog, but terrified that if I looked like I wasn't really trying they would turn their aggression onto me. (Would it be, "Go get a garden hose"?) So I pretended to enter into the "fun" and aimed carefully to "just miss" the poor creature, hoping they would not detect my ruse. Fortunately the frog deflated before anyone "'sploded him" as they were gleefully egging each other on to do. And it made a quick getaway once its legs could touch the water again.

Almost every day at Stewart Heights brought similarly weird experiences. A boy and girl in my fourth grade class told us they had started having sex. Most of the rest of us had only a vague idea about the mechanics of sex so we all gathered around demanding details. No one knew there might be duration involved. We thought it occurred in a flash like a lightning strike. When the couple explained it went on for many minutes, I stupidly asked the boy what would happen if he had to pee when he was up inside her like that. He told me he didn't know. He never had to pee while they were having sex. Maybe he'd just "pee inside her." When my classmates accused him of making it all up, the couple offered to demonstrate, but only in exchange for our lunch money. That began an almost daily routine where toward the end of lunch period the couple would go off into the woods next to the school with two or three hungry classmates in tow, everyone emerging red-faced ten or fifteen minutes later. I really wanted to go with the group to watch, but I could not pay and never had the chance to witness the spectacle of the pre-pubescent copulating couple.

All the other Heights boys gambled for marbles. I did not have any but almost everyone else had big bags full. They were used in a game played in a circle scratched in hard dirt on level ground. Every player had to contribute an agreed upon number of marbles to the circle. If you could fire a "shooter" marble with your thumb from the circle line and knock one of your opponent's marbles outside the circle you got to keep it. If you failed to knock an opponent's marble out, your shooter marble had to be left behind in the circle adding to the pot.

As the Fourth of July approached, I learned that the marbles were an important component of another "game." For a week or two before the holiday most of the boys had a good supply of firecrackers. Not wimpy little "ladyfingers." But big one- and two-inch devices with waterproof fuses. They were called "Cherry Bombs" back then. I think my classmates were stealing these from their adult male relatives. Whatever the source, they were being hoarded for the "great war." Nobody explained to me what was about to happen but I got caught up in the preparations anyway. All the boys, across all the grades, naturally divided themselves into two groups—spontaneous, ad hoc gangs. As nearly as I could tell there was no ideological basis for membership. It was just all the boys in the school split into two groups almost at random.

My gang leader told us to find pipe. As much as we could get. Any length. One inch and three-quarter inch preferred. I found some pipe in a trash heap and brought it to my gang assembling on one side of the school playground. The other gang was feverishly preparing on the opposite side. We cut the pipe into three-foot lengths and began burying one end in the ground. Most of it was buried at a 45-degree angle aimed toward the opposite side. We put some pipes in a dirt bank, tilted only slightly upward from the horizontal, aimed toward the other gang.

When everyone was ready, war was declared and the guys with firecrackers began lighting them, dropping them into the pipes, and pouring one or several marbles in after. BLAM! The firecracker went off at the bottom of the pipe and the marbles exploded out the end. In a few minutes marbles from the other side were falling out of the sky like hailstones. They hurt like hell and made it hard to light the crackers and drop the marbles. But we persisted through the pain and did our best to inflict even more on the other side. Occasionally the explosion would shatter a marble and it would come out of the pipe in a spray of glass shards. Some of the shards would embed themselves in the back of the kid who had just dropped the marble and twisted away with his fingers in his ears. There was a first aid crew on each side assigned to tweezing out the chards and dabbing at the blood with an iodine swab. We imitated lines from war movies. "Medic. Medic. We need a medic over here." The war lasted until everyone ran out of firecrackers and marbles, probably not even a full hour. But it was intense, noisy, exciting and painful while it lasted. It was about the most fun I ever had up to that point. Probably because it was a real spectacle. And not one that

I just watched. It was a real spectacle and I got to be right in the middle of it. The pall of gunpowder smoke hovered over the field until morning of the next day. There was no interest on either side about winning or losing. Really. It was not whether you won or lost. It was how you played the game.

Also at Stewart Heights I was shown a dead dog buried in the common area behind my family's unit. It was a large black and white collie in a shallow grave with a piece of plywood on top of the dog and a few shovels of dirt on top of the ply. For several months, with two other neighbor boys I undertook to open the grave every Saturday morning to examine the process of decomposition. Each week when we closed the grave back up, we said a few words for the dog that none of us had known in life. It was a bit sacred to us, like The Tomb of the Unknown Dog. One of the boys inexplicably brought a toothbrush every week and cleaned the dirt and rot from around the dog's gums and jaw before we reburied him. I didn't ask if it was his toothbrush or one of his parent's.

Uncle Eddie, his wife my Aunt Betty, and their daughters, cousins Janie and Cynthia, lived in Stewart Heights for several months when we did. He was driving a delivery truck for a magazine distributor and part of his job was picking up the unsold comic books and destroying them. The company held that they were effectively "destroyed" if he tore off their covers leaving the rest of the book intact. So, in addition to drawing paper, Eddie brought me hundreds of "destroyed" comic books and I became the Stewart Heights project librarian. It was a popular posting. My personal favorite genre was not superheroes. It was horror. I loved Tales From the Crypt. The only superhero I liked was Plastic Man. Wouldn't it be great, I thought, to be able to reach anything I needed in the house and yard, even the whole neighborhood, without getting out of my chair?

With hundreds of comic books at the foot of my bed, I got to meet almost every kid in my section of the project. One of the girls a year or two older than me offered to exchange sex for my entire collection of Romance comics. I did not like the Romance genre so I gave her almost my entire stash. For free. I asked for nothing in return. She thought I was weird.

I do not remember the name of any kid I met at Stewart Heights except for Scott Robinson. We walked together to school a few times and I learned that his father was also a University of Washington student. Medical School. Robinson told me his dad was issued a cadaver to dissect and he brought the dead body home and let Scott and his brother play with it. I did not remember Scott's name until we reconnected at Cornell in the graduate program in anthropology. It is a small world. I used to say if you sit on a bench in the Paris Metro for a few days, everyone you ever knew will come by. Scott remembered walking to school with me in Stewart Heights in 1950 but nothing about the cadaver. He is a professor in Mexico now and we correspond occasionally.

A few months before we were able to leave the Heights, Eddie moved his family out of the project to a nice single-family detached rental house in Seattle's South End. He involved me in packing and unpacking for the move. He rented a box truck and 'allowed' me to ride in the back on our return trips to get more stuff. It was pitch black inside the box and he drove fast around curves tossing me about like a ragdoll in the dark. It was probably dangerous but we both thought it was hilarious fun. I got a few bruises but no cuts or broken bones. It was the closest thing I got to a carnival ride as a child. Eddie knew it, too.

The Only Violence We Experienced Directly Was Perpetrated by My Father

The only violence my family experienced in our year in the violent project was perpetrated by my father. Seeking separation (mainly symbolic) from the other families, he installed a four feet tall hog wire fence around a small part of the common area outside our back door. It effectively gave us the only "private" yard in the project, about ten-by-ten feet enclosed. My mother planted bulbs inside the perimeter of the fence. My parents did not discuss it as a beautification project. They made it clear to my brothers and me that it was their way of showing that we were not the same kind of people as the other Stewart Heights residents. In the spring, soon after my mother's bulbs flowered, two boys in their early teens came by. They sneered at our "private" yard and proceeded to lean over the fence and systematically yank out the blooming daffodils and tulips. My father saw them from inside the house and burst out the back door silently but at full speed.

I watched from inside the house as the boys turned and ran. My father was faster than a streak of blue shit. He vaulted the fence in perfect high-hurdles form and caught them in less than fifty yards. He grabbed them both by the backs of their shirts, one in each hand, and dragged them kicking and screaming back to the fence just outside our "yard." He beat them both to the ground screaming in their faces about having respect for other people's property. He did not kick them, but he hit them both several times full force with his fists until they were crying and begging for mercy. He finally let them up and told them to go home and tell their parents what they had done.

The severity of the beating, I suspect, was intensified by the fact that he had ripped his only good pair of pants and lacerated his inner thigh on the top of the fence as he cleared it in a single bound.

Later that summer my father was arrested, tried, and sentenced to one night in jail for battery on a minor. The arrest, jail sentence, and time served occurred when I was at my Great Grandmother's, and no one spoke of it. I did not hear the jail part of the story until several years later when Bill let it slip. I am sure my father defended himself in court and convinced the judge that he had done nothing wrong. Not really. Not when you pull back and take the whole situation into account. Because my father never did anything wrong in his entire life. He was always very convincing about that. One night in jail seems light for the violence I witnessed.

My year at Stewart Heights was mainly unpleasant, but it had its enjoyable moments, and I learned a great deal about variation on the spectrum of humanity, two or three standard deviations away from the merely mean.

8

1950-1951 Cedar Vale Projects in the Seattle North End

IN THE SUMMER OF 1950, a unit opened up in a small project in the North End of Seattle. I was glad to get clear of Stewart Heights. Our new home in the Cedar Vale Project was incongruously embedded in the upper-middle-class North End of Seattle. Our unit was exactly the same as at American Lake and at Stewart Heights except for one important amenity. The stove in the kitchen did not burn coal. It burned heating oil. A fifty-gallon drum hung high on the exterior wall outside the kitchen. It supplied oil to the stove through a copper line. It was great for my mother because oil burners are much more controllable than coal and wood burning stoves. My reader should know that while it was a major improvement for us, cooking on an oil burning stove was still close to the bottom tier of domestic amenities. Anyone with any money was already cooking with gas or electricity.

Burning oil was fabulous for me because it meant my coal wrangling days were over. At Stewart Heights I had grown large enough to carry a full scuttle but in winter I was still making several trips a day. At Cedar Vale my parents shifted my main chore from keeping the scuttle full to keeping the bathroom clean. The shift from coal to oil alerted me that if my future was to be a laborer, I could easily be replaced by technology. Sometimes not very much technology. In this case it was by ten feet of copper tubing and a shut-off valve. It was a small thing, but a large revelation.

Cedar Vale was scheduled for demolition. We knew it meant another move at the end of the year, but it was worth it. It was close to the University. Instead of more than an hour each way around the Lake, my father had a fifteen-minute bus ride. Cedar Vale was gang free with little domestic or other violence. No finger-cutting or frog-'sploding. The land under us was ripe for real estate re-development into middle class, single family detached houses. While the project was demolished at the end of our year living there, by a quirk of fate its demolition did not end my strong connection to the place.

I Encounter My First Classmates Who Were Growing Up Middle Class

Our Cedar Vale unit after a rain. Note the barrel supplying oil to the stove. Whoever was responsible for grading and drainage didn't do their job properly. But the kids loved it.

I attended View Ridge Elementary for fifth grade. There was a surrounding social context. View Ridge was one of the nicest upper-middle-class neighborhoods in the city with a country club, golf course, swim club, etc. Cedar Vale was the only housing blight for miles around. And I was the only kid from the projects in my class. My classmate friends included Guy Moen whose father was about to invent and patent the world's first one-handled faucet for mixing hot and cold water. And Albert Balch II, "Berty" Balch. Balch Sr. was an innovative real estate developer who built almost the entire middle class North End of Seattle after World War II. I didn't know it, but it was Berty's dad who had optioned the purchase of the Cedar Vale project. Every other kid in my fifth-grade class came from families that were comfortably at the top end of the middle class or slightly above.

My family had not been able to afford a used car, new clothes, telephone, newspaper delivery, or fresh milk for more than a decade. Now hanging out after school with a friend meant

I was visiting in multi-storied homes on large lots with garages bigger than any housing unit I had ever lived in. Oh, and servants. Bert's dad purchased a new Lincoln sedan every other year and owned a color TV in 1950 when the only broadcast in color was a half hour of nightly news on NBC. Color transmission was the origin of the NBC peacock icon. Wow! Colors.

The Balches Welcome Me Into Their Home Life

Far from discriminating against me because of my low social standing, Mr. and Mrs. Balch took me under their wing and strongly encouraged my friendship with Bert. Bert was not a bad kid, but at age 10, he showed no interest in anything. Not school. Not friends. Not sports. Not anything. His parents noticed that I threw myself fully into a wide range of pursuits—drawing, contraption-building, violin playing (View Ridge Elementary had a music teacher who helped), theorizing about life, etcetera.

Mr. and Mrs. Balch went out of their way to welcome me into their lives. I visited Mr. Balch in his offices and joined the family on their weekend outings. Perhaps it was partly out of pity. If it was, it never came through in their interactions with me. I felt no condescension. They clearly hoped that my enthusiasm for life might rub off onto Bert. Their door was always open to me after school and on weekends. After school they made sure I ate a healthy snack with Bert. I was still pretty scrawny. Mrs. Balch pulled some strings at one of her charities and caused the Seattle Milk Fund to drop a free bottle of fresh milk on my parents' doorstep every morning. One thing I am sure about: I would not have been welcome in the Balch home were it not for the manners my great grandmother taught me.

The Balch home sat on several otherwise undeveloped woodlots. Albert Sr. had his crews build his children a playhouse in the woods that was only slightly smaller than the project unit my family lived in at the time. The contrast between my unit in the projects and the Balch home where I spent most of my time after school and on weekends seems quite stark to me now. More so than it did at the time. Bertie was rich and lived in a big, detached house. I was poor and lived in a Cedar Vale row house unit. It did not seem to me to be a very big deal. It did not affect

The Balch home in View Ridge where I visited after school and weekends. Note the treetops in the woodlots Albert Sr. preserved around the side and back of the house.

the games or the things we invented or how we related to each other. Having a maid make us big fat sandwiches to eat on our arrival after school—that was a big deal.

Albert Sr. always called me "Sunny" because of my disposition. But I sometimes heard "Sonny" and perhaps a wish that Bertie had my drive. Mrs. Balch planted carrots for us in her mini-forest. She observed that the carrot tops looked exactly like small ferns so they would not spoil the natural landscape. Her carrot covered forest floor provided us with an endless supply of healthy vegetables to eat when we played outside. We pulled them up, wiped the sandy soil off on our shirts and chomped down.

Taking Things Apart and Putting Weird Stuff Back Together Again

Bert and I were joined by another kid from our class named Richard (always "Richard," never "Dick") Ronning and the three of us began to dig deeply into everything electrical and mechanical. We were all a little bit outcast. Richard had heart trouble, Bertie did not like people very much, and I was, well, I was me. The three of us got on very well together. In the early 1950s kids could find thrown-away tube-type radios, wind-up mechanical phonographs, broken wind-up alarm clocks, etc., in almost every clump of bushes. We fished out anything that looked like it might be interesting to take apart. When I discovered there were miles of thin copper wires winding the transformers in old radios, I built a series of electromagnets, experimenting with different ways of winding the wire around large iron nail cores. I discovered that if you wrap each layer of winding with a single thickness of waxed paper before winding the next layer, the power increases substantially. Together we figured out how to use our home-made electromagnets to make buzzers and eventually an electric motor. It was small and very weak but functional. It spun so fast we couldn't see its armature. We tried to build a double magnet solenoid actuator, but it defeated us.

We soon discovered that cast-off appliances were sources of motors, solenoids, switches, gears, etc. and began scavenging for ready-made useful bits. I figured out how to make universal joints out of rubber tubing to re-route power to wherever it might be needed. Richard got hold of a spark coil from an old car. We used it for all sorts of hijinks. We shocked the crap out of classmates and ran sparks through Richard's aunt's cigarettes creating thousands of invisible holes in the paper so when she tried smoke, all the air would come through the sides and the cigarettes would never light. She knew we had sabotaged her somehow when we took a great deal of interest in watching her try and fail to light up. She could see we were straining our guts not to blow up with laughter. But she never figured out why her cigarettes would not light.

The following year when I started earning money babysitting, the first thing I bought was two heavy-duty "Burges Number 6" dry cell batteries with screw terminals that I could wire in series to give my projects a 12-volt jolt.

I Pitch Myself Through My Bedroom Window and Nick an Artery

My life has been generally free of accidents but at Cedar Vale I had a strange one. Except for falling off a mountain once, it was the worst accident of my life, and it left a scar I still have. It happened when I was sound asleep. On a warm spring afternoon while my father was in classes at the University, my mother, my brothers and I were napping. I was in my upper bunk in the boy's room and my mother was in my parent's bedroom. I had some kind of nightmare. I do not remember it. But apparently I convulsed violently and pitched myself out of the bunk. The room was small and the window was on the same wall as the bunkbed. I fell out of the upper bunk on the wrong side. Through the window into the yard outside the house. A kid flying out through a glass window crashing into the yard would have been a terrible sight if a person were to see it, but there was nobody around. Several neighbors heard the crash and came running.

I was still asleep as I crashed through the glass, but wide awake when I landed on my face on the ground. A fall to the floor inside the house would have been five feet. But the row house sat on a perimeter foundation that added an extra 18 inches to the fall outside. The glass fell before me, and I landed in hundreds of sharp shards. I reflexively put my hands out to break my fall and received several cuts on my palms and fingers. Most were superficial but we do have an artery at the base of our thumbs.

When I pulled the biggest shard out, I had about a foot-high squirt of blood with each heartbeat. I immediately put my other thumb on the leak as I had been instructed by my Uncle Ed and squeezed hard enough to shut it off. My mother stumbled bleary-eyed out into the sun to see what the commotion was all about. She was about to yell at me for breaking the window but quickly surmised that I had been in some kind of weird accident and that I was hurt.

I kept the pressure on my palm very consciously minimizing the drama of the moment. My mother told the neighbors that everything was fine, nothing to see, and took me by an upper arm and fast-walked me back inside. Over the kitchen sink I took the pressure off and sprayed a couple of squirts before quickly stoppering it up again.

My mother, still woozy from her nap told me I had cut into an artery and she could not deal with it. I would have to take care of it myself. And with that, she stumbled back into her bedroom laid down and went back to sleep.

To this day, I do not understand what happened to her in that moment. She was usually more than competent to handle emergencies. Okie enough to set bones and bind wounds if needed. Bill once cut his chest open on a barbed wire fence and she stitched it up with a sewing needle and thread. But that afternoon, in the shock of the moment, it was like, 'I'm sorry. Too much blood. You broke a window and cut an artery.'

And back to bed.

In addition to his emergency advice ("If you get shot or stabbed, stick your thumb in the hole") I remembered the First Aid merit badge requirements in the Boy Scout Manual Uncle Eddie gave me. I knew to apply compression and to keep my hand above my heart. I got a wad of clean gauze from the bathroom cabinet, squeezed it into my palm and held my hand above my shoulder. I knew that if I could not staunch the flow I would have to apply a tourniquet. I found the stick and cord I would need in case. I sat quietly applying pressure for more than an hour until my father came home and my mother got up. They asked if I was still bleeding. I checked and I wasn't.

Cedar Vale, View Ridge, Richard, Bert, Mr. and Mrs. Balch, my up-close exposure to what middle-class comfort looks like, and the establishment of my career as a bricoleur—it was a great year. In the summer of 1951 we moved a few miles away to married student housing at the University of Washington. But I did not have to break off my friendships at View Ridge. The Seattle dump was adjacent to married student housing and I built myself a bicycle from discarded parts I found in the dump. On my rattletrap bike, I could get back to Bert's house in about 20 minutes. With the mobility the bike gave me, I was beginning to feel powerfully in charge of my own life.

While I continued to spend several afternoons a week at the Balches, I still had no idea that it was Albert Balch Senior who had purchased the Cedar Vale project and evicted us. Nor could I have known the magnitude of the impact on my life his purchase of Cedar Vale would have. Two chapters ahead in the section on "The Model T Ford" I will tell how the Balch purchase of our project was one of the luckiest things that happened to me in my entire life.

9

Union Bay Village—University of Washington Married Student Housing, 1951-1954

The Importance of Turning Eleven

WHEN WE MOVED TO UNION BAY VILLAGE in 1951 I was still two years short of being a teen-ager. But already there was an organic change happening. It did not feel hormonal. It was more like something happening in my brain that was urging me to do more. I did not stop reading, drawing, and playing the violin. But they were no longer sufficient. I felt an almost instinctual drive to try to figure out new things. Things I had not contemplated before. Sometimes seriously complicated stuff like model cars of my own design powered by rockets. A growing proportion of my drawings were blueprints for my strange projects and experiments.

Does every child enter a similar larger metaphorical room at about age eleven? A sudden awareness of human-accomplishment-in-general accompanied by a need to join and contribute to it? At about this age, I think there is a rush of awareness of the great potential that resides in us just by virtue of our being a human among humans; a species-defining burst of energy and curiosity and stamina and drive and focus. I believe that twelve-year-old children are capable of successfully embarking upon just about anything. At least I thought that about myself in 1951.

There were a number of other things going on in my life, but the change of consciousness that shifted my entire being on its axis, was this: whatever I did now, I held myself to an adult standard. If I painted or drew or built a model, the results had to be as good as could be accomplished by any adult around me who undertook similar pursuits. I was through with kid's stuff. I did not try to do everything that I noticed adults doing. It was only, if there was overlap, mine had to be as good as the adult version. Or better. Like my Lincoln drawing.

Ming Kipa scaled the highest peaks on all seven continents including Everest before she turned 15. The summer before his senior year in high school, Bob Feller, age 17, pitching for the Cleveland Indians in his first Major League game, struck out 15 batters. I was not interested in trying to replicate others' accomplishments. But I fully identified with those who had a burning desire to master whatever tool or discipline they picked up and carry it through to its highest expression. At age eleven, I built intricate model cars and thought about the next steps I would need to take to build a real one. I knew the only thing that would stop me from getting there would be my own decision to do something else instead.

My Very Specific Need for Money

Every dream comes with a price tag. About my eleventh birthday a realization descended upon me with almost physical force: MONEY. I needed money. My reader might be thinking, that is not a very imaginative idea. How American can you get? My need for money felt different, not the way it is framed in American mythology. I had no interest in becoming rich, or in wealth as an abstract construct. I did not envy or desire the lifestyle of my middleclass friends who got allowances and were given lunch money so they did not have to scrape plates in the school cafeteria to eat. I assumed that kind of wealth, where your parents would simply buy you a bike when you reached a certain age, would be forever beyond my reach.

Here is what I needed money for. I needed money for food. We were still starving, and I was starting to grow taller and hungrier. I needed money for store-bought clothes so I would not shock the parents of my school pals who had never before seen a child outfitted from church rummage sales. I needed money for balsa wood, X-acto knives and blades, glue, dope (that was not slang for narcotics, it was the proper name for airplane paint in the 1950s), electric motors, rocket motors, and gas engines for model building. I needed strong batteries to power my growing inventory of inventions. I was able to get enough parts out of the dump to build a bike for free, but I needed money for tires and innertubes. I needed a puncture repair kit. My need for money had zero abstract qualities. It was concrete, empirical, very specifically tied to what I was interested in doing at the time. And as certain as I was that I needed money I was even more certain that my parents could not begin to spare even a nickel. It would be entirely on me to figure out how to get it.

Even before I conceived of this need for money in such an absolute way as to shape my life around it, throughout my childhood I had always been on the lookout for any chance to earn a dollar or even a dime. From age eight, there were occasional short duration babysitting gigs for my mother's friends. When we lived at American Lake, these were often for barter. No one in the projects had any money after paying rent and buying food. Not even a dime. When I was eight, the first payment for services I ever received was a scented bar of soap shaped like a woman's hair bow. It had obviously been a gift to my client that she never took out of its box. At about the same time, many years before I would wear my first tie, in exchange for feeding a dog for two days, I was given a tie pin. I mowed lawns, used my skinny arms to retrieve things that got stuck in toilets, anything that might provide me with some small change. When I visited her, my Grandma Fran paid me a dime for every gallon of rocks I collected from the "lawn" she was trying to create by mowing the weeds on her 21 building-lot property in Tacoma.

Sometimes I wonder how my life would have been different if, at eleven, I had not become single minded about acquiring money. Would my dreams and projects have been any different if my parents had been able to supply me with the food, clothing, tools, models and model parts I needed? Were my horizons limited by the projects I could afford to pursue on what I could earn as an eleven-year-old? If I did not pay my own way from the start, I may well have ended up a very different person. I'll let my reader decide. One thing is certain. By paying my own way from an early age, I alone decided what I wanted to do with my money. There was no adult frowning at me about my choices or encouraging me to do this instead of that. My father once noticed I bought a model airplane engine before I had built any models that required gas power. It was an expensive purchase. He asked me "Why?" since I had no need for it. I told him I would figure it out. He said, "Ridiculous," and turned away without further discussion. It was my money and my engine. I eventually used it to power a model airboat I designed and built.

Before I became single-minded about obtaining the money I needed for my projects, I spent the small change I earned on candy bars and rolls of caps for cap pistols. I did not own a cap pistol but I liked setting off single caps by burning them with a magnifying glass, or an entire roll of caps by smashing it with a hammer. A whole roll would produce a really respectable bang like a large-bore rifle shot or a car backfiring. With a nickel box of caps I could scare the crap out of an entire neighborhood. As much as I loved a loud bang or a candy bar, I would not consider wasting money on kids' stuff like that after I turned eleven and conceived of my need for more serious earnings.

I Start Two Successful Businesses

Union Bay was a large project with several thousand people. It was almost 100 percent WW II vets like my father. But they had waited until after the war to get married and have babies. It was definitely baby boom time in Union Bay. Every other unit had children ranging in age from infants to five years old. At eleven, I was the oldest kid in the project and I hit pay dirt.

Babysitting was my first business. I charged 20 cents an hour and could sit every night of the week. The demand was so great that I could batch different family's children together in a single unit and earn 60 cents to a dollar an hour. Better than minimum wage. During football season, about ten of my clients reserved a Common Room in the project Administration Building and left me in charge of almost 20 kids ranging from infants to school age for the duration of every home game. I kept the older kids entertained while bottle-feeding babies and changing diapers. I charged $10 a game equal to $97 in today's money or $40 an hour.

I soon gained a project-wide reputation for being able to control unruly children better than their parents could. I became the "Child Whisperer of Union Bay." My main method was by storytelling. I could bribe them to settle down by promising them a story if they did. I borrowed heavily, re-telling children's classics I got out of the Bookmobile, but about half was stuff I made up on the spot. Some stories were a mélange of classics with my own additions and twists. There were a few families where the kids were almost feral and I had to resort to more imaginative methods.

My Village Laundry Business

In the afternoons after school, there were no lawns to mow, but I was able to start a lucrative laundry business. A huge centrally located laundromat served the entire Village. The place was filthy with scum, soap powder and cobwebs, and unbearably hot in the summer. Lint from the dryer vents coated the weeds, bushes, and trees for 100 yards in all directions. The student wives of Union Bay hated going there but no one could afford to send their laundry out for professional washing. I restored a cast-off American Flyer wagon I got from the dump and trundled through the project on different daily routes calling out "Washing, washing." Every household client knew what day of the week I would be coming by and had their washing sorted by color and packaged in pillowcases equal to one load per case ready for me to pick up.

The laundromat charged 25 cents for a load of washing and 10 cents for ten minutes of drying. My terms were easy to communicate and understand. I simply doubled the machine rates. If they gave me two loads to wash, no drying, I collected 50 cents for the two machines and 50 cents for myself up front. If they wanted their washing brought back dry, it was the same deal. (No folding.) For every dime for the dryer there was a dime for me.

Model Building and Inventing Stuff

Before long I was making as much money as my father got from the G.I. Bill and his student assistantships. I could have supported my entire family as well as or better than he did. But I did not. When my earnings started to add up, in addition to batteries, I spent good sums on balsa and paper model airplane kits that I assembled, flew, and experimentally modified for better (usually worse—but I learned) flight. I built model cars and model boats powered by 0.49 and 0.32 gasoline engines.

A company named "Jetex" sold reusable solid fuel rocket motors that could be attached to anything that might fly. I mounted my single pellet Jetex 50 on a miniature model car I built and modified for this experiment. With the kids I babysat gathered around, I lit it up and sent it whizzing down an alley. It had not been my intent to build a flying car. I had bench-tested the motor and timed the duration of the burn and enjoyed the loud hissing sound and sulfurous smell it made. But I had no idea of how powerful it was. My tiny car gained incredible speed, almost too fast to see. The first small bump sent it airborne. It left the ground at about a thirty-degree angle and flew toward the sky straight as a bullet. The kids screamed in delight to see it take flight. It continued to accelerate and did not lose an inch of altitude for about 75 feet before smashing into the project administration building just under the eaves at the second story. It exploded on impact and fluttered to the ground in many more pieces than it was originally made of. If it had gone straight up it might have simply disappeared into the firmament. At least it looked like that to all the witnesses. The admin building survived without a visible scratch. I was hugely relieved it did not hit a window or one of the kids. My audience was enormously appreciative. I told them not to tell their parents about the demonstration.

The "Child Whisperer of Union Bay"

In my work as a babysitter I rarely met a kid that I could not persuade to obey me in a few moments. But it wasn't always so easy. Especially with kids whose parents could not control them. Some of my charges presented real difficulty. I sat a slightly obese woman's five dirty kids, all pre-school. They were totally out of control. There was no man around and she was not a student. The student-father had dropped out of college and abandoned his family in Union Bay and the woman just kept paying the heavily subsidized rent without informing the project administration of the change in her situation. The first day I sat for her she told me I must not allow the kids to annoy the neighbors who might inform on her and get them kicked out.

The minute she left they began running wild, screaming at the tops of their lungs and peeing on the neighbor's porches. I dragged them all back into the house and locked the doors, but they only escalated, screaming even louder and throwing anything they could get their hands on. I cast my eye over to her treadle-type sewing machine sitting ready for use in a corner of the living room. I told them firmly that if they did not stop throwing stuff, and settle down and behave themselves, "I'll run your hands through the sewing machine and stitch them together." Now they screamed in genuine terror. I was unknown to them. They had no idea about whether or not I was a maniac. They immediately began to obey my every command. I made them clean the house—or at least pickup their own messes. "Or else it's the sewing machine for you, kid."

They informed me that they were going to tell their mother when she got home, and I would never babysit them again. I told them, "Fine by me" and continued staring at the machine. They were little angels all afternoon. When their mother came home, she was shocked to see the tidy house and her kids playing quietly together. They made good on their promise, "Mommy! Mommy, he said he would stitch our hands together in the sewing machine."

"If they continued to misbehave," I explained.

"You threatened to run their hands through the machine?" She asked.

"Yes, I did."

"And they settled down?"

"Yes, they did."

"That's brilliant," she said. "Why didn't I think of that?" When she said it, the screaming really started. "Quiet down or you'll get the machine," she yelled. Instant silence. I continued to sit for them—now among the best-behaved kids in the project.

I built a contraption I called "The Bad Child Electric Cor-rectic." It was a wooden box with a red light on the top, a buzzer inside, a menacing looking large dry cell battery strapped to the side with coiled red wire leads. And finger holes. I carried it with me to all my sitting jobs. Kids were very curious. I explained that some of the children I sat— "not nice ones like you, but the bad children"—had to be disciplined by putting their fingers in the holes in the side of the box. I told them it would not kill a child but it would inflict serious pain. Then I would demonstrate by putting my finger in one of the holes. The light flashed, the buzz-er made a zapping sound, and I would yank my finger out with a blood curdling shriek. "See, it's perfectly safe," I would yell while pretending to be a bit dazed. "Of course, you would never do anything to cause me to use the box," I would say. I never had any discipline problems. Ever. It was just storytelling, playing with their toys with them, helping them draw, and the Correctic box sitting unused on a table.

I saved about half of my earnings for larger purchases and spent the other half on model kits and supplies, and food. I built working models by the dozens that I could fly or send roaring across ponds of water or whooshing up alleys. And I also built non-working models for display. In the early 1950s hobby stores sold many nice "shelf" model kits of WW II airplanes. These were not 100 percent plastic. That came later. They were composed of rough, pre-shaped pieces of balsa wood—usually the fuselage and wings—and some parts made of molded plas-tic—canopy, engines, pilot, guns, bombs, landing gear. I as-sembled and painted these kits meticulously. I primed, sanded, painted, and sanded (again) the balsa parts with as many coats as needed so no wood grain was showing; until it looked like painted metal. I trimmed a small paintbrush down to four or five hairs so I could paint the details including the faces of the pilots—eyebrows, pupils, nostrils and lips in 1/64th scale, smil-ing out through the clear plastic canopies of the planes. 1/64th means the pilot's head is smaller than a peanut. Not Mr. Peanut, shell and all, but a single peanut kernel.

My models conformed to an adult standard, or beyond.

Learning the Importance of Not Taking Credit

My model building expertise led to another one of those life-changing moments. I conceived of a scheme to trade my finished P38 Mustang and Naval Corsair for three new unbuilt planes with the owner of the small variety and hobby store where I bought the kits. The store owner thought they were beautiful and readily agreed to my trade so she could put them in her window to lure other customers. For me, the joy was in the building, not in the display, so we both got what we wanted.

Her display of my Mustang and Corsair caused me to learn this lesson about showing off my skills. One Sunday, I happened to walk past the store. It was closed and there were two men kneeling with their hands cupped to the glass admiring the models. I stopped and went up to them.

"Are you looking at the planes? I built them."

They stood up, turned, and looked at me contemptuously. "You lying little shit. Are you trying to tell us you made those planes?"

"Yes. I made them and traded them with the store owner for some new kits."

"No kid could have done that. Look at the detail. They were probably made by a man who flew those planes. Didn't your people tell you you're not supposed to try to take credit for something someone else did?"

My mind flashed back to Stewart Heights the poster contest, the gang, my fingers. I began to back away quietly.

"That's right. Slink away like a dog. Get the hell out of our sight. What kind of people births a turd like you?"

My parents never specifically taught me not to take credit for other peoples' work. To the contrary, almost daily, I witnessed my father taking credit for things other people did and getting away with it. I always felt slightly revolted when he did this. It was only because of his negative example that I knew better. What I learned from the variety store window incident and a few similar encounters during my childhood was something quite different: The wisest course is never to call attention to your own work. Sometimes it is crucial not to take any credit for it. For high accomplishment it is usually better to off-load most of the credit onto someone else. There is a fairly common personality type in the United States—those who hate any outstanding work that is not their own. My mother was like that. I should have known better.

In the course of my lifetime I have been fortunate to win some important prizes and awards. But I did not put myself up for any of them. The nominations always came from someone else, and I was usually unaware that I was being considered until the winner was announced. It makes for a pleasant low-key career. I have the two nasty men at the Variety Store window to thank for securing this important lesson.

Enjoying Playing in the Dump

About a half mile from campus, Union Bay Village and the main Seattle dump sat adjacent to each other on the shore of Lake Washington. No one used the term "landfill" back then. It was "the Dump" and it was completely open access. Anyone, not just the city garbage trucks, could drive up and dump there. It was the best playground and salvage center any eleven-year-old kid could imagine. When I was not working or building models, I could go to the dump. It was endlessly entertaining. There were always other kids romping around in the trash finding fun stuff to play with. It was our playground, museum, and porno shop. We found and divided a huge stash of 1950s "girlie" magazines. No nipples or pubic hair showing, but everything else on display including truly grand canyons of cleavage.

When I pulled it from the dump, my laundry wagon was rusted with a missing wheel. But I found a larger wheel set that I could adapt to its axles by making bushings out of copper tubing. I bought new cotter keys to hold everything together, repainted the wagon with white enamel, and started my business. My Grandpa Ross admired my wagon restoration, especially my solution to the bushing problem. He told me my work was "creative" and "sound." I made my first bicycle by combining frame and mechanical parts from two lightweight bikes, and buying a new chain, tubes and tires to get it up and running. A Union Bay neighbor helped me assemble everything into a serviceable machine. He took care not to do the work for me, but to explain the principles of bicycle assembly and maintenance.

About a year after I "discovered" the dump, a middle-aged African-American man moved in. He built himself a home at the entrance from materials he found in the dump. He began his own salvage operation. He made stacks of automobile wheels, copper pipes, wiring, radio tubes, bicycle frames, etc. His displays of sorted junk at the entrance were very similar to those I saw much later in the parking lot of the Istanbul bazaar. He allowed kids to continue to use the dump as a playground but not for scavenging. If we wanted a bicycle frame, we had to buy it from him. Since we knew he got it for free, we could usually knock him down to a few nickels for just about anything we needed.

Once Again, My Housing Project Was Adjacent To An Upscale Neighborhood

The neighborhoods to the north and east of Union Bay Village were very posh. The Laurelhurst district, just up the hill from Union Bay, and downwind from the smell of the dump, was actually one of Seattle's toniest. Unlike View Ridge, developed by Bert's father as merely upper middle class with nice pattern book housing, Laurelhurst was definitely another cut above. There were no pattern-book houses. Every house was individually architected--one of them, I later found out, by my Grandfather MacCannell. My school for sixth grade was Laurelhurst Elementary, located deep inside the fanciest neighborhood. It was at Laurelhurst that the other violinist and I entertained the teachers on their breaks playing Mozart duets.

There were no other poor kids from the Village in my class and I was not especially welcomed among my classmates. I did make friends with a Jewish kid, Bill Moses. A boy named John Bradley's mother heard me play the violin at a school assembly and tried to form a "band" with John on clarinet, another kid on guitar, and me. I have no idea of what kind of music she envisioned for clarinet, guitar and violin. The trouble was that John and the other kid were just starting to learn their instruments, and none of us knew the inherent limitations of a b-flat clarinet. We thought that if John played a note on clarinet and I played the same note on the violin they would actually be the same note. But there was a half-tone difference between the two instruments and the result was a horrendous cacophony. So we gave up.

My babysitting and laundry businesses thrived, and I was quite well-to-do. On my way home from school, whenever I wanted, I could stop off at a drugstore lunch counter and order myself a club sandwich and a coke. I bought all my own clothes including quality shoes and wool slacks. My Grandpa Ross told me that I should always buy the very finest clothing that I could afford. While my independence was very rarely questioned no matter what I got up to, the staff in the up-scale clothing stores where I shopped were not prepared to deal with a twelve-year-old boy buying clothes without his parents. At first, they refused to sell me expensive items like a quality pair of shoes or a three-quarter length wool winter coat. They were concerned that my parents might not agree with my choices and hold the store responsible for selling a little kid stuff that was too expensive. I had to reassure them that my parents trusted my judgment and were always happy with my choices. I did not disabuse them of their assumption that I was just a neglected rich kid with a really big allowance. They liked the fact that I always arrived with a large roll of cash secured with a rubber band that I snapped onto my wrist as I peeled off the bills to pay for my purchases. I had learned from experience the risks involved in telling them I earned it myself. They steered me toward a kind of ultra conservative British Prep school style before it was a "style."

I saved enough to buy myself a brand-new English lightweight bicycle with four gears, generator head- and tail-lights and a leather saddlebag, the finest available at the time, better than the bikes of most of my wealthy classmates. No one could tell me to spend a little less on a perfectly good bike. I wanted the best. My bike cost me $80.00 or $775.00 in today's money. Not quite fitting into Laurelhurst "society" was non-problematic. I could clothe and feed myself nicely. On the weekends I would bike three miles to View Ridge and visit the Balches and the Ronnings.

Except for the woman with the five feral kids there was a college student, and sometimes two, in every project unit. My misgivings about my own parents' prolonged college educations aside, I found the population of the Village to be a delightful demographic. There were no children my age, but I was able to make a number of friends among the adults. Some of the men began to give me the kind of attention and guidance I never got from my father. They were probably looking forward to the day when their own children would emerge from early childhood and develop more mature interests. I was like their "starter" male youth for mentoring.

My new lightweight bike and preppy clothes

The man who taught me how to be a bicycle mechanic also gave me a used left-handed baseball mitt and showed me the basics of pitching. Learning that there was such a thing as a left-handed mitt was a true revelation. I just assumed that all mitts were right-handed, i.e., worn on the left hand. Wearing a right-handed mitt meant that after I caught a ball, I would have to fling off the mitt and transfer the ball to my throwing hand to try to make the play. I was rarely able to accomplish this quickly enough to get anyone out. Until I got a proper mitt.

The 1952 Presidential Campaign

As the 1952 presidential campaign heated up, the entire village erupted in a frenzy of support for Adlai Stevenson. Every row house in the Village became papered top to bottom and side to side with Stevenson / Kefauver signs. There were lawn signs in front, window signs in every window, huge placards on every door. Not an inch of tarpaper siding was left uncovered. Every unit was completely hidden behind the enthusiastic red, white, and blue cardboard display. Except mine. There, in the sea of posters, was our drab dun colored unit with zero display, as conspicuous as a naked man in a crowded stadium at a ball game. This was my first lesson in Semiotics 101. In an instant I learned that the absence of a sign can be far more meaningful than the presence of a sign. I was afraid I might be stigmatized by my parent's right-wing political beliefs and lose laundry business. So I affixed "I Like Ike" and "Stevenson / Kefauver" bumper stickers to my wagon to try to hold myself outside the fray. I did not suffer any loss of business.

The Blow of Seeing My First British Car

It was another one of those instantaneous "blows" that turned everything I used to think inside out. I fatefully saw my first foreign car. It was an MG TC driving down the street with its 19-inch-tall wire wheels and cycle fenders like a very old car but low slung with racy lines, i.e., also futuristic. Very old and futuristic. What was that car? I wanted to know. Needed to know. There were a few on the streets of Seattle in the early 1950s, brought back from England after the war by American G.I.s.

One of the things that made me hyper-curious was every TC was driven by a woman with a male passenger. Or so I thought. It was several months on the lookout before I found one parked and discovered their steering wheels were on the "wrong" side. This cleared up the mystery of the women "drivers."

I bought an issue of *Road and Track* magazine in 1952 and began the research that

1949 MG TC

would clear up the many mysteries forming in my head. In England they drive on the other side of the road. Holy crap! I was inexorably pulled into the mystique surrounding these cars.

Austin Healey 100-4. Again, not a line wasted.

The sighting of that TC framed my consciousness for the next several years. It compelled me to face my commitment to beauty. Anything, even utilitarian transportation could come in beautiful and ugly variants. Whenever there was a choice in the matter, I would live my life on the side of beauty.

I have gotten a bit ahead of myself, but it is important for my reader to know that everything I did for the next several years was inflected by my attraction to European cars.

If I built a model plane or worked on a fishing boat, e.g., I would wonder how the knowledge I gained might be transferable to high-performance cars. If I installed a gasoline engine in a model car I wondered if it would go faster if I mixed some acetone in with the gas? (It does.) If I used my mother's perfume as fuel? (It does not. But it actually did sputter to life for a moment.)

One of my neighbors in Union Bay Village was Phil Freeman, a brilliant graduate student in physics. His first faculty position after he got his Ph.D. was in the Physics Department at Berkeley where half the senior faculty were Nobel Laureates. That is how evidently brilliant he was. At first, I babysat for Helen and Phil and did their laundry. Their sons, Mark and Aaron, were still in diapers. Phil was the one who taught me how to make gun powder and anything else about the physical world I expressed an interest in. In response to my queries he was able to explain to me exactly why bicycles and motorcycles topple over when stationary but not when in motion. Things like that.

Phil hired me as his apprentice installing Freeman Metal Marine Pilots on fishing boats. The device ("You set your course and it keeps it") had been invented by his uncle Wood Freeman who was a chemistry professor and a commercial fisherman. Freeman Metal Marine Pilots were very expensive but were regarded as essential by the demanding commercial fishermen in the Pacific Northwest. Uncle Wood was six feet five inches tall and straight standing. He always wore a white shirt and tie when assembling the Pilots in his basement workshop. But he was too old to go to the docks, do the installations, then head out to open waters to test them and show the fishing captains how they worked. Installation, testing, and teaching fell to Phil and me. I loved roaring around Puget Sound on big salmon trawlers, listening to the rough talk of the fishing captains. What 12-year-old kid wouldn't?

I remained close with Phil through my teen years, through my undergraduate years at Berkeley, through graduate school at Cornell, until his untimely death in the 1970s. I once confessed to him that my parents had discouraged me from going to college. He said, "When I met you, you were about ten or eleven. After we spoke, my first thought was not whether you would go to university. I was mainly curious about which graduate school you would eventually choose to attend. And in what field?" He never said as much at the time. But obviously I was getting a better and more encouraging vibe off of him than from my parents.

Nathan Eckstein Junior High

After sixth grade at Laurelhurst, while still living in the Village, I attended Nathan Eckstein Junior High School for two years. Nathan Eckstein was several miles north of Union Bay Village and wonderfully, from my standpoint, it drew from both Laurelhurst and View Ridge Elementary schools.

That meant I was back in school together with my friends Bert and Richard.

In seventh grade we had different classrooms and teachers for different subjects, girls with little and sometimes large breasts, gym with showers, hair in new places, jockstraps, enforced academic and athletic competitiveness, athlete's foot, the works. Mixed into this hormonal witches' brew, how you dressed and what your father drove, began to figure into the pecking order.

My family situation did not lead to me becoming stigmatized in what was probably the most upper-middle-class middle school in Seattle. My earnings enabled me to mask my family's poverty. I could buy everything I needed and pretty much anything I desired. And as I paid for my wardrobe myself, it was entirely of my own choosing and uncompromisingly "in style." Most importantly, I no longer had to slop plates in view of the entire student body. My parents could not, but I could pay for my lunches and any "extras" I wanted.

The unspoken arrangement I had with my family was whatever I earned was mine to keep and to spend as I wished. I had no thought to pitch in and help out with family expenses beyond what I saved them by buying my own food and clothing. And they expressed no interest in me contributing part of what I earned to the household budget. It seemed a sufficient boon to them that I was eating less from the family larder, costing them no weekly "allowance," buying all my own clothes, especially shoes, and never asking them for anything expensive like a bicycle or, eventually, my first car that I bought when I was 15. My father more than once remarked that I was eating better, dressing better, living better than they were but his irritation never grew to the point that he asked me for money. Later, I learned the hard way that eating extra food I purchased in his presence could throw him into a violent rage.

When I found out that children in poor immigrant families sometimes bring their earnings home to their mothers, I understood. It made sense to me that if there were strong bonds of love in a family, the children would want to contribute to its general welfare. I would have gladly given every cent to my great grandmother or, if they needed it, almost any other member of my extended family. I never felt any tug to share with my mother and father beyond the relief I brought by paying my own way. And, after the "room of my own" incident when I was four, they never again presumed to ask for my help.

I Cure My Classmates' Athletes' Foot

My search for innovative ways a kid could earn a dollar was unrelenting. One day I walked through a marsh between the garbage dump and a shallow edge of Lake Washington. It was no doubt heavily polluted and overgrown with mutated cattails much taller than I was. When I got home and took off my wet shoes and socks I discovered my chronic case of athlete's foot (the gym showers) was cleared up. Instantly. Something about the chemical composition of the polluted marsh water had attacked the foot fungus killing it completely. To make certain it was not a fluke I re-infected myself and tried the cure again. Sure enough, the marsh water worked a second time. I bought a dozen quart-sized mason jars, bottled the water as my "miracle cure" and sold it to my classmates for a dollar a bottle—with 25 cents return for the mason jar. They knew I was always experimenting with machines, electricity, and chemicals, so my claim to have discovered a "wonder drug" made perfect sense to them. I gave free treatments to a couple of friends to start the buzz. It worked and I had a waiting list for the next available jar. I made money hand over fist until, after about ten days, everyone's athlete's foot came back with a vengeance. When I realized it would require continuous multiple treatments to keep it under control, I told my customers the truth about my "secret ingredient" and led a few of my close pals through the marsh. I did keep some regular customers who were rich enough they could not be bothered to go to the marsh for self-treatment. When my Grandma Fran heard of my Athlete's Foot Cure business she hooted with joy: "You're going to be just fine, sprout."

The education delivered by the public schools I attended was top notch. And Nathan Eckstein was even a cut above that. The projects where I was living happened to be in the wealthiest, most privileged, heavily supported public school districts in Seattle. In those days, we were not assigned homework until high school. We did everything in class during the day. So my sometimes heavy work schedule did not interfere with my schooling and I continued to follow all the lessons closely. I had no consciousness of grades. My motive was to get the work done correctly, not to get a grade. I got all "A"s and "B"s. Mostly "A"s. My parents were even less concerned about grades than I was. They barely glanced at my report cards and never commented.

Because of my "Miracle Cures" and some other things I had a quirky reputation at Nathan Eckstein. I was able to make exact copies of typewritten hall pass notes freehand with a ballpoint. My "typed" counterfeits were good enough to get us by the cursory glance the hall monitors gave the notes. I never sold these but gave them out as favors to friends. We could leave class anytime we wanted.

Experimental Instruction in Spanish

One of the history teachers at Nathan Eckstein was a young Mexican who told us the story of his family's swimming across the Rio Grande when he was five years old. When we complained about the rigor he demanded from us, he countered with "Imagine what it would be like if I taught you in Spanish." He explained that he entered first grade in Texas before he knew a word of English. He painted a vivid picture of what it was like for a young boy to be trying to learn English at the same time as trying to learn to read it and write. We identified so strongly with his struggles and eventual success that we begged him to teach us Spanish. I became a ringleader in the effort to persuade him. The idea of learning a foreign language was intoxicating to me. I did not care what language. Any language would do. Just as reading was my first passport to elsewhere, acquiring a foreign language could land me elsewhere with competency to understand what was going on there. It was another of those transformative moments. I was all in.

Our charismatic history teacher got permission to start a special class of Spanish language instruction that, if successful, might be incorporated into the regular curriculum. He selected me to be one of the 10 pupils in the experimental class. He taught us enough Spanish in eighth grade that when I moved to San Diego three years later I was able to understand and to make myself well-understood in the Spanish-speaking communities I encountered there and in Baja California.

My lucky-break Spanish language instruction occasioned one of my father's thoughtful and positive interventions in my life. One day, on his return from his classes at the University, he gave me a used, but good condition copy of Appleton's New English-Spanish and Spanish-English Dictionary, revised and enlarged third edition with supplements. It was the finest book I owned up to that point, not a student edition but a serious tool: 539 pages of fine print translation. My father told me that he had spotted it in the university bookstore and thought I might be able to use it. How right he was. It is sitting here beside me on my desk as I am writing this. I continue to use it in my correspondence with Spanish-speaking scholars and my dealings with the super men who assist me with my landscaping and carpentry.

"We're Running Away"

Moving to Union Bay turbo-charged the tension between my mother and father over his wandering eye. Almost every unit had an attractive twenty-something woman student or student's wife. It was never possible to know what it was about my father's infidelities that would set my mother off. She openly expressed her strong feelings to me and I don't know how many others. Sometimes she was out-of-control screaming about one of his girlfriends, not caring who heard her—her children, her relatives, our neighbors. At other times she seemed to be gal pals with the other woman, never registering a complaint. The amount of her pique did not seem to be correlated with the intensity of the alienation of my father's affection. She was as likely to shriek out her anger if she caught my father ogling a woman in the street as for a full-blown affair.

Throughout my childhood she over-shared the most lurid details. There were no discreet words like "erectile dysfunction" back then. She complained to me that while he was having an affair with a fifteen-year-old, my father was not able to "get it up." With her, my mother, not the fifteen-year-old. I didn't even know what she was talking about. Whatever it meant, I thought it was wrong for a mother to be telling her son about something like that. She demanded my sympathy. But I never gave it. My unvarying response was to sit stoically and passively absorb her harangues with a rigorously neutral attitude. She took my neutrality as treason. She was trying to get me to comfort her. My lack of sympathy was not motivated by solidarity with my father. He was a jerk. I was angry that she would come to me with complaints that she should have directed first to my father and then to other adults, not her young son. The more she emoted, the less loyalty or closeness I felt to either one of them. As I entered adolescence, each ugly revelation was like another brick in a wall between me and my parents. It was about this time that I decided neither of them had even a single worthwhile quality. As an adolescent, my judgment was total. I thought they were both completely worthless. As an adult I did not back off much. Even now, I continue to believe their character was irredeemably flawed. Some of their professional accomplishments demanded rigorous application on their part. But their efforts to "better themselves" did not turn them into worthy human beings.

In the Union Bay project when I was twelve, my father began eyeing a neighbor woman named Marylou. I babysat for Marylou so I monitored his flirting closely knowing where it might lead, and I made an early determination that his advances would get him nowhere. Marylou was flattered by his attention, but too close to her husband and children to succumb to his advances. She was amused, but I could see, long before my father could, that she had drawn a line. This did not stop my mother from going ballistic. Probably my father's persistence in the face of Marylou's resistance is what set her off. It was like Marylou, by resisting his advances, was insulting my mother for having a creep for a husband. If Marylou had succumbed to his advances my mother's position as alpha female would have been restored.

One evening, mother came to me sobbing. "Get your coat. I can't take it anymore. We're running away." It was an order. I didn't dare disobey. But I also knew she was a hysteric—always fully satisfied simply to have made a dramatic scene. Spur of the moment, with no suitcases or money, leaving my brothers behind, I knew she had no intention to follow through. So I got my coat and we "ran away" into the night. She said, "Hurry, I have to get away from here." We had gotten almost to the garbage dump when Marylou, her husband, and my father came screeching up in a borrowed car. "Fran. Fran. What's wrong?" My mother just kept sobbing incoherently. "I think she's a little tired," I managed to say, adding, somewhat out of character for me, "Maybe she's sick and tired." Few other words were exchanged as we drove back to the project. The next day and ever after I was treated by all the parties as though I had not been there, like nothing had occurred. My mother knew what she was doing. That night marked the end of my father's attention to Marylou. As with all her sharing on such matters, I wished she had figured out how to handle it without putting me in the middle.

My Father Continues in Graduate School and Family's Poverty Begins to Ease

As I prospered at Union Bay, so did my parents. While I was in seventh grade, my father transitioned from being an undergraduate education major to a masters' student in mathematical statistics. The G.I. Bill would go on endlessly so long as he was making normal progress toward some degree. With a K-12 teaching certificate in hand they shifted gears. How about shooting for an advanced degree, maybe even a Ph.D.? They discussed it in guarded and hushed tones. It might not work out, but if it did it would be the grand prize and worth all the time and trouble. They called the Ph.D. degree the "Union Card." Along with many of his G.I. Bill peers in graduate school, he regarded his K-12 certificate as giving him a safe fallback position. He would just keep going until someone told him to stop.

Now, as a graduate student, he got his first teaching and research assistantships. And my mother, who until that time had been averse to working outside the home, trained as an IBM keypunch operator and went to work for General Insurance of America in their accounting division. "Just to get us over the top while Earle is earning his Ph.D.," she explained. She had been attending the University of Washington part-time and arranged with General Insurance to be excused from work for four hours a week so she could continue taking one class each quarter. For the first time since I was three years old my parents had enough money for a modestly normal almost middleclass life.

We could afford milk delivery without Mrs. Balch's intervention, a subscription to the Seattle Times, store-bought haircuts, a telephone, a 21-inch black-and-white Packard Bell television set, and a vacuum cleaner. "There's no dust bag to empty when you do it with a Lewitt." And, 'ta da,' in 1953, a new car. It was a bottom-of-the-line six-cylinder, excrement-brown-colored Dodge Meadowbrook sedan. But it was a Dodge—a half step above the cheapest "big three" Ford, Chevy, and Plymouth. So both my father and mother could really think they were somebody. A new car, and not the cheapest one available, either. And to top it off (literally) my father demanded that the dealer paint the top beige, to make it into a "two-tone," then an option that was regarded as higher class.

With the New Car Came Camping Trips
Almost Every Weekend

The Dodge brought a big change in the pattern of family activities. We were able to go camping on weekends and holidays. Both my mother and father were enthusiastic campers, al-

Fran MacCannell poses proudly with the new Dodge on a camping trip in 1953

most to the point of fanaticism. They bought two umbrella tents. Eight by eight with a center pole for the three boys, ten by ten with corner poles for the two of them. And a Coleman lantern and two-burner kerosene Coleman stove, sleeping bags and air mattresses. With that initial investment we hit the road almost every weekend even during Washington's famously rainy winters. Washington state has hundreds, perhaps even thousands of campgrounds, many of them sited and designed by my grandfather. We all felt very much at home in the woods. I liked it a lot. Especially when it was rough and stormy like at Iron Springs on the Pacific coast where we went for several years in a row between Christmas and New Year's.

We became so well-off that every Saturday afternoon, my father gave me 10 dollars to take the bus to the Pike Street Farmers Market downtown and buy the family groceries for the week. The Market was closed on Sundays. My parents discovered that if you shopped late Saturday and bargained with the farmers you could get what was left in their stalls at greatly reduced prices. Often less than half price. They instructed me to bargain hard and come back with as much food as I could. I usually managed several bags, enough to cause me to make more than one trip up and down the bus steps on my way home. I occasionally treated myself to a baby shrimp cocktail in a snow cone purchased with 25 cents of their money, not mine. Yes, I still feel a bit guilty about it.

Even though I was mainly self-supporting I benefited a great deal from my parent's new affluence. We had been so poor just the year before that instead of being sent to the Pike Street Market on Saturday, I was sent to Golden Gardens Park on Puget Sound. My contribution was to harvest limpets to make a stew that we could eat for a couple of days. There is precious little meat in a limpet, so I had to get a big bag full for enough to feed five people. It takes a lot of prying to get a limpet off a rock.

This was profoundly embarrassing for me as Golden Gardens in the summer months was a favorite date and hang-out beach for my classmates. When they saw me, they correctly surmised what I was up to. In spite of the fact that I could dress as well or better than they did, and rode a better bicycle, they knew. They knew I lived in the projects. They knew exactly where I was coming from and what I was doing. My family was so poor I had to forage for limpets. In 1954 we were poor no more and we moved out of Union Bay Village into a real house.

10

We Move Out of the Projects into a Real House 1954-56

IN 1954, MY PARENTS BOUGHT a 1920s era, comfortable two story, five-bedroom, 2.5 bath, house with a detached garage on 8th Avenue N.E. in Seattle for $8,000. They had zero savings, so my Grandma Fran loaned them the down payment. I got a room of my own that I did not have to pay for and so did Bill and John. My room was in a finished basement. It had narrow slit, armored-car-type windows close to the ceiling. I could stand on my tiptoes, look out and see people's feet and ankles as they walked by. Some natural light came in and it had a small closet and room for a bed and a worktable.

In the Village I had to pack my projects up every evening, put whatever I was working on and my tools away, and stow my foldup table. My work area filled the entire space between the bunkbed where Bill and I slept and the army cot that John slept on. I had to sit on Bill's lower bunk to work. Every night I packed everything away so we could get in and out of bed. After our move, I was able to spread out my modeling and drawings and leave them in place until I completed them. That was a definite improvement in my quality of life.

My mother and father were able to buy stuff to go with the house. Like a washing machine and dryer, a stove and a fridge all in a matching yellow non-color that I think was called "Harvest Gold." This was pretty heady stuff after more than a decade of abject poverty. But the move was not all to the good.

My Family's New Affluence Meant Worse Schools

What was not an improvement was my new school district. The deepest irony of my childhood and youth in Seattle is the schools I attended while living in the projects were vastly

superior to the ones I attended when we moved out of the projects into a nice neighborhood with single family homes. View
Ridge, Laurelhurst and Nathen Eckstein by happenstance were
the best schools in the city. How Cedar Vale and Union Bay
Village ended up in their districts, I'll never know. When my
parents became homeowners we moved to the Wallingford district. Wallingford was not a bad neighborhood. It was middle- to
lower-middle class detached homes, well-kept and comfortable
like ours. But it was economically several cuts below View Ridge
and Laurelhurst. Because of my family's new affluence, I had to
leave the Nathan Eckstein catchment area and enter Alexander
Hamilton junior high.

Richard, Bert, Guy Moen, and my other pals at Nathan
Eckstein would eventually go on to the then top-ranked Roosevelt High. From Hamilton I would go to Lincoln High, not
the lowest ranked academically, but somewhere in the middle
of Seattle's eight high schools. I was unaware of the difference a
school district makes until I suddenly experienced it. I had never thought about education quality before, but I could tell right
away that my new school was not a quality place. The problems I
experienced in Stewart Heights I attributed to my teacher, Mrs.
Boley, not to the school. My new school was interesting but far
from excellent. Some of the teachers had seriously strange personality quirks. My journalism teacher played Edith Piaf records
during class, refused to read anything we wrote and gave us all
Bs. Weird.

My social studies teacher was an out lesbian —"out" to us,
her students. This was also very strange at the time. We used to
tease her in a friendly way, "Hey, Miss Pease, why don't you get
married, ha ha." And she would cheerfully answer back, "What?
And have another mouth to feed?"

In my journalism class I learned zero about journalism,
but the class launched in me a life-long love of Piaf. Hearing Piaf's voice altered my consciousness much as my first sighting of
the MG TC had. Suddenly there before me was this wonderful
sound. I could not understand a single word. But I was felled by
the weight of emotions and intellect carried along on the voice
alone. I was compelled to realize how much more of our human-

ity the voice can convey beyond the meaning of the words that come out of our mouths. My sense of the importance of beauty now extended to the human voice. From that moment I have always listened for the sound of "freedom" in the voice, for evidence of an ineluctable human spirit that cannot be denied. That stupid class without a wit of journalism nevertheless changed me.

Starting with Piaf, I have never stopped listening for intonation that can change everything, power revolutions, rescue souls from the depths of despair, express universal sadness, ecstasy, a dream for a better future.

At Hamilton and later at Lincoln High, I encountered classmates who were open about their intent to pursue criminal careers as adults. I made friends with some of the future criminals, who were called "the hoods," as well as with those who were destined for squarer adult lives. The hoods adopted me as an honorary member of their gangs, explaining that I was "smart" and would probably end up as something like a lawyer or a politician. They did not expect me to join them in their petty larceny. They openly cultivated my good will, telling me to remember them and come to their aid when they got in trouble in our adult lives. I briefly considered a career as a master criminal but gave up on the idea as quickly as I got it. My red hair. Wherever I went, I was the one everybody noticed and remembered because of my hair. Not understanding how line-ups worked, I was certain to be picked out of any line-up, I thought.

Even though we were destined never again to be in the same school together, my old classmates at Nathan Eckstein who went on to Roosevelt continued to be my closest friends. I began skipping many of my parent's camping trips so I could spend the weekends with Bert and Richard. When I asked if I could stay home instead of going camping with them, my parents were always quick to say yes. When I stayed behind, Bill was given his choice to go with them or stay with me. John always went with them. They seemed to prefer camping without Bill and me. Bill, eleven at the time, had friends in our new neighborhood to hang out with while I was in View Ridge. My parent's only condition was that I make sure Bill was fed—that I would fix at least one meal a day for him. We ate some wondrous concoctions that year.

I Adapt my Businesses to Our New Neighborhood

My family move caused me to lose my lucrative Village laundry business. But I was able to more than make up for it as a landscaper and handyman. My gigs babysitting almost every evening continued unabated. After our arrival in a neighborhood of single-family detached homes, I added yard maintenance to the services I offered and quickly developed a far-flung clientele. I had enough households on every two-week schedules that I could work between two and four hours after school every day mowing, weeding, raking leaves, etc. One very old widow hired me to wrap every lump of coal in her bin in newspaper bound with twine. She stoked her own furnace, but she didn't want to touch the coal. So I made her these clean, neat little bundles to throw in her fire box.

Soon I was making as much money as I did in Union Bay Village. Many of my baby-sitting clients drove me back and forth to my old haunts in the Village so I could continue to sit for them.

My personal style began to evolve. I bought myself a high-quality wool tweed, three-quarter length "car coat," then the height of school fashion in Seattle. It was moderate and taste-ful. But not my pants. At the urging of my new proto-delinquent friends I purchased a pair of canary yellow "peggers," zoot-suit type pants with a blousy pleated waist and tight cuffs that, even though quite ghastly, were the most desired by the "hoods" at the time. I also bought myself a pair of "salt and pepper" peggers that could almost pass for a normal pair of pants.

The Invention of Long-Playing Records and Rock 'n Roll

About this time, coincident with the first appearance of Rock 'n' Roll music, vinyl long-playing records (LPs) began to replace the old 78 rpm shellac disks. The old format could only hold about 2 minutes of music on each side. Smaller 45 rpm vinyl disks could hold about five minutes on the side. And large format 33 and 1/3 rpm vinyl LPs could hold about 20 minutes per side. For the first time it was possible to have classical music recordings that did not need to be interrupted and flipped or changed every two minutes.

I bought myself a small portable LP player.

My first LP record was a two-disk recording of the sounds of Grand Prix cars, the precursors to Formula 1—interviews with drivers, and one-minute segments of the engine sounds of Ferraris, Vanwalls, Jaguars. There was a one-minute track of each of the cars at idle and another one-minute track of them at full speed in top gear down a main straight.

At a time when my male classmates were teaching themselves to speak exactly like Donald Duck, and propositioning girls in Donald Duckese, I was teaching myself to produce the sounds of Ferraris. I could make the sounds of each different car at speed by biting my lips together and forcing air out. The sound of a small displacement 12-cylinder Ferrari at speed was tenor, like ripping canvas. I could make the Ferrari sound, the base roar of a Jaguar, and everything in between, with sufficient accuracy that my pals could name the car I was imitating.

My classmates were buying Rock 'n' Roll 45s as fast as they could be produced. *"Rock Around the Clock,"* *"Ragg Mopp,"* and soon the early Elvis were transforming my entire generation's consciousness. I was still playing the violin but not for much longer.

All of my violin training had been in the classics. I enjoyed Rock 'n' Roll, but my first LP music purchases were Debussy's *"Children's Corner Suite,"* and Mozart's *"Eine Kleine Nachtmusik."* Today, these seem to be somewhat juvenile classical music choices, but I should probably cut my 14-year-old self some slack.

My Grandma Fran Loved 'Race Music'

Rock 'n' Roll didn't knock me over the way it did my classmates. And not because of any snooty preference for classical music. Again, I have my Grandma Fran to thank. In the late

'40s she became a fan of "race music." Radio stations were racially segregated, and the music played on Black stations was proto-Rock 'n' Roll, Rhythm and Blues with a back-beat. My grandmother never listened to race music in my presence. But I soon discovered, when she left me alone in her car, if I turned on the radio it would be tuned to a Black station. In the late 1940s I could belt out the lyrics,

> *"Hambone, Hambone where you been? / Around the world an' I'm goin' again. / What you gonna do when you get back? / Take a little walk by the railroad track . . ."*

I could sing "Hambone" five years before Bo Didley recorded it as a Rock 'n' Roll hit in the early 1950s. I turned the radio off when I saw my grandmother coming back to the car so my knowing her secret became my secret. I would have loved to listen with her and sung along together. But the world was just too stupidly segregated for there to be even a small place for a white Okie grandma and her skinny redheaded grandson singing race music duets in the 1940s. We might have pulled it off alone in her car with the radio playing. I wish we had.

> *"Hambone, Hambone, pat him on the shoulder If you got a pretty girl I'll show you how to hold her . . ."*

In school, I was not "popular." I was acceptably just inside the weird line and had no trouble making other slightly marginal friends and even dating some of the "popular" girls. Smart girls, I soon discovered, were much more to my liking than popular girls and I found them easier to approach and more receptive to my interests and ideas. Beginning at age 15, I had a series of teenage-serious, "going steady" type relationships each of several months' duration, all with straight-A students. I was not focused on their grades. It was their more agile and flexible minds that attracted me. Their GPA was incidental. Most of my girlfriends were a year older and a class ahead.

II

Learning From the Model T

DURING THIS PERIOD by far the most formative experience was caused by Albert Balch Sr.'s intervention in our (Bert's, Richard's, and my) lives that went far beyond a wealthy doting father's normal generosity. He created the conditions for us seriously to pursue automobile mechanics and restoration to an adult standard. Here is what he did.

Remember Cedar Vale Project, slated for closure and demolition when we moved out and that Bert's father owned Cedar Vale and planned to replace our row houses with substantial up-scale single family homes? I had visited him in his offices on many occasions and without knowing what they were I had probably seen the blueprints on the wall, but he never mentioned his plans to me. After evicting us, and every other family, Balch Sr. bulldozed Cedar Vale off its foundations and sent the entire project to the dump, leaving only the grid of streets—about twelve square blocks. He then erected an eight-foot-tall cyclone fence with a locking gate around the perimeter, and near the middle of the planned development he built a very nice model home with a detached multi-car garage connected to the main house by a covered breezeway that could accommodate two additional cars.

Albert Sr. told us he would delay further development of the property for two years so we, Bert, Richard, and I, could use it as an off-road place to drive before we would qualify for learner permits. We could drive there until we were old enough to get our drivers' licenses.

Mr. Balch found and purchased two Model T Fords, neither of them running, and had them delivered to the display home's garage and breezeway. Model T Fords are universally recognized as "the car that put America on wheels." Fifteen million "T Buckets," or "Tin Lizzies" were built and sold between 1908 and 1927. In 1927 a new Model T cost $300.00. In the 1950s they were totally anachronistic but there had been enough of them built that we could spot one on the road every two or three weeks. Non-working examples were everywhere. A short drive into the countryside would turn up several non-running Ts sitting in farmer's fields, most available for sale for ten or twenty dollars.

We were not allowed to enter any room of the model home except one of the bathrooms to clean ourselves up and the kitchen to fix snacks. That kitchen was the most magnificent I had ever seen. In addition to the two almost complete cars, Albert Sr. gave us a Model T parts catalogue and told us he would order the parts we needed. If we could make one running Model T from the two broken ones and a few new parts, we could teach ourselves to drive and use my old project's gridded street system for our motoring pleasure. Even though he was not my dad, I was able to benefit magnificently from the super-dad who evicted my family.

Our car was originally a four-door phaeton like this one. Only we stripped off its body and fenders, leaving only dashboard, steering and other controls, and seats. Even if it looked this good (it didn't) it still was totally anachronistic even in 1954.

Because it was on private property, it was completely legal even though we were only 14 years old, something we had to explain through the fence to bewildered Seattle cops on more than one occasion. Bertie was instructed to tell the police that his dad owned the property, that they would have to serve his father with a search warrant to enter, and to hand them one of Albert Sr.'s business cards if they had any further questions.

It took only a few weeks of motivated problem solving for us to get a rolling chassis and a running engine. With the bodywork still off, we taught ourselves how to drive. All we needed were seats and a steering wheel. Bert and Richard did most of the mechanical work because they could come directly from school every day. My contribution was limited to weekends. I read and interpreted manuals and parts lists. Richard was the only one of the three of us with sufficient upper body strength to crank the engine. His doctors had him on an exercise regime because of his heart.

One of the hardest parts was getting gas for the car. We had to walk ten blocks to the nearest station then carry five-gallon Jerry Cans back to the property. Five gallons of gasoline in a heavy metal can weighs almost 40 pounds and is a big load for a skinny 14-year-old. We had to trade off every fifty feet or so to get the fuel to the car. In those days there were no self-service stations. The attendants were almost always bad boys in their high teens—17, 18, 19. Not much different in class or capability than the young men who would begin "knocking over" (robbing) gas stations and liquor stores at about the same age. Armed robbery was a seriously considered career option for white working-class teen-aged males in the 1950s. Probably better than digging ditches.

After about our third trip, the guys who pumped our gas became curious about what we were up to. "What are you kids doing with all this gas. Not for a lawn mower. Are you planning to blow something up?" When we told them what we were "up to" they were incredulous. Later that day two of them appeared, watching us intently through the cyclone fence as we chugged around the streets of the old project. We drove over to them cross-country to say "Hi." They hung on the fence shaking their heads in disbelief. One of them told me, "If I'd had something like this, my life would have turned out completely different." Amen, brother. He was absolutely right. My life turned out "completely different."

Driving A Model T Is An Existential Challenge

Its gear changes are foot actuated with two pedals, its clutch and neutral gear is at the end of the pull on the handbrake, and both the fuel feed and spark advance are on the steering column where the turn signals and lights are today. "Spark advance"? In order to get more RPM and power from an internal combustion engine you need to feed it more fuel and make its spark plugs fire faster. Automated spark advance was one of the miracles of automobile engineering in the 1920s. On a Model T, spark advance was manual. It was and is hard for me to believe that this was the automobile that put America on the road. It is proof that Americans will accept almost any torture and master really complicated procedures, for the sake of their mobility. Two years ago, a close friend told me his father, a very famous scholar, was supposed to learn to drive on a Model T. He got one block before running into a stone wall and that block was the only time he drove for the rest of his life. If you try to drive a Model T you will understand completely.

Today, we pull up to a stop by removing our foot from the gas and putting it on the brakes while steering into the space. This same maneuver is accomplished in a Model T as follows: Using one hand you steer into the space; using your other hand you pull down on the throttle; using your third hand you retard the spark; using your fourth hand you pull up on the handbrake. As the car slows to a stop you fully engage the handbrake which also puts the car in neutral gear. This sounds silly but it is perfectly accurate. To operate the machine your hands do a ballet across four different sets of controls that must be adjusted more or less simultaneously. To get going again you push down on the hi-lo pedal to engage low gear while slowly releasing the handbrake that also engages the clutch. Then repeat the above process in reverse, feeding more gas and spark while accelerating to about five miles per hour at which point you release the hi-lo pedal to engage top gear. Then it's more gas and spark up to its top speed of 45 MPH. Oh, and don't forget to steer.

I was the worst driver of the three T-kids because I became obsessed with getting the right fuel feed and spark setting. Failure to get the spark right could result in killing the engine. If we killed the engine, it would sometimes take hours to get it going again. In the beginning, getting it re-started sometimes required a partial teardown of the engine, or at least the carburetor. So I had to make a choice between keeping the engine running smoothly, i.e., focusing on the spark and gas settings, or focusing on the road. Adjusting the throttle and spark advance at the same time requires taking both hands off the wheel. Skilled Model-T drivers can intuitively hit the right gas and spark setting in an instant and get their hands back on the wheel before the car has travelled more than ten or twenty feet. When I didn't hit the spark and gas mixture sweet spots right away, with my hands off the wheel I sometimes wandered off the road. With its 19-inch wheels and huge ground clearance the T Ford was perfectly comfortable off road. And with the houses bulldozed out of the way, there was nothing left of my old project for me to run into. I always steered very clear of the beautiful model home. Even though staying on the road did not matter either to the car or our surroundings, my clumsy driving perturbed especially Bert.

Getting the engine started before we had everything sorted was a pain. Richard could turn the crank several times but we worried about his heart. When Richard was not with us, Bert and I could sometimes get it going by standing on a front tire and jumping onto the crank. But for this method to work it had to start on the first half turn. There was also the risk, if the spark was too far advanced, that the engine would backfire, explosively reversing the direction of the crank. This was the number one cause of broken arms when hand cranking was the norm. And if it happened when we were using our "jumping onto the crank" method it could pitch us on our heads into the weeds beside the road.

A Car of My Own

From that T-Ford, I learned the basics of car assembly, repair, and restoration. In less than a year, before my 15th birthday, I had saved enough money to buy my first car. This was an important fork in the road where the paths were different. Because Bert was a rich kid he was stuck with the car his dad gave him. Since the likelihood that my dad would give me a car was less than zero, I could have any car I could afford. The car I bought was a clapped-out nine-year-old Ford Tudor, army grey. I acquired it from a sociology graduate student friend of my father's. Instead of biking over to View Ridge to work on the Model T, I began spending my weekends and every non-work hour after school restoring, lightly customizing, and hot-rodding my Ford—rebuilding its transmission and brakes, fitting it with a straight-through muffler, and de-chroming, reupholstering, and repainting it gloss black.

A 1946 Ford like my first car. On mine, I removed the hood ornament and chrome stripes down the sides and above the wheel wells, and filled in the holes for 'smoother,' 'less cluttered' lines.

I was far from alone in finding the chrome on the exterior of Detroit cars, including my Ford, busy and distracting from their honest uncluttered form. Most high school hot rod owners in the 1950s stripped their cars back to the unadorned body. Taking the chrome stripes off the trunk and removing the hood ornament and filling the holes was called "shaving the hood and deck." Undertaking these simple operations was just as natural to me as modifying the look of something I was drawing.

There was a fifty-foot dirt driveway beside our house leading to a shack-type one car garage in our back yard. My father ceded the drive and garage to me, preferring to park his car, his still newish Dodge, in the street in front of the house. Our driveway was not exactly the street system of the Cedar Vale project but I could legally "test drive" all my mechanical work by roaring forward and reverse up and down beside the house. By 1946, Fords had automatic spark advance and a conventional set up for the clutch and manual gear changes, the "H" pattern on the steering column.

Bert tried to re-kindle my interest in the Model T by driving it on the streets from View Ridge to my house in Wallingford when he was 15. He was arrested, of course. Three years later I would occasionally see him, presumably with a valid driver's license, motoring along the streets of Seattle in his very incongruous vehicle. I pulled him over a couple of times to chat and catch up. He enjoyed pointing out to me all the necessary modifications he had done to make the Model T street legal—head and taillights, fenders and a windshield, etc.

During this same period, when I was getting my own car ready for when I could drive it legally, I helped a kid on my block (he was about 17 and already had his license) restore a 1939 Packard 120 convertible coupe. His dad bought it for him to mess around with. It was a pretty car and once we got it running, I enjoyed riding in it. It was the first Packard with independent front suspension. My Grandma Fran said cars with independent front suspension had "knee action."

While my 1946 Ford was a respectable hot rod for the era, I had very mixed feelings about it. I was already so smitten by English and European exotics that every modification I made to my Ford made me a bit sad. It was not an MG, a Jaguar, a Porsche or an Alfa Romeo, or even a Volkswagen. When I saw one of these cars buzzing down the street, it was like love at first sight over and over again. When I found one of them parked, I could stand and admire it for half a day. Well, maybe not the VW Beetle. If I was destined to become an automobile mechanic, at this point in time a highly probable adult vocation for me, I wanted to be working on these cars. When I spotted one of their owners getting in or out, I always engaged them in conversation. If they were not in a hurry, they were usually very generous, describing their cars' design and mechanicals in detail. I got an entire education about the advantages of rack and pinion steering, four-speed transmissions, synchromesh first gears, and other design features that Detroit had never considered.

12

My Father Hires Me to be
a Census Taker

MY FATHER'S POSITION weith the Population Laboratory was to manage disputes between the towns (more precisely, "incorporated places") and the State government. Each incorporated place would receive an annual allocation of State tax
money based on its population size. For a small town, an extra
one hundred people could make a big difference in their budget.
The towns would usually pad their population growth estimates
to try to get a bigger slice of the tax pie. The baseline was the
decennial Federal Census that provided the last accurate headcount. A rural community might report to the State that "in the
1950 census we had 1,322 people but today in 1953 we estimate
that number has grown to 1,705."

My father's job was to visit the town, talk to people, read
the local newspaper, and drive around looking at fresh graves
in the cemetery, "Help Wanted" and "House For Sale" signs
and other indicators of increasing or decreasing population. He
would prepare a draft report of the Population Lab's estimate.
He might concur that the town's estimate seemed reasonable or,
if it seemed too high, he would counter it with the State's estimate. For example, he might say, "There has been some growth,
but not to 1,705. The state estimates the current population to
be 1,500."

Because budget allocations were at stake, a disagreement
about population size set in motion a negotiation whereby the
State and the town would arrive at an agreed upon number. If
they could not agree, things got interesting. A special census
would be required to provide an empirically accurate basis for
the allocation. These head counts were costly, involving state
census enumerators knocking on every door in the town and

interviewing every family. The allocation would be based on the results of the actual headcount. Here is the interesting part: which number, the town's original estimate, or my father's, was closest to the actual count determined which jurisdiction paid for the census. If my father was closest, the town had to pay the full costs of the census. If the town's estimate was closer than my father's, the State had to pay.

An agreement was usually reached without an actual headcount. Neither side liked to gamble the cost of a census. However, on several occasions the Population Lab had to go out into the boonies and conduct a special census.

Here is another quite wonderful thing my father did for me for which I will always be grateful. He got the Lab to hire me to be an enumerator on a special census.

Half-way through my 15th year I had grown to my full height—six feet plus a fraction. My father told his colleagues that with a suit (I already owned two) and tie and an official looking clamp-board, I could pass as a college student. From his perspective, he was not doing me any favors. Enumerators got paid by the head, not by the hour. The graduate students took the plum neighborhoods in the center of town where the houses are packed together, and they could rack up the numbers quickly. No one wanted to work the small farms on the edge of town with half mile walks between houses, dusty dirt roads, and vicious dogs. That would be my beat.

I loved that day. I loved the randomness of knocking on every door. I loved the great variety of humanity I encountered. I loved the rigor and the tricks of the trade. "Your job is to find and count absolutely every living person. When a father has given you the name, age, and gender of his last child, you must ask 'what about the baby?' Most fathers forget to mention their last-born child."

I did not mind the challenges of my beat. Not the long walks between houses. They were called "domiciles" on the census forms because many of my families did not live in houses. There was always something interesting to look at. Like Model T Fords without wheels sitting in the middle of wheat fields. I did not mind waiting for a "head of household" to come out and tie up his pit bull. I did not mind that I could make much more money doing my regular other jobs. I was 15 years old and out in the field actually doing social science.

The First Door I Knocked On

It was a hoot. Made more so by an incident that happened at the very first house. It was definitely a domicile, not a house. A converted chicken coop, actually. I saw the tell-tale signs of habitation I had been told to look for—children's toys in the yard, a stove pipe routed out a window. When I entered the yard a large multi-breed dog came out from under the coop barking with its ears laid back. An adult male appeared. He was wearing bibbed coveralls over a "union suit." (Okie for "longjohns," or one-piece male underwear with a trap door at the rear.)

His strange attire didn't bother me. It happened also to be Ross Meskimen's default outfit. But this guy had shoulder-length hair and a waist-length beard. That kind of hair and beard I had only seen in cartoons depicting people crazed by religion. Every male in the 1950s had close-cropped hair. And I had never seen a man with a beard of any kind. Not in real life, only in period-piece movies. This beard was beyond strange. It was scary.

The man did not grab the dog by the collar or tie it up. He picked up a tree branch and hit the cowering dog, sending it weeping copiously under the house. The whack and the weeping seemed to be an oft repeated ritual exchange between man and dog. The blow was little more than a tap, and the moaning of the dog was clearly a case of over-acting.

The man turned and went back in the house and shut the door behind him without looking twice at me. It was like my being in his yard was none of his business and maybe if he ignored me, I would go away. The dog stayed hidden under the house and stopped moaning.

Rattled but resolute I crossed the yard and knocked on the door. It was a "double Dutch" door that opened separately on the top and bottom. While my knuckles were still raised, the top part swung swiftly inward. The bearded man stood close but said nothing. He just gazed intently waiting for me to speak.

I could see past him into the interior of the coop. Standing motionless, staring at me through the gloom, there was another adult male who was almost a duplicate of the one at the door. Same outfit. Same beard. Same intense eyes. The only light streamed through a window. I had already noticed there was no electrical hook-up. There were several children and infants playing on the floor.

Hanging back in the gloom was a woman in her 20s wearing a flour sack dress. Literally. It had the name of the mill upside down across her belly. Her head and neck stuck out of a hole cut in the middle of the sack's bottom which was the top of her dress. Her arms stuck out through smaller holes in the sides. It was my first glimpse of people who were poorer than I had ever been. Until that moment I had no idea there was a clothing threshold lower than church rummage sales.

The man at the door continued to give me a hard stare saying nothing. I had memorized my spiel:

"Good morning. My name is Dean MacCannell. I am an enumerator for the Washington State Population Laboratory. We are here in Okanogan today conducting a census of the population. Our count will be the basis for the town's budget allocation from the State. So, it is important that we get the names and ages of everyone living here. Can you tell me the name of the principal family that resides here?

The bearded man leaned forward an inch or two. His mustache quivered and he snarled,

"RAT!"

I had to make a quick decision: to retreat, to take off like a striped-ass ape, or to stand my ground. I thought of the dog under the house. I wondered if it discharged its other duties like biting the census taker in the ass with the same skill as acting contrite. I decided to take my chance with the human being in front of me and stood my ground.

"So would you spell that R a t t, Ratt?" I asked taking out my pen.

Did I detect a half-smile of appreciation? I think I did. "No," the bearded one replied. "That's Dub-yeah Aar Aah Gee

Haitch Tee. RAT."

He knew perfectly well that his Appalachian holler pronunciation of "Wright" would be heard by me as "Rat." I caught
on immediately. This guy got a big kick out of producing confusion and fear when a northern bureaucrat or cop, or whomever,
asked his name. 'No, I wasn't trying to be smart-ass officer, I
was just telling you my name as you asked.' What he enjoyed
even more was my refusal to take the bait. An immediate bond
formed between us. I may have been the first northern person
he met who did not cut and run when he barked "RAT" at them
or start to arrest him.

I would have liked to introduce him to my Uncle Doc
as another master of the eggcorn. I would have loved to stick
around all morning and tell him how Doc would explain why it
is so difficult to get through to a politician. It is because they are
surrounded by sycophants. But in Doc's pronunciation it was "a
sicko-fence." Or how Doc's son Jimmy always called my mother,
his Aunt Frances, "Aunt Rancid." There was so much we could
have discussed, but I had a job to do. I collected a lot of names
of the "Ratts" of Okanogan out of that chicken coop that morning—his, his younger brother living together in the coop with
their young wives and nine kids between them.

Smiling, I set off for my second house. The Academy
Award-winning dog stayed put. Every house was easy after that one.

13

Adolescent Ups and Downs—April to July 1956

VATS OF INK HAVE BEEN SPILLED and forests cut for descriptions of the angst of adolescents. In the spring and summer of 1956 I experienced a gamut of emotions as fully and deeply as any Holden Caulfield or young Werther. These included 'You are about to die' terror, a strong sense of accomplishment, rapturous joy, total relief, utter disgust, the giddiness of real freedom. These were not free-floating or in any way inexplicable. Each one had a clear and obvious cause, and they were not mixed together. None of them settled on me as a semi-permanent anxious, manic, or depressive state of mind. They came and went as I was bullied by a vicious youth my age; my brother John almost died from eating peanut butter; I got my first regular job, 20 hours a week, part-time after school as a night truck mechanic; had sex for the first time; escaped my father's grasp as he tried to kill me; was informed by my mother that she was having an affair; witnessed my parents engaging in a wife-swapping scheme; and moved away from home. All of this in a five-month span of time. Some life-altering changes come quickly. Especially when you are an adolescent.

My Bully

At my new school, I have mentioned, there were boys who had already decided on criminal careers. The worst of the bunch was a family of five boys by the name of Aure. (Pronounced Oarie.) They lived in a house like mine in my neighborhood about five blocks away. The youngest Aure was named Jens. He was the only one of the five who had not been expelled from school. Jens was in my grade, but we shared no classes together. His four older brothers were already dealing drugs, robbing gas stations and liquor stores, stealing cars, pimping out their girlfriends, and doing time. Every kid for miles around knew to avoid "Aure Ally" that ran behind the Aure household. The word was they would beat to near death anyone who came into their alley. No one was brave enough to test whether or not this was true. We did know that if you drove or walked down the street in front of their house, they would shoot you with air rifles and pellet guns.

Jens strongly disliked me. No incident preceded his attitude. He simply decided that I should be tortured and terrorized just for being who I was. He confronted me in the halls at school, in the streets of the neighborhood, and at public events like school dances. He would come up to me and say, "We need to settle this once and for all. Meet me at the _____ after school. I am going to give you the beating you deserve. I'm going to beat the shit out of you." I had no idea what "this" was, but I was frightened. Jens was a bit taller and heavier than me and already battle scarred. I did not weigh my options or consider what was the worst that might happen to me. A broken bone or tooth? Being maimed and crippled for life? Killed? It all ran together as sheer terror.

I stayed as far away as I could from the meeting places he designated. This only made things worse. The next time he saw me he would snarl, "You didn't show up. What are you, chicken?" Then he would crow and cluck loudly and call out to anyone standing nearby ridiculing me for being a yellow-bellied coward. He once told me "You've been avoiding me. No one turns their back on me. The next time you turn your back I'll bash your brains out with a rock." If I was carrying a notebook (no one had backpacks in the 1950s) he demanded to see it. If it contained a completed homework assignment, he would take it out and study it for a moment. He would either take it for himself or tear it up. If I was carrying any of my drawings, he always tore them up. "Jens took my homework," was an acceptable excuse at Lincoln High. The teachers would say, "It's okay. Do it again in study hall and turn it in at the end of the day." I bought myself a nice "letterman" type jacket but not in Lincoln High's red and black school colors. It was tasteful light grey wool with white leather sleeves. I had it for two days before Jens came up and said, "Give me your jacket. Take it off. Hand it over." I did as I was told. He said, "This is a gift, right? I didn't take it off you. You want me to have this. Right?"

For several weeks I was frightened to leave the house except to hurry back and forth to school. It interrupted my yard work and reduced my income. He had successfully reduced me to zero. It did not enter my mind that Jens never actually laid a hand on me. He had grabbed me by the shoulder once or twice to turn me to face him. He robbed me more than once, but never actually hit me. It was all words and sneering facial expression. If he had beaten the crap out of me, I probably would have gone home, nursed my bruises and thought "It wasn't that bad." Ninety-nine percent of terror is your own imagination screwing with you. The other fifty percent is the risk that you will suffer real harm.

Which perhaps explains why my retaliation was overkill.

As a trusted student, I was often called upon to carry messages between the administration and the teachers while classes were in session. As I entered a classroom on one of these errands, there was Jens sitting in the front row with the other boys who needed to be closely watched by the teacher. He did not see me as I came in the door, so I carried the note to the teacher's desk without incident. I could feel his eyes burning into my back as I dropped off the note.

I was certain that he would thrust out his leg to trip me as I left the room. I do not know what possessed me, but my next moves entered my mind with high resolution clarity. I purposefully walked close enough to the front row to guarantee his success tripping me up. His leg came thrusting out like a frog's tongue as I knew it would. I hesitated less than half a beat, leapt high into the air and came down on his exposed shin full force with both feet.

I had not rehearsed this move in my mind or planned it before I spontaneously executed it. I am sure if I had thought about it, I would not have done it. I did not break his leg or dislocate his knee, but I might have. When I landed on his shin, he cried out so loudly that he was heard several classrooms away. His screams caused everyone in the room to lift half-way out of their seats.

All eyes shot toward Jens. I took full advantage of the moment and flung myself onto the floor yelling, "Hey! Jens tripped me."

Jens was badly hurt. He was not visibly crying but tears of pain were streaming down his cheeks. He had not tripped me at all. I anticipated and avoided his move. I also smashed his shin with great force and my ruse of laying on the floor and blaming it on him was successful. Jens' screams turned to groans. The teacher yelled, "Shut up Jens, don't try to deflect the blame." She came over to help me up. She apologized to me muttering something about his being incorrigible and how this was "the last straw." I cut the last class of the day and ran home and hid. I was pretty sure I was a dead man walking.

What happened as a result of his "tripping" me was he got sent to the principal's office. He was on his final warning. I did not know this—it was confidential. The police were called. He was taken to juvenile court and sentenced to Reform School. This was all done on the teacher's say-so. I was not called into the proceedings. Jens was gone. I was free to walk the streets again. To carry money in my pockets again. The length of his sentence never entered my mind.

Until.

Until six months later I was walking down the street and saw him, free as a bird, walking toward me on the opposite side. My blood ran cold. Okay, now I am dead. As soon as he spotted me, he angled across traffic and positioned himself directly in my path. I slowed and he kept coming. When we were face-to-face at about three paces he stopped and extended his hand. I stopped but did not offer him my hand. What's he going to do first? Yank my arm off? "How have you been?" He asked.

Me: "Er. Okay."

Jens: "I haven't seen you in a while. I've been away."

Me: "I heard."

Jens: "Just thought I'd say hello."

Me: "Okay."

Jens: "See you around. Take care."

And ever after that, whenever Jens Aure saw me, he always

gave a little wave, or called out, "Hi." He never threatened me again.

I do not know what happened. I have two possible explanations. One, he had a really good guidance counselor in Juvie [Juvenile Hall or "kids' jail"] and it actually worked as a Reform School. Or two, Jens had an almost perfectly constructed authoritarian personality. I intentionally hurt him. I successfully made him carry the blame for the incident. I got him sent up the river. Ergo, I was to be accorded absolute respect. I do not know the right explanation, but I'll take whichever it is. After that, neither Jens, nor anyone else, ever bullied me.

Perhaps when we are in our mid-teens, life reveals more of its serious sides. Before Jens, I do not recall any earlier incidents that were overshadowed by concerns about life and death. And yet, almost every memorable incident around my 16th birthday came with life-altering consequences attached.

John's Near-Fatal Misadventure With
Army Surplus Peanut Butter

Sometime late in my 15th year, my brother Bill entered his adolescent growth spurt. He became ravenously hungry. He did not have any after school odd jobs that might provide him with money to buy his own food. So he just starved. My father noticed before I did and actually took pity on him. His solution was to buy gallon cans of Army Surplus peanut butter and huge rounds of Danish Rye tack. He told all of us, not just Bill, if we got hungry we could eat as much peanut butter on rye tack as we wished. I tried it. The peanut butter coming from the Army was not adulterated or extended with anything that commercial peanut butter companies were putting in their products at the time. I found it delicious compared to Jiffy or Skippy. But the ultra-hard rye cracker put me off, so I ate a couple of bites and that was it. I could and did buy better snacks

Not John. He hadn't yet entered adolescence, but he was mightily attracted by the idea of getting to eat as much as he wanted, whenever he wanted. I observed him on several occasions eating a full 14-inch round of rye tack with a quarter inch spread of peanut butter on the top. I thought nothing of it. I was actually glad for him. Until. One day while I was fixing dinner for the family, he began stumbling around talking nonsense. By the time my parents arrived home he could not walk. His temperature had dropped into the high 80s and his pulse was thready. My father rushed him to the hospital. They found that his stomach, small intestine, and large intestine were all completely blocked with a cement-like mixture of hard tack and peanut butter. He was close to death. They somehow managed to extract enough of the stuff from both ends that he was able to start digesting again. I cannot imagine what procedures they used to accomplish this feat without cutting into him. But they did. They saved his life. He was home in a couple of days with an admonition to lay off the peanut butter and rye tack.

My First Real Job

In the middle of my sophomore year, one of my high school classmates told me about a job opening for a night truck mechanic at Troy Laundry. Troy was one of the biggest businesses in Seattle with a large fleet of trucks plying regular pick-up and delivery routes in the city and surrounding suburbs. My classmate's dad was a Troy laundry driver/salesman. Troy was having trouble staffing the night position. It required a basic knowledge of light truck maintenance, but it was only half-time—20 hours a week Monday through Friday from 5:00 to 9:00 pm. It should have been a union job, but Troy was one of the only non-union shops in Seattle. And it should have been a man's job, but the economy was still working for the working class, and no men were looking for half-time. I took the bus downtown and asked to speak to Walter Hagen, one of the two brothers who owned Troy.

Hagen interviewed me at length, seemed to enjoy my earnest, skinny, six-foot-tall, redheaded combination of chutzpah and politeness. He quickly discerned that I was not running my mouth; that I knew what I was talking about when it came to light truck maintenance. He hired me on the spot a few months shy of my sixteenth birthday. He knew I would be driving their trucks all over the place without a license. Even though Troy was self-insured, he told me, "Get your driver's license on your sixteenth birthday or I'll have to let you go."

My First Sex

In the mid 1950s, youth in their early teens experimented with cross-sex intimacy—boys and girls hung out together, talked a lot about their thoughts and dreams, kissed and fondled each other up to the edge of no turning back, fell into and out of love. Young, exclusive (at least for the duration of the relationship) couples shared secrets, becoming progressively more intimate physically and emotionally, enjoying getting each other sexually aroused, usually on the back seat of the boy's hot rod, stopping just short of "going all the way." Until we did not stop just short.

There were no half-measures. Sex meant intercourse. None of us had ever heard of oral sex. Had anyone floated the idea of a girl performing oral sex on a boy, it would have been regarded as bizarre and disgusting. By both the boy and the girl.

So how did it work exactly—sex between inexperienced, consenting minors in the 1950s? I can only speak for middle-class white kids in the North End of Seattle, but here are the basics. First, the girl had to trust the boy completely that he would never do anything to harm her. This included her certainty that he would never brag or gossip about what they did together. And especially that he would never slip up, lose control, or otherwise do anything that might get her pregnant. This was usually an unspoken trust, but it had to be absolute.

Avoiding pregnancy was not as big a problem for us as has been widely touted. There was no easily available contraception or sex education in the schools, and our parents didn't talk to us about it. Other than my mother's ongoing complaints about my father not being able to keep it in his pants, the only conversation about sex I had with either one of them occurred when I was five years old. I asked my mother, "How does the baby get into the mother's stomach?" Her immediate reply was, "The same way it gets out." This was accurate as far as it went, but to a child with no knowledge of female anatomy it was completely meaningless. Well, not completely. It was a strong signal to me that I shouldn't be asking about such things. And I never did again. Nor did either of them volunteer any information or advice.

Sex education was not a part of any curriculum. But that didn't stop us from educating ourselves. Along with all the other teenagers in my high school, both boys and girls, I closely studied medical and biology texts. We collectively developed expert knowledge of the physiology of conception. We shared the latest research findings about "safe days" before, during and after menstruation. We knew about temperature changes during ovulation. We knew to keep ejaculate away from any mucus membranes. We knew the difference between popular myths about sex and research-based medical findings. Starting about age 15, next to auto mechanics, it was the most important complex and detailed body of knowledge that we gained and shared. And it was entirely off to the side of any curriculum or parental advice.

My first sex happened in the early summer of 1956. It was certainly one of those moments that changes everything. I wrote as follows about it when Bennett Berger asked me to contribute to his edited volume, *Authors of their Own Lives: Intellectual Autobiographies of Twenty American Sociologists* (1990):

I was so enormously frustrated when it finally did happen, at sixteen, that I actually lost my virginity twice in quick succession. The first time I thought I did it I narrowly missed (it was in the dark on rough terrain—how is a boy to know?) The girl, a year older but as inexperienced as I, never let on until, on the occasion of our "second" time, I blurted out, "Hey, it didn't really happen last time." "I know," she said. "You were so happy I didn't have the heart to tell you." I could not then, nor can I now, say which of the two times was better. My girlfriend had a clear opinion on the matter, however.

When I showed my contribution to the Berger volume pre-publication to my brilliant graduate student, Adele Krueger, she brought the typescript to me with her finger on this passage and asked me if I really wanted to be sharing something this intimate? I explained to her that I had given it some thought. When preparing to write my entry, I read several autobiographies of people who were a bit older than me and still alive. I noticed that the women like Betty Friedan and others, especially in the women's movement, always included a passage about when and how they "lost it," and how they felt about that moment. But none of my male near contemporaries ever did. This puzzled me at the time and still does. Stereotypically, American males keep their feelings to themselves. I told Adele that I would leave the passage in my chapter to try to supply some gender balance to this confessional form.

I might have told Adele that I left most of the intimate details out of my account for *Twenty American Sociologists*. The "whole truth and nothing but the truth" about sex can never be told, but here is one additional bit. As we snuggled together, my girlfriend asked me, "How do I know you won't take advantage of me if I get too excited?" It was well after dark, and we were almost naked in a sleeping bag in the arboretum behind the Seattle Museum of Science and Industry. "Easy," I told her as I unhooked her bra. "Just keep your panties on. I'll reach inside. But I won't take them off. And as long as you have them on, I can't take advantage. You know I wouldn't." I pulled off my shorts and patted her reassuringly on the outside of her panties. I don't know how long we enjoyed each other that way but at some point, she suddenly pulled out of my embrace. I was alarmed that I might have offended or frightened her. To the contrary, she had pulled back in order to wriggle out of her panties. No words were needed. Her gesture of affirmative assent was eloquent and completely unambiguous. And a moment later I was no longer involuntarily celibate. Or so I thought until the next time.

There were only a few repeats with this lovely girl whose name was Sandra. We got together when we could find precious privacy. But her parents noticed her newly calm demeanor and on the last day of school packed her up and sent her to live with an aunt in Cincinnati. She was the only child of a high executive in one of America's largest railways. Even though it was dazzlingly untrue for the emotional gap between us, we always knew that the social gap was ultimately insurmountable.

Fortunately, neither of us happened to be the love of the other's life. There was no tragic exchange of letters or expensive transcontinental phone calls. Her parents allowed her to come back to Seattle briefly at the end of the following academic year before she left for college in another state. We met for lunch in the elegant dining room of Seattle's downtown Bon Marché department store. We held hands but that was all. We had both moved on and were glad for each other. I noticed that her vision correction for near-sightedness had become stronger. I paid for our lunch and that was the last we ever saw or heard from each other.

Our affair was brief, but it taught me something that has stayed with me and proven true for the rest of my life. My sexual enjoyment is entirely contingent on the enjoyment of my partner. If she is not as eager as I am, I have no interest in pressing the matter. Of all the sudden revelations I have experienced, this is the one that has led to my greatest happiness.

My Father Came After Me With Intent

While we were still very poor, I knew not to buy food for myself and eat it in front of a family member who couldn't afford to supplement their diet. But after we bought a new car and moved out of the projects, went grocery shopping regularly and were eating much better, I became less circumspect. One hot spring Saturday afternoon, after working all day on my Ford, I bought myself a 16-ounce bottle of ice-cold Coca Cola. I slumped into a living room chair, pried the top off and started to drink from the bottle. My father walked over and stood menacingly in front of me and demanded, "Give me that." His attitude made it clear that he thought I was intentionally insulting him by drinking the Coke in his presence.

He snatched the bottle out of my hand with more than necessary force, tilted it up and began to gulp it down, watching me closely out of the corner of his eyes. His head was tilted all the way back with the coke near vertical. I leapt up from the chair. My Coke was draining at a rapid rate and was almost half gone down my father's gullet. It was clear he intended to leave me none of it. He was not just taking a swig. He was chugging the whole bottle and leering and gloating at my growing agitation.

Without any thought of consequences, I grabbed the bottle and pulled it out of his mouth. I just wanted my Coke back before it was all gone. Of course, given the intentionally dramatic way he was drinking, with the bottom of the bottle pointed at the ceiling, the effect of my action was to cause the remainder of the Coke to pour into his nose and throat, all over his face, soaking the front of his shirt and pants. He fell into a choking, screaming rage. He grabbed the now empty bottle from me and threw it at my head. I was already on the move, and he missed. The bottle smashed into the wall beside me. His face turned purple, and his eyes bulged out of their sockets. His nostrils flared, his upper lip curled, and he let out a blood curdling roar.

Bear in mind that my father never lost his temper. Ever. Until that moment. He could take hours of screaming accusations from my mother without mumbling a word in his own defense. He was Mr. Taciturn. I had never seen him like this. Maybe when he beat down the boys who pulled the flowers out of our yard at Stewart Heights. But no. Not really. Even then he was not this crazed. I was overwhelmed by an existential fear that if he caught me, he would kill me. His anger went well beyond the deed that provoked it. The face splat punishment he got for stealing my Coke was actually more comic than tragic. It was obvious that his rage was fueled by pre-existing hatred. He lost all control. He wanted to erase my existence.

I ran for my life out the front door and down the street. Over my shoulder I saw him in hot pursuit. I heard my mother screaming from our front porch, "Earle! Earle! Stop. Come back in the house!" He didn't turn back. He continued to chase me. "I'm ordering you to stop," he yelled. I had never disobeyed a direct order from either of my parents. Not even once in my life. Disobedience was unthinkable. But in this case, I made an exception and kept going like a streak of blue shit.

I was 15, almost 16, and he was 37. It may have been the first moment in our lives that I could outrun him. After about three blocks he became too exhausted to pursue me further and broke off. I continued running, turned the next corner, and slowed, cautiously looking back. When he didn't appear around the corner, I continued walking fast, looking back over my shoulder. And I walked like that into the night, with every step carrying me ever further away from my house.

Around 11:00 pm I called home from a pay booth. My mother picked up the phone on the first half ring. I did not have to say anything. She blurted out that I could come home. She'd made him promise to forget the whole thing, to never mention it. So I returned home. No one greeted me at the door, and I went straight to bed. At breakfast the next morning, it was as though nothing had happened. My brothers were looking at me, I thought, with new respect.

The Steinburn Affair

Sometime shortly before my 15th birthday, Tom Steinburn came into our lives. He was a widely acclaimed mountaineer. At first I thought this was a positive thing. He joined us on camping trips and was eager to teach me the fundamentals of rock climbing and kayaking in rapids. Whereas before, when my parents went camping, I often stayed home, when Tom came along, I eagerly joined the MacCannell/Steinburn excursions that took place about once a month.

Tom taught me how to care for a mountain coil, to tie a bowline, the required communications when on belay for protected climbing, how to chimney, rappel, set a piton, etc. He took me to the Seattle Mountaineering Co-op to outfit me with hiking boots, rock climbing shoes, day pack rucksack, pitons, a hammer, carabiners, a wool sweater, socks, and mittens from Switzerland, everything I needed as my skills progressed.

"On belay" on a gentle pitch. Tom Steinburn shows me the ropes, 1955

The Seattle Mountaineering Co-op was in an office in a high rise building in downtown Seattle. If you were a member you had a key to the office. No one minded the store. It was a membership honor system. You let yourself in, turned on the lights, and began plowing through the European ice axes, crampons, Primus stoves, et cetera that were stacked everywhere. There were no US manufacturers of this type of equipment and no importers at that time. The entire stock of the Co-op had been bought by members visiting Europe and brought back to Seattle as luggage. Everything had a price that reflected its cost in dollars plus any import duties. When you selected what you needed you totaled up the value of what you were taking from the store and put the money, cash only, in a metal box. If you could not find what you needed or saw the store was running low on an item, you noted this on the "Wish List" tacked to one of the walls. When a member traveled to Europe for any reason (it was usually to climb in the Alps) they would take the cash from the box and the wish list with them and replenish the supply. This was globalization in the 1950s. With Tom's guidance, I bought a bunch of interesting stuff that none of my family, friends, or acquaintances, had ever seen or even heard of. [As a footnote, the Seattle Mountaineers Co-op morphed and evolved into REI, Recreational Equipment Incorporated, a global retail chain. Globalization in the 2000s. It sweetly retains a trace of its original set-up.]

My Mother Flaunts Her Indiscretion

After we moved to a real house on 8th Avenue, my mother rode the bus home every day from where she worked at General Insurance. One day, as her bus travelled through the University District, she chanced to look out the window to see my father walking up the street romantically entwined with what was then called a "co-ed"—a female student. This was the occasional cause of one of her loudest flameouts. When my father got home, she really let him have it. The main theme of this harangue was not his infidelity per se, but how cruel and inconsiderate he was for having an affair when she was working to help support the family while he finished his Ph.D.

"What am I working for? To pay for your screwing around?"

My father, as always, just paced back and forth with a blank expression on his face, not responding to anything she said until she screamed herself out and fell exhausted and silent.

This particular yell-fest occurred coincident with my growing awareness that Tom Steinburn was using my mountaineering lessons to get close to my mother. I suspected something. Once, I came home unexpectedly and found my mother and Tom sitting opposite each other at our dining table. There was something about the way they were looking at me, and each other. I thought maybe they had suddenly changed positions when they heard me coming. Something was off.

It was not in keeping with what I thought I knew about my mother. Infidelity was my father's department. Not hers.

Until.

One evening, she announced to the whole family at dinner that she and Tom would be going away together for the weekend. She did not say why, and no one asked. We knew. Her blatant admission was almost triumphal—she might as well have said it outright, 'No one here has any standing to question this hugely transgressive act that I am about to commit. By putting up with you lot, I've earned the right to transgress without penalty.' I felt she was including me and my brothers along with my father in the group of men who had made her life a living hell and entitled her to a free fling.

It was my misfortune to bear witness to my father's agony that weekend. He paced around the house day and night, groaning like he was having a painful bowel movement. Then he had several painful bowel movements. He shaved compulsively over and over again and growled at my brothers and me. He ordered me to cook him special meals. His most repeated words were, "That lousy son-of-a-bitch." (My father never swore. Never even said "damn.")

Shaking with rage he told me, "I had a great thing going until Steinburn came along and ruined it. The man has no morals whatsoever." Did I mention that my father was always hyper-moralistic when it came to everyone's behavior except his own?

Late Sunday night, my mother came home. My father had been watching out the front windows all day. Steinburn dropped her at the curb and sped off. She was glowing and happy but mainly interested in putting on a big show for my father's benefit of just how glowing and happy she was. She made no effort to hide that she had revenge on her mind. Her gloating was oddly reassuring to my father. What she had done was still all about him. Or at least enough about him that he was still an essential part of the act.

Immediately everything seemed to return to normal. Two weeks later, about the time of my sixteenth birthday, another Steinburn-MacCannell camping/mountaineering lesson trip was planned. I thought maybe her revenge infidelity had effectively turned things around. Perhaps she had even figured out how to block my father's future infidelities. We went in two cars because, for the first time, Steinburn brought his wife, Annie. I rode in the Steinburn car. Annie was a stern looking woman. I thought, "This is great. There won't be any funny business this weekend with her around."

I Could Not Have Been More Wrong.

Saturday morning, as usual I got up before dawn and was sitting "Indian-style" on the end of the heavy Park Service picnic table in our campsite. On the table itself, not on one of the benches. For a few minutes I had been enjoying the sight of first light filling the night sky. The tent I shared with my brothers was behind me. The adults' Steinburn tent and MacCannell tent were set up side-by-side facing me. I saw some rustling of the tents and heard a mumbled verbal exchange between the men. The two tent flaps opened and my father wearing rumpled pajama bottoms stepped out of the Steinburn tent and Steinburn in jockey shorts stepped out of the MacCannell tent. They crossed paths wordlessly returning to their own domains.

They both looked over and saw me sitting there staring at them. Neither of them appeared to be at all concerned that I saw them. No one spoke. I was shot through with revulsion. It was not because I had just witnessed a wife-swapping with my mother a party to it. At that point nothing my parents did could have shocked me. What revolted me was the off-hand way they exposed me to it. What shocked me most was that they were okay with me knowing; that they were so casually willing to take a chance that I (and my brothers!) would see what they were up to. That it was so flagrant. They knew I was always the first one up in the morning. It was more likely that I would have been out of my tent than not. That they would so thoughtlessly include me in their dirty secret disgusted me.

That was the last time I had anything to do with Tom Steinburn and the last time I went camping with my parents in the Pacific Northwest. The risk of more revolting revelations was simply too great. I felt bad for my younger brothers but needed to be rid of my parents.

All the signs were pointing in the same direction. Eighteen was still two years away but it was already time for me to clear out. A few weeks later I got my wish.

14

I Join the Labor Force and Leave Home

ON MY SIXTEENTH BIRTHDAY about a month after I went to work at Troy, as demanded by Walter Hagen, I got my driver's license. I was no longer self-employed. But I had not joined the proletariat on the lowest rung of the ladder either. I was not a sweeper or a dishwasher. I did not flip burgers.

My job at Troy was based on my knowledge of automobile maintenance and repair. During my lifetime, cars and light trucks evolved into almost maintenance free appliances. Anyone born after about 1980 cannot imagine what cars were like in 1956. A young person in 2020 might not even know how to open the hood of their car. My teenage engagement with auto and light truck repair and maintenance will seem extreme today. In the 1950s it was only slightly more intense than the norm for American males in all but the highest socio-economic classes. We all had to know how to fix cars.

Before computers, mid-twentieth century assembly-line fit and finish tolerances were so variable that cars began falling apart after 25,000 miles and were completely worthless after 60,000. Even when new, there were no integrated engine management systems. This meant that any one of dozens of things could routinely go wrong and stop your car. A cold morning or heavy fog could prevent the car from starting. A hot day, steep upgrade, or traffic jam could overheat the engine or cause fuel-line vapor lock and kill the engine. A steep downgrade could easily overheat the brakes causing fade and even failure.

Every driver had to be a skilled diagnostician. You had to be able to recognize and anticipate myriad but not unusual problems; determine whether the strange sound or shudder was something you were competent to fix on your own, or whether you needed a mechanic. Jaguar would not permit an engine tear-down under their new car warranty (six months or 5000 miles) unless engine oil consumption exceeded three quarts in a thousand miles. Two quarts in a thousand miles was considered normal oil consumption for a new Jag. Cars that "burned oil" fouled their spark plugs. You had to remove the fouled plugs, sandblast, re-gap, and re-install them to get the engine running again. Unless you were wealthy and could hire a mechanic to replace them with a new set.

If you were not wealthy you did all routine maintenance, lube jobs, oil changes, and tune-ups yourself. Probably half the men in the US were competent to rebuild manual transmissions, replace clutches, and rebuild the brakes on their cars, without professional help, in their own driveways or garages. If you did not know how to rebuild the master cylinder in your brake system, there would usually be a friendly neighbor no more than a few doors away who could coach you through the job.

No car today requires that every moving part of the suspension and the drive-line universal joints have be hand-lubricated every thousand miles. Every car and light truck in the 1950s had to be "lubed" with a grease gun usually about once a month. Again, if you were not in the upper ten percent, you crawled under your car and did this yourself. Some of the more complex systems had as many as 30 grease nipples to hit. These nipples were always covered with grease and caked with road dirt to the point of sinking into invisibility. Missing a single nipple could be fatal to your suspension or your drive shaft. For an owner not to be under the hood and under the car several times a week to keep it going, you had to buy a new car every two or three years. Or buy a Mercedes Benz or Rolls Royce that were hand assembled to much higher standards and might last five or ten years. We had to know our cars and their individual quirks the way people in the 19th century knew their horses. In the winter, my Grandma Fran soaked a towel in boiling water and wrapped it around the throat of her carburetor every morning to get her old Oldsmobile started. Even though I have had little use for them in 25 years, I still own three almost complete sets of automotive tools in metric, Whitworth, and SAE sizes.

Troy paid me $1.25/hour well above the then hourly minimum wage of 75 cents. My job was to keep their 40+ truck fleet on the road. —engine tune-ups, points, condenser and plugs replaced, lube jobs, oil, filters and tire changes, tire pressures checked, fuel topped up, trucks washed, wheel bearings repacked and drawn up, brakes and clutches adjusted, and brake shoes changed, tire chains on and off as needed in the winter, annual license tags changed and registration renewals properly installed on the steering columns. I worked alone for four hours weekday nights in a well-equipped shop and tried to stay ahead of the needs of my forty plus trucks.

Like every other Troy employee, I lined up at the pay window Friday afternoons to collect my weekly earnings. It was old school. We were paid in cash. In a brown envelope that opened at the end, not the top, with our name written on it in long hand, filled with crisp bills and a few coins.

Seattle was a union town. Even though Troy was almost uniquely a non-union shop, every Troy worker loved the unions. Why? Because when the Teamsters, or Machinists negotiated a higher wage, the Hagen brothers topped it by ten percent in order to block any organizing at their businesses. So we were all doing better than we would have done if we were organized, plus we did not have to pay union dues. Every one of us praised and supported the unions every chance we got. We knew our prosperity depended on organized labor even more than it would have had we been organized ourselves. And in the few labor actions I got caught up in, the union guys understood Troy exceptionalism, i.e., they did not beat me up when I had to violate picket lines to retrieve our trucks from striking union machine or body shops.

The Troy drivers sent me in armed with a modified baseball bat with ten-penny nails protruding from the head. The union guys just made some jokes about my medieval weapon, laughed and threw me the keys.

One night I was driving a Troy truck back from a minor breakdown and I was forced off the road by a Teamster boss driving a new Cadillac. He knew Troy was non-union but when he saw one of our trucks being driven by a kid, he thought he'd have some fun with me.

"Show me your union card."

"I haven't got one."

"You can't be driving truck unless you are
   a Teamster."

"I know."

"So what are you doing driving truck, then."

"I stole it."

I knew if he called the cops on me, the bosses at Troy would tell them I was their employee and had their permission to drive the truck. The union boss knew I was playing with him the same as he was playing with me. So he just gave me a long dirty look and got back in his Caddy.

When I arrived at work every day at five o'clock in the afternoon, the place was in chaos. The drivers' shift was ending, and they were all speeding into the lots at the same time to offload the city's dirty laundry. We used the large, rolling canvas laundry baskets that still today figure in crime dramas as means of escape from prisons, and from hotels or hospitals under surveillance. The trucks were roaring in and the bosses, secretaries and other daytime employees were hurrying to get out. Giant baskets, trucks, and employees' cars hurtled about in every direction. The employee parking lot was separate from the truck lots, but it shared the alley that ran down the center of the city block occupied by the facility.

To prioritize the maintenance work that needed to be done across the fleet, I had to talk to the route drivers as they came in at the end of their shift. So I did a cross between a jitterbug and a ballet to avoid the moving trucks and cars. The route drivers were trying to get home as fast as possible and also to tell me what their truck needed. Our conversations were short and to the point. The drivers liked me. When you have red hair, everyone knows your name right away. It's "Red." "Hey, Red, you think I can get new tires on the rear tonight?"

In a large motor pool the moving vehicle has absolute right-of-way over anyone on foot. The pedestrian has better vision and hearing than the drivers in the trucks, and better maneuverability. The trucks are bigger and faster, but it is your job as a pedestrian to anticipate their movements and stay out of their way. The drivers are not required or even expected to be aware of your presence. Should they become aware of your presence, they were as likely playfully to aim for you as to swerve or brake to avoid you. This kind of game is part of the fun of a blue-collar job. At least it was for me. Sometimes I would burlesque a matador in front of an oncoming truck.

There was another red headed guy who arrived at work the same time as I did. He was an after-hours sweeper. He was not adept at negotiating the chaos. Every other week or so he got hit by a truck. Nothing too serious. Maybe a broken arm, but mostly just bad bruises. He did not last long at the job. But while he was there, the drivers differentiated between the two of us. I was called "Red." And he was called "Stupid Red." To his face. No one was PC back then. Even Stupid Red assumed it was proper and was good-natured about it.

Cadwallader's Success

I worked unsupervised at night after everyone else had gone home except a middle-aged Black woman janitor, the red-headed sweeper and his eventual more agile replacement, and another boy a year or two older than me who cleaned the soap trap sumps under the two dozen washing machines that were the size and shape of cement mixer trucks.

The "night staff," as we called ourselves, often paused to marvel at the mystery of a 10-foot-by-20-foot blackboard with a giant grid of data on the back wall of the interior garage. Each driver's name was painted on the left vertical axis, and the days of the week were painted on the top horizontal axis. The cells for each day of the week after a driver's name were filled in with the dollar value of the laundry and cleaning he brought in that day. On Friday the cells were tallied. A final vertical column contained the weekly total for each driver. There was a good bonus paid to the highest grossing driver each week.

The mystery was this. One driver, Ray Cadwallader, had the highest total every week, without fail. How did he do it? He was a little older than the other drivers. Probably in his 50s while they were in their 30s and 40s. Presumably one of the ambitious younger drivers would have the energy to hustle up the highest score, at least occasionally. But it never happened. Cadwallader always won. All our queries about Cadwallader's success were met with stony silence. Like it was something we should not be asking about.

Since I had some hold over the drivers, I was delegated by the "night staff" to extract the secret of Cadwallader's success. I had quite a bit of control over whether they would be driving a clean truck; or one that you did not have to crank for two or three minutes and risk "flooding" the engine before it would start; or one that's brakes did not squeal. So the drivers would at least pretend to take my queries seriously. Did Cadwallader have a better route with more affluent customers? No, his route was actually considered to be a bad one. Was he more handsome and charming than the other drivers? No, they were conventionally 1950s good looking younger men, and he was an ugly cuss with a kind of abrupt personality. So how, I persisted, how can he get the highest tally every week? I finally wore them down. It was like, "The answer is staring you in the face. Do we have to spell this out for you?" Yes, you do. They finally revealed the secret. Cadwallader was the only driver who did not have regularly scheduled trysts with one or several of the housewife customers on his route. "Yeah, we all lose, on average, about two hours a day off our regular routes. We'd all get the same numbers as Ray if we stopped screwing around. You can't tell anyone." I did not tell. Until now.

As Soon As I started Working, Leaving Home Felt natural and Seamless

From age 14, when my mother was working at General Insurance and until I got my job at Troy, I had been preparing the evening meal for my family. Every morning my mother would write out the menu with any special preparation instructions. When I returned from my after-school handyman odd jobs around 5:00 or 5:30, I cooked the meal and set the table. I did my school homework on the dining table, while waiting for something to bake in the oven, or after hastily whipping a salad together. Both parents got home around 6:00 and the whole family immediately sat down to eat together. My brothers did the washing up and drying.

It must have been irksome when I went to work and was no longer available to cook. But no one complained. My mother stepped in to do it after she got home.

For my first couple of months at Troy, even though I would not be home until 9:30, they set my place at the dinner table and served my portions onto my plate. We were more affluent, but we maintained the poverty tradition of dividing every last bit of the food into five precisely equal portions. There was no such thing as "left-overs." Ever. My mother often ridiculed women who prepared "too much" food when "most of it would just get thrown out anyway." Each member of the family took turns serving, getting the scoops of mashed potatoes, salads, etc. divided by five, exactly. Anyone could trade with the server for his or her portion if they believed it to be bigger than the one they got. This practice caused the servings to be unerringly accurately equal.

While I was at work, my food was scooped onto my plate at the beginning of the meal just like everyone else's, and it sat there in front of my empty chair until the end of the meal. After dinner, someone put my plate on a warming shelf above the kitchen stove where I would retrieve it and eat it when I got home from my shift. It was not very palatable. Everything was exactly the same temperature. The main dish was too cold and the salad too warm. But I ate it and was grateful even though I noticed that my portions kept getting smaller as I wasn't around to challenge the server. That was okay by me. I was supplementing my diet almost every day with snacks, and occasional entire restaurant meals.

Paul and Valerie Hanna, the Car Club, and the Family I Chose

A few months before I went to work for Troy, hanging out one day at one of my favorite car-spotting places, the sidewalk

1955 Triumph TR like the Hannas' car

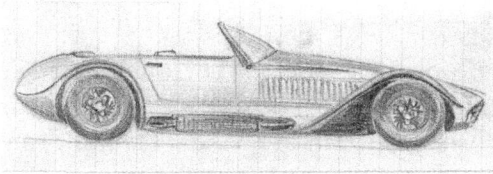

My 1956 concept sketch of a TR 3 fitted with a lightweight racing body

in front of Seattle British Motors, I met Paul Hanna. He drove up and parked his sparkling new, sky-blue Triumph TR 3 roadster. He greeted my staring at his car with a friendly smile and conversation. Paul was a union bricklayer, a racer, and a total car nerd. He could talk about the different chemical compositions of engine oils and their relative advantages and disadvantages in the stresses of competition. I was a perfect foil for his arcane knowledge, taking it in as fast as he could dish it out. He took an immediate liking to me and invited me to his house to meet his other vehicles—a VW drop-side flat-bed pick-up with Conestoga top, an MG TC, a Lambretta 150 cc motor scooter—and his lovely wife, Valerie.

Valerie Hanna was a recent immigrant from bombed out and impoverished post-war England. She was the first English person I ever got to know. She was initially attracted to Paul because he was so unusual for an American guy in the 1950s, driving an MG TC. So we had that in common. Far from being stereotypically "cold" and "aloof," she was warm and attentive. I loved learning her names for everyday objects like "torch" for flashlight. Especially car parts, such as "hood" was convertible top and not the engine cover as in America. And the trunk of the car is the "boot" in British English. She did not mind my querying her about these and many other intra-English language differences, and she loved telling English jokes. "I say, have you heard about Chumley . . .?" She was a skilled surgical nurse fitting the pattern of what I considered to be the "normal" adult females in my life, working like my Great Grandmother Emily and my Grandma Fran.

Paul was an admirer of my drawings of experimental car mechanicals and body designs that I was churning out at a rate of two or three a day. The Hannas took me to my first sports car race, included me in meetings and parties of the Northwest Chapter of the SCCA (Sports Car Club of America), and in a matter of weeks provided me with a vast network of contacts in the foreign car community.

Valerie was the chief operating theater nurse for Seattle's best ophthalmological surgeon. She had to appear every day in a perfect, white nurse's uniform head to foot. She sent her uniforms out for cleaning and pressing, going through several a week. Her laundry costs took a substantial bite from her pay.

One of the perks I enjoyed at Troy was my own numbered Safety Pin. I could put anything I wanted washed or dry cleaned in a large mesh bag, seal it with my numbered Pin, and throw it into the day's haul. A few days later everything would appear in my locker washed and cleaned, pressed and starched, hanging or neatly folded and wrapped. It was free of charge and because it went through the process marked as from a Troy employee, it got VIP treatment. Everything was super white and super crisp. If my work coveralls became permanently stained with grease and oil, my laundry would yield a brand new gleaming white pair, always with "Dean" stitched in cursive in red thread on my left breast pocket.

As soon as I heard about Valerie's laundry problem, I offered to include her uniforms in my bag with my mechanic's coveralls and paltry other teen-aged boy cleaning. It was a good arrangement. I instantly got unearned credit from the Troy drivers for the hot nurse they assumed I was dating.

The more I said "No, no, she's just a friend," or "No, no, she's married," the more they thought I had a great thing going. So many nurse's uniforms to clean every week. Wow! "She probably isn't even a nurse." What kind of hot sex were we into?

"Here, Let Me Fix You A Proper Meal"
One night, I stopped at the Hannas' after work to drop off

her uniforms. We got caught up in conversation, as we always did, until I mentioned I should get home and eat my dinner. "Is your mom making it for you? Yes, of course, you should go."

"No. No." I explained how it got dished out three or four hours earlier and was waiting on the warming shelf over the stove. Valerie, the nurse, immediately voiced her objection. "You could get sick from eating something like that. Here, let me fix you a proper meal." And with that she went into the kitchen and quickly put together a delicious dinner. From that point it was, 'You bring me a clean uniform and I fix you a nice meal.' And we could talk cars far into the night.

Valerie was always right in with the men for the car talk. She had even done a few hot laps on a racecourse in the Paul Hanna MG TC ending in a fender-bender that was not her fault. One of the other racers, assuming it was Paul under the helmet and behind the goggles, put a move on her that was not allowed. He knew, or thought he knew, that Paul was skillful enough to avoid his aggression. Valerie was not. She ended her racing career on the spot. No one was hurt and the body damage was minimal, but Valerie did not fancy being on the track with aggressive bastards who didn't obey the rules, even if they happened to be close friends. The contrite aggressive bastard friend made them a nice coffee table from the broken rear wheel of the TC. The Hannas eventually gave the table to me. When we were first married, Juliet and I used it through grad school. We then passed it on to our friend Alan Nagel who coveted it. Alan is a professor of English at Iowa. The table, witness to thousands of intense all-night conversations ranging from horsepower to Hegel, may now be sitting in the middle of a cornfield somewhere in the middle of America. That is where I would like to think it ended up.

Before long I was eating with the Hannas every evening and sleeping in their spare room. My parents did not register any attitude one way or the other about my nocturnal absences. I informed them that I might be sleeping over at the Hannas occasionally and that was accepted as a blanket explanation of why I did not show up for breakfast. Had they said anything I would have reminded them about "18 and Out" and simply claim to be following their playbook on an accelerated schedule. That is exactly the way it felt to me. I was now self-supporting and "out." The Hannas were not charging me rent, but if they had I could afford it. I was out of there. Gone. Kaput! And it felt great. My little speech for my parents was well-formed and memorized but I never had to deliver it.

It was a seamless transition. The Hannas' house was only about a mile away from my parents'. Once I was completely moved in, Valerie invited my mother over for a meal to meet her, to let her know I was being properly fed, and to allow her to inspect my room. My mother expressed no interest in any of it except the meal that she ate with relish. I visited my brothers after school when my parents were at work. But I was now on my own and it felt as wonderful as I always thought it would. I assumed I had broken free of my parents' control forever. I was wrong, of course.

The Hannas imposed no rules on me, no curfew, no mess abatement, no nothing. They did not have to. I was neat and polite and whenever I left, I told them where I was going and why, and when I expected to be back. Except for my dating, most of our social life was together, centered around the car club and its activities.

Paul and Valerie gave me free use of all their vehicles—the MG, the Triumph, the VW, and the Lambretta. There was no hesitation on their part about my borrowing their cars. Even if I had no clear purpose other than just cruising around for fun, they did not mind. If they were not driving one of the vehicles, the keys were in a bowl in the living room and I could take it. Since there were only two of them and four vehicles, something interesting was always available. If I went on a date and it was free, I could take the Triumph. If my Uncle Ed needed help moving furniture, I could take the VW truck. My Ford hot rod may have had more cachet among my 1950s high school peers. But I vastly preferred to be behind the wheel of any Hanna vehicle.

E.R. Nottingham's Boat Works

Soon after I moved in with the Hannas, when school got out for the summer, I got my second regular job at E.R. Nottingham's Boat Builders. It was a temporary (summer) job with regular hours from 9:00 to 5:00. I got permission to leave 15 minutes early so I could clock in on time at Troy, a short hop across town. Having a full-time job and a half-time job seemed perfectly natural to me. My Meskimen relatives always worked 12 to 15 hours a day when they worked. Both Troy and Nottingham's were interesting enough that I did not find my 12-hour days the least bit tiring. Everything I had to do at both jobs was pretty much the kind of things I might have been doing if I was just messing around on my own.

Nottingham's employed about 12 men including Mr. Nottingham's ne'er-do-well son. The company was transitioning from wooden boats to fiberglass construction. Nottingham the elder hired me, again above minimum wage, I think it was a dollar an hour, to shadow him in the front office and to assist at the various workstations around the shop. I learned how to deal with the sail makers, how to sand and varnish ships' wheels and tillers until I could see my face in them, to do inventory of all the fittings in the storerooms, help wrap large boats in layers of cardboard and trailer them to the rail yards to be shipped to customers and to boat shows in other states.

I do not know who recommended me for this interesting job. It may have been my new friend Bert Chambers who I met through the Hannas. Bert raced an XK 120 Jaguar and owned a little pretty Nottingham cat-rigged sailing dinghy. Nottingham did not tell me what he had in mind when he hired me. He

1954 XK 120 Jaguar. In 1961 I was able to purchase a used one for $1000. It looked like this, black with red leather trim. I sold it in 1963 for $1000. It was the first of four Jaguars I have owned over the past 55 years. If I bought it today in reasonable condition, I would have to pay $150,000.

made me take phone calls, sort bills, grade and sort mahogany and teak, run a drill press for simple repetitive operations, handle pick-ups at suppliers. Soon I had at least a superficial working understanding of everything going on in the shop and yard. I could not do every job in the shop, but I could ably assist and I knew how they all fit together.

In late July or early August E.R. took me aside and explained that he and his wife were going to spend the last two weeks of August cruising, sailing their forty-foot yawl in the San Juan Islands, his first break in 20 years. The reason he hired me was to have someone to sit in the front office while he was away, answer customer queries, and handle any other phone calls, do pick-ups and deliveries, assist the men on the floor as needed, prioritize the bills for him to pay on his return, and mainly not let his 30-something son do any of these things. If his son started to order the workers around, I was to let them know they should resist any of his demands that were weird, unreasonable, or incorrect. And that I spoke for Mr. Nottingham, the elder, on that matter.

It was a brilliant plan. As a 16-year-old kid I had zero authority. I could not give orders to a 70-year-old master boatwright and would never consider doing so. It was the other way around. Everyone was looking out for me, afraid that I might screw-up. They were aware that E.R. had entrusted me with keeping the shop going in idle mode and maintaining an even keel while he was away. They certainly would not do anything wrong that might get me in trouble. The boss might check in once or twice, but before cell phones and the internet, gone was gone. Even his son stayed on his best behavior. Had the father brought in someone the son's age to do my job there might have been conflict. But who could pick on an earnest, skinny kid who would never overstep any bounds?

The sweeper at Nottingham's was named Cecil Smathers. He looked to be around 60 years old, but he might have been younger and simply worn out. I am pretty sure his ancestors fought on the losing side in the Civil War. He was even skinnier than I was and had only a few teeth left in his head. He bragged that the only job he'd ever been fired from in his life was ditch digger for the Works Progress Administration. He said, "It was the middle of the Depression and there was no work. I heard that you could go down to the WPA, sign on, and get a paycheck for leaning on your shovel. So I did. And they took me out to a jobsite and showed me this ditch to dig and I said 'Fine' and just leaned on my shovel like the feller said. And the boss came along and told me to get digging and I said I heard the WPA paid you for leaning on your shovel. And he told me I was fired." I learned quite a bit from Cecil, but the important lesson was not to take right-wing propaganda seriously—it could cost you your livelihood. He may have made up the story and that was his intended lesson.

Cecil gave me instructions on how to ride the rails to several key destinations in the United States—Los Angeles, Denver, St. Louis, New Orleans, Chicago, New York. I knew at the time that I would likely never ride the rails, but I kept detailed notes anyway. He described the freight yards at each transfer point; which direction to look for the railroad cops; whether you had to jump off the train outside the yard while it was moving or could ride it into the yard, wait until dark, and change to the next train. He told me how to count the tracks I crossed to make sure I was getting onto a train that would carry me closer to my destination. He warned me that if I ever got into a boxcar and there was only one guy sitting silently in the corner, I should get off immediately. If there were several guys in the car who greeted you, that was okay. But the one silent guy in the corner will "slit your throat when you go to sleep, take your shoes and anything else he needs, and throw your body into the weeds beside the tracks." Cecil had been one of the "lost boys" of the Depression who crisscrossed the U.S. by rail looking for work in almost every state. He had a lot of tattoos. The most memorable one was a series of blue dashes from earlobe to earlobe across the front of his neck. Just under the dashes, following their contour was a fine print instruction: "Cut on dotted line."

When I returned home to the Hannas in the evening after work at Nottingham and Troy, even though it was late, between 9:00 and 9:30, as often as not, there would be a house guest, or guests. I always knew in advance because there would be one or several exotic cars parked out front. Before long, I knew who was visiting from the cars. Almost all of the guests were car people and the conversations would go past midnight. The Hannas introduced me to their friends in such a way that I was immediately included. Even though the company was mainly in their thirties and forties, I was never made to feel like a 16-year-old kid. For my part I was always careful and measured about anything I added to the conversation. I made sure I had something to say; that I didn't "run at the mouth." When the guests saw that Paul allowed me free use of all his cars, they offered me "seat time" in cars I had not driven before. Every car had a different "feel," a different way of connecting to the road, that was much discussed. Everyone's opinion was sought and debated. Including mine. I was considered fresh and unbiased, not committed to praising the car I had purchased.

The Hannas' Wall of Penguin Paperbacks

It was in these late evening discussions that I discovered people bonded over literature. This was a revelation to me. While it was true that the Hannas' friends were more bonded over cars, almost every conversation contained some observations about a book one or several in the assembled company were reading or had read. Whether it was "good" or not, and why, or "disgusting." I remember one of the racer's girlfriends opining that *Lolita* was "disgusting." Of course, I grabbed it and read it right away.

My parents never discussed books and never encouraged me to. I almost always had a book going—popular fiction and pulp paperbacks mostly. But I never considered reading as other than a private act. That books might be a basis for sociability was world-changing for me.

I was passionately interested in knowing what was inside the books under discussion and being able to take part in the conversation. On one wall of the Hannas' living room was a floor-to-ceiling and wall-to-wall bookcase Paul had built with narrow shelves. They were spaced to fit Penguin paper backs. There were several hundred of them. The entire wall was shaded the bright and faded orange color of the spines of the Penguin books. There may even have been a thousand of them, including every classic, modern and historical. It was after these late-night conversations that I found my way to Thurber, Melville, Orwell, Mailer, Hemingway, Dostoyevsky, and, of course, the disgusting Nabokov. I found he was not quite disgusting enough for my adolescent taste. This was not exactly a deep dive into literature, but it was enough to secure my life-long indebtedness to the insights the classics contain. An indebtedness that I shared with my future friend and mentor, Erving Goffman.

Whenever an author was mentioned, I would pull the books off the Penguin shelf and carry them to my room. I knew I could not catch up, so I usually chose a book by an author that was different from the one everybody was talking about. After an evening discussing *1984*, I grabbed and read *Keep the Aspidistra Flying*. Instead of reading *The Naked and the Dead*, I read *Deer Park*. This stratagem assured that I could add something quirky to the conversation, but it kept me from some important works. Today I have read all of Orwell except *1984*.

I was completely knocked over by the opening lines of *Moby Dick*. "Call me Ishmael." It was not a demand to read. It was a demand for me to speak. It establishes the reader as an interlocutor in the narration to follow: the most economical expression of the truth of the relation of author to reader anywhere in literature. I was so thrilled by it I immediately conceived of a new business plan. I would write first lines and first paragraphs of novels and sell them to real authors. How about,

"I was born on 'death row.'" [$25.00]

"Do you think God gives a rat's ass about whether or not you believe in Him." [$50.00]

Needless to say, I gave up on my plan to be a ghost writer of first sentences for pay as soon as I hatched it, probably faster than I gave up on the idea of becoming a master criminal.

It only occurred to me much later on how weird it was that I never heard any discussion of works of literature until I moved in with the Hannas. The only books my parents ever read were their university course textbooks which they always sold back to the store at the end of the term. The only fiction at my house was a bound set of the collected works of H. Ryder Haggard that my father said he enjoyed as a teen-ager but never discussed with me or anyone else in my earshot. All he needed to do to guarantee that I would never read Haggard was to praise him. (I confess that I have enjoyed movies like *King Solomon's Mines* based on Haggard's writings.) *All Quiet on the Western Front*, which had such a profound effect on me when I was six, disappeared from the household several moves back.

The indelible life lesson I learned from my first real exposure to the classics at the Hannas is this: no one can learn from direct experience everything they must know to be fully present and aware in the lives we are living. If you depend on your own experience for life's lessons you will always be one step behind, and your life will pass you by and for the most part will go unnoticed and unlived until something literally or figuratively smacks you up alongside the head. It is called the "school of hard knocks" for a reason. The only way anyone ever got a firm prospective grip on their own life is by close attention to the stories told by others. Our most precious resource in this regard is our literatures great and small, storytelling in all its forms written or oral.

Early summer of 1956, a certainty settled into my soul. I was not conscious of it at the time, but I know it took firm root then: if I was ever to be so lucky as to have a life partner, she would have to love literature. In my wildest dream I could not imagine how fortunate I would eventually be.

15
Summer, 1956 Continued

PAUSE FOR A MOMENT TO PICTURE the universe contained inside a gasoline engine at 3000 rpm. The pistons, going up and down in the cylinders, are reversing direction 25 times each second. In your mind, try to divide a single second into 25 equal increments. It challenges human imagination. Now consider the difference between a huge piston weighing five pounds and a little piston about the diameter of a silver dollar that weighs only a few ounces. Shake the heavy one four inches back and forth 25 times a second for an hour and try not to shake the universe apart. Your engine cannot exceed 3000 rpm by very much without destroying itself and probably anything nearby. Also try to slow it quickly. You can't. There is too much metal in motion.

This is the difference between torque and horsepower. The big heavy pistons are good for engines made to pull heavy loads at low speeds—trucks and tractors.

The screaming little pistons could spool up to their 7000 rpm redline in an instant without harming themselves. Torque versus horsepower is like the difference between the "thrump thrump thrump" of a pile driver versus the vibration of a violin string or a hummingbird's wing. Reversing direction of the lightweight pistons in a racing engine is a piece of cake. It can spool up to a redline of more than double a truck engine and back to idle in an eyeblink and provide the horsepower and flexibility required to hustle a sports car around a track.

This is why American cars in the 1950s were mostly used for drag-racing but not the kind I got into. The industry here had only advanced far enough to create big truck-like vehicles that could at best achieve a high speed while driving in a straight line. I was never interested in drag-racing. European-style sports car racing, which was just beginning to penetrate the U.S. in the mid-1950s, was an art of finesse and balancing tradeoffs rather than a contest of brute force. To whatever extent I have been a competitive person, I have set myself against the challenge of dealing with complexity itself rather than a group of peers among whom I yearned to be fastest, biggest, best. Nowhere has this distinction been more apparent in my experience than in the world of motor sports.

Tom Carston's Cadillac-powered Allard raced in class A Modified. Carston owned the largest meat packing company in the Pacific Northwest. His driver was Jerry Grant who went on to compete at Indianapolis. Carston and Grant tried to turn a Cadillac engine into a racing engine by lightening its pistons and flywheel, enlarging its valves, etc.

The engine exploded right next to me. You can see one of the holes ripped in the bodywork between the first and second vents on the hood. A piece of red-hot shrapnel the size of my fist almost hit me. I used it as a paperweight for many years. That was the closest I came to being injured at a racetrack.

Club Racing In The Pacific Northwest in the Mid-1950s

Monday through Friday from 8:00 am to 9:00 pm I was at work at my two jobs. The weekends? I was at the sports car races.

In the 1950s, amateur club racing in the Pacific Northwest was done mainly at county airports, the kind used by small private planes. The car club would rent the airport for the

1955 Alfa Romeo Giulietta Roadster with a 1.3-liter four-cylinder engine. Unmodified, this car would race in the F Production class.

1955 OSCA purpose-built to race in class F Modified. Not to be messed with by you and your Alfa or MG. Unless . . .

1955 MG TD 76 running in F Production

weekend. The race organizers laid out closed circuit courses with one long straight on the main runway, and several short-er straights connected by left and right turns of varying ra-dii. The turns were called "corners" no matter whether they were 90 degrees, "U" shaped, or gently sweeping. The longest straight would permit most cars to reach their top speed, usually followed by a brutally sharp corner. The courses were marked off on the airport runways using hay bales and traffic cones to create the corners. The goal was to reproduce the twists, turns and straights of actual roads. But runways are perfectly flat, and roads designed for driving are not. The "camber" or pitch of turns on an engineered road is a big part of what keeps cars on said road, and the courses we laid out had none of it.

The rules of racing were not complicated in those days. Cars did not come equipped with them at the time, so aftermarket seat belts were required. If you were running an open top roadster, a roll bar was required. And everyone had to have a quick-release fire extinguisher bolted in the passenger foot-well within easy reach of the driver. The race scrutinizers checked your brakes and tire tread depth. Other than that, with a helmet or "crash hat" we were good to go racing. We raced the cars we drove every day, Porsches, Alfas, Jags, MGs, Triumphs, Austin Healeys, often with zero or very few modifications.

With a little tweaking they could be turned into potent racing machines.

Unmodified, most of them were "redlined" around five thousand rpm. The "red line" is the rate of turnover at which the engine is in danger of exploding. If you have an old-fashioned analog tachometer on your car you can see the literal red line somewhere around 4 or 5 o'clock on the dial.

Some cars raced as "production" models, i.e., the way they came from the dealer; others as "modified." Because there are so many things one can do to increase the performance of a car, the isolation of modi-

1964 Porsche 356 Coupe—the body unchanged since 1955

fied cars in their own class made racing fairer.

The characteristics of each production vehicle were well-known to everyone, so a win against a stronger car in the "production class" was a clear demonstration of the skill of one driver versus another. Some production Porsches had the same engine size as MGs, but the Porsches were more expensive, more powerful and had four-wheel independent suspension that gave them an advantage in some corners. Even coming close to a Porsche in an MG could mean glory to the "loser" and dishonor to the "winner." You didn't have to win to win. The underdogs could "win" by putting up a good fight.

What were we competing for? Little brass participation plaques we could stick on our dashboards. And reputation within the club. There was no press coverage and almost no audience. The straggling few who came to watch (the clubs were non-profits so there could be no admission charge) were almost always outnumbered by those of us who came to race—the pit and corner crews, owners, and drivers.

That wonderful summer before my sophomore year of high school, I had a few friends among my classmates. My larger primary group, the people I hung out, visited, shared meals, and drank with, were all adults—most of them over 30. If you can call someone who loves cars as much as they did 'grown up.' They were all connected in some way to the sports car scene—race drivers, race drivers' girlfriends, shop owners, car builders, machinists, mechanics, everyone in the Pacific Northwest whose life was mainly organized around their ownership and racing of a European car.

Paul Hanna and my other car friends were especially eager to show me how to hustle a car around a racecourse. First there is a great deal that must be talked through. Second, we would venture out onto an isolated road with me in the passenger seat and an experienced driver demonstrating technique. Ultimately, I was invited behind the wheel to take the experienced driver out for a ride and "seat-time" instruction.

Paul somewhat quirkily added that one who drives cars owned by others is technically a chauffeur. And that meant I had to be trained as a master chauffeur. He told me to visualize a

Miles' 1955 Flying Shingle, MG TD based special running in F Modified. This was one of the most successful cars on the 1950s racing circuits. Ken turned the tables on the rich guys in their Ferrari's and Lotus and OSCA cars. They couldn't catch him in the "Flying Shingle."

princess in the passenger seat, very sensitive to every stop, start, turn and bump in the road. He taught me to bring a car to a halt so imperceptibly that he, as a passenger with his eyes closed, could not tell the moment we came to a complete stop. That took a lot of practice. He also made me drive around the block with a half-full mug of water balanced on the transmission tunnel. My driving inputs had to be so gentle that it didn't fall over. "Good. Now decrease your lap time by five seconds."

When he thought I was good enough to get a job driving for an important English family he said I was qualified to be a "chauffeur" and to drive other people's racing cars.

Here Is How You Get A Vintage 1950s
Sports Racing Car Around The Track

Driving a sports-racing car in competition in the 1950s was among the gentlest of the gentle arts. There were no computer-controlled, traction sensing devices or big fat sticky tires. It was just you, the driver, mechanically communicating with the engine and four skinny, skid-prone tires. You pressed on the brakes, clutch and gas. Power was delivered to the rear wheels, and you steered the front.

The following instructions do not apply to modern cars. Do not follow them unless you have a vintage 1950s racing sports car.

To drive competitively, you must enter each corner at a speed somewhat higher than your car can manage without breaking free of the surface of the road. In layman's terms, every corner involves a purposefully induced "skid." Your ability to live with and control high-speed slippage across the pavement is what determines your prowess as a driver. Once your tires stop tracking and begin to move across the pavement it is crucially important that all of your driving inputs—steering, acceleration, braking—are gentle, almost imperceptible. Even though you are about to fly off the track, your goal is to make it through the turn pointed up the next straight. The princess sitting next to you should not be aware of what you are up to.

There are three ways to lose control and leave the track. If your front wheels fly off first and you leave the track facing forward, this is called "understeer." If your rear wheels break free first and you "spin out" and leave the track backwards, this is called "oversteer." If you fly off the apex sideways so your car is no longer tracking front-to-back but moving laterally across the pavement, this is called "neutral steer." And you might roll over.

When they become unsettled in a corner, every car has its own tendencies. Porsches oversteer. Jaguars understeer. (Once again, bear in mind this only applies to the 1950s models of these cars.) Before you try to control it, you must know and understand your car's natural tendencies at speed when it is only partially connected to the road.

To prevent a violent departure from your racing line in a corner, you must establish the speed of entry the instant before you turn the steering wheel. You have been hard on the brakes approaching the turn. Having set your speed for the turn, you lift gently off the brakes just as you enter the corner. A sudden lift-off can induce violent oversteer or understeer depending on the tendency of your car. The instant you initiate the turn your right foot must move from the brakes to the gas. If you coast through the curve your car will become unsettled and want to leave the track. You gently power through the turn maintaining or slightly increasing your speed.

If you have done everything correctly, you will have induced a controlled drift, ideally with some oversteer, i.e. the back of your car is going around the corner slightly faster than the front of your car. It is crucial to keep your adrenaline under control. Harsh braking or hitting the gas while in a drift will break your car loose and send you off the track—frontwards, backwards, or sidewards. Your best outcome if you screw up is a 360-degree spin that leaves you on the track and you can proceed. Embarrassed but pointed in the right direction. That is, if you didn't hit another car in the process of being clumsy in public. Even if you didn't cause an accident, the corner worker will have radioed your safety violation   to

Spotting and flagging on a corner, 1956 club race. That is an Alfa Giulietta Sprint Coupe in a high-speed drift.

race central and if you make two more mistakes you will be "black-flagged." Your race will be over. Unless, of course, the corner worker happens to be a close friend in a generous mood.

A successfully controlled drift is a kind of kinetic poem. Some oversteer that does not take you off the track is actually decreasing the radius of your turn—your rear is swinging out slightly—and helping speed you around the corner. When you get everything perfect, and your car has enough power, you can "steer" through the turn using only the gas pedal. Without moving the steering wheel, you can bring the back end further around by applying more power and bring it back in line by applying less. That is how to get through a turn as quickly as possible.

Here is how you compensate for error. If the rear swings out too far and you start to spin you must not take your foot off the gas. A sudden drop in power at the rear will make matters worse. If you applied a little too much power, you compensate by steering gently in the opposite direction of the turn. That should bring your car back in line.

There is more to learn. There is always more.

You are nearing the end of a straight and have achieved your maximum speed. In a small displacement 1950s sports racing car, say about 100 MPH. You know that you will need to halve that speed to get through the upcoming turn. You have selected a marker—a tree or a haybale—something that does not move—as the last possible braking point to get your speed down. You hit the brakes as you pass your marker, taking care not to lock up. Still on the straight before the turn, the instant you hit the brakes you begin to downshift. You are in fifth gear and you will need to be in third to power through and out of the turn.

As you are passing through neutral on the way to fourth, then third gears, with the same foot that is hard on the brakes, you must swivel your heel over to the gas pedal and press it hard enough to raise the engine speed to match the car's speed in the lower gear you are selecting. It is called "heel and toe braking," and it is awkward but essential. It is an instantaneous blip of the gas pedal in the midpoint of the shift. There are two reasons you must do this. In the 1950s, racing cars still had drum brakes that are prone to fade and even failure when they become overheated. Closed-circuit racing is almost guaranteed to overheat brakes. So you save your brakes at every opportunity by using the engine's compression to slow the car. Engine braking is the first reason for "heel and toe." Second, if you de-clutch in a lower gear without raising the engine speed, you risk engine compression induced rear wheel lockup that can be even more unsettling to the car than panic breaking.

In practice sessions, I would position myself in a lonely place between widely spaced cars so I could refine my skills in private. Once I got everything sorted, I would pull in behind an experienced driver in a similar car and try to maintain the same drift lines and speeds.

In competition you are often alone on the track with the car in front and the one in back barely visible. And you are also often in high-speed traffic jams with six or eight cars diving toward the same apex at the same time.

This is when you find out if you can continue to be gentle while trying to maintain composure and position. How do all the smooth moves you just taught yourself hold up when you are pressed on all sides by others' desires? It is a good lesson for life.

Pete Lovely owned a Volkswagen Porsche dealership in South Seattle. In the 1950s, he was incontestably the fastest, smoothest driver in the Pacific Northwest. He went on to a successful professional career in Europe. When I was learning, he took me aside and said, "The secret to becoming a successful racer is to drive as slowly as you possibly can. [*pause*] And win."

At my first two races, Paul made certain that I had a pit pass and job as a corner flagman. When I was well enough known that I could walk past security no-questions-asked I began hanging out in the pits. The "pits" were not anything, actually. Just spaces chalked off on the side of the runway along the main straight near the start-finish line. You looked for your car number and class designation chalked between two lines. Each "pit" had enough space for two or three support vehicles, tools, hydraulic jacks, and three or four guys to work. There were no walls and no shade unless you brought a temporary shade canopy.

Pete Lovely with 1955 Corvette racing in B Production. Pits such as they were..

Almost everyone on pit row wore old and ragged clothes that they wouldn't mind throwing out if they got too much oil or grease on them. I wore pristine white super-clean coveralls fresh from my Troy locker. As young and skinny as I was, my gleaming coveralls with my name gave me a more official look than anyone else on pit row. Like it was my job to be there to take up the slack in everyone's pit, as needed.

I had already met many of the racers at home at the Hannas' so they were quick to ask my assistance as a kind of floating gofer among the racing teams doing everything from last-minute oil changes to going into town for sandwiches. I painted professional-looking numbers on the cars with tempera that could be washed off after the race. Some teams used masking tape to put crude, notchy numbers on their cars. My painted numbers were preferred. I carefully taped over headlights so if there was contact on the course the broken glass wouldn't fly around and hurt someone.

Before each race there was a drivers' meeting and technical inspection. The main discussion at the drivers' meeting was what constituted unsafe driving. The corner workers were connected to race-central by walkie-talkies. The drivers were allowed two infractions and given yellow warning flags. If they committed a third infraction, they were black-flagged. Their race day was over.

What was an infraction? Nothing so fancy as an "unsafe racing move" determined by televised instant re-plays as in Formula 1 today. Our "unsafe racing moves" consisted in losing control of your car and spinning or leaving the track. What "leaving the track" means might seem unambiguous, but it wasn't. There was always debate about how many wheels had to stay on the track in order for you to have "stayed on the track." "If only one wheel leaves the track [it was usually the outside rear] is it fair to say you left the track?" The drivers had to agree in advance of the race whether one wheel, two wheels, or three wheels off the track were permitted as "safe driving." There was a cadre of drivers who always voted for three wheels off as within bounds, and another group that maintained all four wheels had to be on. The larger, more flexible group in between the "hairy" drivers and the cautious drivers generally considered local conditions. If there were boulders or large trees near the runway—anything immovable you might hit—a zero- or one-wheel policy was adopted. If there was nothing but dirt clods, blackberry brambles and scotch broom or other shrubs to hit, a more liberal two or three wheels off was often permitted. The arguments did not usually last very long because everyone was eager to race and willing to compromise.

To race you had to join the Club and pay "start money"—$30-80 per car per weekend. There were no commercial sponsorships. Some rich guys with real race cars were out there on their own. They sometimes brought small teams with volunteer or even paid mechanics. But as often as not it would be a man alone in the pit—just him and his car.

My father wrote a "To Whom it May Concern" letter giving his permission for me to drive in sanctioned road races so long as no liability I incurred came back on him. By the end of that summer, I had been behind the wheel of exotics including Ferrari, Lotus, and C-type Jaguar. A few of the owners who thought I was faster and easier on their cars than they were gave me the

1955 Lotus 11 built to run in F Modified. The Production MGs and Alfas built for everyday use with similar sized engines didn't stand a chance. Hence the division of the F class (and all the engine size classes) into "Production" and "Modified."

keys for the race.

My first true love was a Lotus. Out on the track in proximity to cars with four times its engine size a Lotus 11 seems to gain horsepower. Its acceptance of driver inputs was so intuitively correct that it felt like I was along for the ride in a machine that had competitive consciousness of its own. Driving an 11 at its limit was pure pleasure. It felt like it went hunting for more powerful cars to embarrass. I never tired of braking late and slipping between other cars heading into the apex of a high-speed corner, rocketing out ahead of much more powerful cars, causing them to get unsettled if their drivers tried to keep up. They always caught and passed me on the next straight. It made it more amusing to do it again at the next corner.

I once took a blown (supercharged) Corvette out for a couple of laps in practice. Given its crude, horse carriage suspension, it had more power than it could ever use, and yank-your-head-off acceleration. But nothing ever beat the thrill of driving ultra-light, hyper-competent very low displacement giant killers like the Lotus 11. My taste in cars was very much bound up with my politics. I am on the side of the powerless unless they have stumbled into right-wing fantasies. This was my 16-year-old way of literally speaking truth to power: pass them in the turns. Power does not always prevail. Not against gentility, balance, subtlety and cunning.

Given the dominance of foreign cars in the U.S. today, it may come as a surprise that in 1956, driving a European import was widely regarded as "un-American." About once a week I got a loud, profanity-laced lecture while getting into or out of a car. I must be a "Commie" for driving a car like that. Occasionally I was told that I was lower than the N word. Our cars were vandalized. Usually smashed headlights. Sometimes keyed paint. We were refused service in filling stations. Fords and Chevys began to wear bumper stickers, "Buy American."

My father was relentless in his ridicule of my interest in these cars. "Why would anybody pay $2000 for an Alfa Romeo when you can get a good real car like a Buick for that kind of money?" When I explained it was all about the driving experience and offered him a ride in the Hannas' MG he declined.

He said, "If I wanted to experience riding in a car like that, I would sit on a hard floor with a fan blowing in my face and have someone throw sand into the fan."

A friend of mine did not help matters by putting a bumper sticker on his new $8,000 Ferrari: "Don't laugh—it's paid for."

A friend of mine? New Ferrari? Yes. In the Pacific Northwest in the 1950s everyone who loved cars was equal. If I was as engaged with the engineering, driving characteristics and potential modifications of the Fiat I drove, I was socially no different from my millionaire friend who owned the Ferrari. In the club scene I was his equal. If he knew nothing about his car and had only purchased it as a status symbol, I was his superior.

Because of the entrée provided by Paul Hanna, and my presence at the track every weekend, I was welcome at car club parties, planning meetings, post-race trophy presentations, and as a drop-in at every foreign car related business in the Pacific Northwest. No one talked down to me or treated me like a kid. I was treated as a part of the conversation, no different from anyone else.

And My Car Drawings

Recall my father's comment when he gave me the Stanford-Binet IQ test that I might succeed as a draughtsman? I followed through on his advice taking the three courses my junior high school offered—beginning, intermediate and advanced mechanical drawing. None of the course exercises involved automobile design but I transferred everything I learned to that field. I don't know how many drawings I produced in my sophomore and junior years of high school, but I would not be surprised if it numbered over a thousand. I loved the design work of Vignale, Zagato, Ghia, and Farina. But I could never leave well enough alone and was constantly pushing the idiom further into the future. My drawings were much admired and in demand in the sports car club scene, to be looked at and discussed.

Whenever anyone saw me with my portfolio under my arm they would demand, "Whatcha got for us today?" Often, some detail of one of my drawings would provoke long and intense discussion.

My drawings were highly regarded as prescient peeks into the future of high-performance car design. "Show us what the next Porsche will look like." I was usually able to capture the spirit of the future evolution of a particular car while preserving its positive aesthetics. Often, I saw too far into the future. My proposed Porsche design features did not appear on their pro-

Porsche styling annoyed me. It seemed too close to its Volkswagen half-brother. They were the most potent cars in F Production, but I thought they needed different bodies.

Below are two of my 1950s sketches for alternate Porsche design.

Dean MacCannell, Variations on the theme of Porsche styling sketches from 1956, 1957.

duction cars until 50 years later.

When summer and the racing season and my job at Nottingham's ended, I continued living with the Hannas, going to high school by day and working at Troy by night. I would drop by to visit my brothers occasionally, timing my visits to when I knew my parents would not be home. I had not been able to speak freely in my parents' presence for over a year. If I ventured any opinion about anything, they would immediately snarl at me that I had "gotten above myself." One day they became furious with me for criticizing the engineering of the popular General Motors "Hydramatic" automatic transmission. I made the mistake of wondering aloud why GM had not included a driveline lock in top gear, a feature of all automatic transmissions today. "It is so inefficient to have the fluid drive torque converter letting the engine turn over faster than the drive shaft," I opined. "Going down the highway in high gear, all that wasted power could be transmitted to the rear wheels if they had just incorporated a simple clutch lockup. The fuel savings across the fleet would be enormous." This set off a firestorm.

My parents joined together and called me a "know-it-all." They screamed until they were red in the face. Literally. I asked them to let it drop, but they would not. Under no circumstances should I, as a 16-year-old kid, be allowed to criticize the engineers at General Motors. "They have college degrees. Who are you to question their decisions? Who do you think you are?"

As a teen, my goal was to reduce my contact and conversations with my parents to the absolute minimum. I did not need or miss their company. I had a second straight-A-earning, girlfriend who was my age and in my class. She was interested in my opinions and had interesting opinions of her own, especially about modern art. She was not ready for sex until Spring but it was easy for me to be patient now knowing some things are worth the wait. When foreplay lasts for six months, it does not take a genius to figure out the "secret" of the female orgasm. I discovered there are few things in life more endearing than sharing that secret. Especially with a girl who hasn't already figured it out for herself.

My girlfriend and I were fans of basketball, probably because that season Lincoln High was a basketball powerhouse, eventually vanquishing every other Seattle school and going on to win the state championship. Because of my Troy job I could not get to the games until they were nearly over, usually around the beginning of the last quarter. My girlfriend would go to the games with her gal pals, and I would find her in the pavilion, sit with her at the end, and drive her home. Because of my work and school, most of our time alone together was talking late into the night in borrowed cars parked down the street from her house after ball games.

I began wearing my Troy coveralls to class so I would not need to change before work. That caused me to seem just a bit weird in the eyes of some classmates and teachers. I told them I was not trying to be "different." It was just my after-school work clothes. This was a generally accepted excuse. Having a regular after-school job in 1956 was widely regarded as honorific.

As my junior year progressed class work became more challenging. I loved plain and solid geometry. It seemed to connect mathematics to the real world around me. Trigonometry was a pain in the ass until I noticed that a previous delinquent had carved the formulas for sine, cosine and tangent into the wooden top of my desk. A primary group of adults did not cause me to shun my high school peers.

I became friendly with a dozen or so kids who were neither popular leader types, nor marginal semi-delinquent types. We tried to arrive a half hour before first period every morning and hang out together over glasses of fruit juice in the school cafeteria. The "hoods" continued to be deferential.

With the approval of the school administration, I was able to skip afternoon classes fairly often. Noticing the sparkling new sports cars that I often drove, the principal named me as the designated driver for students who became ill during the school day and needed to be taken home. "Ill during the school day" was most frequently menstrual cramps. So my driving assignments and interesting cars gained me a few girl pals. Even though I had quite a bit more going on, my junior year felt a bit like "textbook" normal high school.

16

Scott Larsen Motors

AT THE END OF MY JUNIOR YEAR. with summer approaching, I thought I would go back to work days at Nottingham. Not as factotum, but to apprentice myself to one of the master boatwrights. I preferred cars, I did not like sailing as much as driving, but classic wooden sail boats were almost as intriguing and beautiful as the cars I was driving. Looking forward to a lifetime of blue-collar work I narrowed my options to designing and building race cars or wooden sail boats. If I could achieve top form in any specialty of either of those fields I knew my life would be full of endless new intriguing challenges and handling things of true beauty every day. I could look forward to a happy adult life.

Before I could present myself back at Nottingham's with my proposal, Paul Hanna told me about a new exotic auto repair shop "Opening in the far north end of Seattle." Scott Larsen Motors launched itself with a democratic (inclusive and egalitarian) series of ads— "All Service and Repair Ferrari. We also service Fiats." "All Service and Repair Jaguar. We also service Austins." "Etc." I had not met them, but Paul told me he knew the guys and they were okay. Paul Scott was an understated Brit with a head for business and a love of Italian cars. Jack Larsen was widely regarded as a genius mechanic of last resort who you took your problem to when no one else could solve it. I knew the type—my maternal relatives. Paul Hanna told me to go out and meet them. If I was planning to apprentice myself at Nottingham's without pay if necessary, why not approach Scott Larsen with the same proposal. That would keep my energy focused in the car world. So I got on the Lambretta and rode out to the "North End."

Hanna had given them a heads up, and they were enthusiastic that I would hang out at the shop, do gofer duty, take up the slack for simple jobs, fetch and put the tools they needed in their hands so they did not have to get out from under the cars. (This was something like Valerie Hanna's job in the surgical theater.) The initial arrangement was that I would work for free to learn the service and repair protocols for the exotics that came through, and I would leave an hour before closing time to get to my paid job at Troy.

My life and my future were completely on track. Or so I believed. At that moment, my break with my family felt complete. It did not occur to me that it might not be so. My plan was to continue living with the Hannas while working nights at Troy, finish my senior year of high school, and spend as much time at Scott Larsen as I could until the following summer. After graduation, I would return to Scott Larsen and pursue whatever projects were most intriguing and rewarding. Like building a Fiat-based small-displacement racing special. I had already started drawing its body shape and drivetrain configuration.

In the beginning, my main task was hustling for parts back and forth between Scott Larsen and the big imported-car dealerships in downtown Seattle. In the morning, after teardown, when Jack and Paul knew what parts were needed to complete a job, I sped into town to get them. I once balanced an engine block for a four-cylinder Lancia behind my calves on the foot pan of the Lambretta. We ate lunch every day at a diner around the corner from the shop where the owner shot dice with us to determine who would pay—him or us. It worked out over time to about a 20 percent discount for our regular patronage.

After I had been doing this for three weeks, one of the guys mentioned to me that they would be coming in on Saturday to clean and paint the floor. The floor of your shop had to be painted glacier white and spotless if you wanted to have any credibility as a serious place for service of upper tier exotics. When I came to work on Monday the floor was beautiful—I could literally see my face in it—and both Jack and Paul seemed perturbed. Why had I not shown up on Saturday? Well, I did not realize they meant for me to help them paint the floor. It was not exactly about learning the trade. I already knew how to paint floors. I reminded them that I was not being paid, was in effect working two jobs, so I needed a day off. They looked a little sheepish and allowed that I had a point. So would a dollar an hour be okay going forward? Perfect. Less than what I was making at Troy but still above minimum wage.

It took only two- or three-weeks watching Jack Larsen at work for me to know I would never be a racing mechanic. I did not have the necessary feel for it. I could take things apart. But I didn't have an intuitive sense of how to put them back together. At crucial steps along the way, I had to make exploded drawings of the arrangement of parts to reassemble them properly. No master mechanic must do that.

It was another one of those moments that turned my world inside out. Perhaps the one that changed my life the most. Had I become stubborn; had I decided I was going to be a racing mechanic no matter what, I am certain Jack would have been patient and done the best he could to teach me. And I am equally certain that I would have been good enough. But just "good enough." Not the first person someone would approach to solve an impossible problem. Not up to the Meskimen blue-collar standard. I knew in my gut my future would be elsewhere. But where, exactly?

Jack and Paul gave me simple hands-on tasks like tearing down carburetors, polishing ports, installing roll bars, etc. In addition to lacking mechanical intuition, my hands and arms were too strong for me to be trusted with some assembly and teardown jobs. My odd handicap was the result of having very long arms combined with years of playing the violin. I had bone-crushing strength in my hands and I rarely lost an arm-wrestling contest to anyone, not even wrestlers.

Early on, when Jack and Paul tasked me with tearing down a Mercedes engine, I sheared off a head bolt and was mortified thinking I had ruined the entire block. Jack was amused, telling me no, the bolt just had to be drilled out and replaced with a re-verse-thread larger one. But in the future, I should not be let near jobs where substantial resistance needed to be overcome. When faced with resistance, I quickly got a reputation for breaking the component. Either that, or the tool I was using. I could not be trusted with the most delicate and expensive machinery, the machinery I most wanted to work on.

A future with a wrench in my hand meant a future as a truck mechanic. After seeing my first OSCA with its body off, the truck option for me shrank to zero. I almost couldn't bear looking at the brakes, exhaust manifolds, rear suspension, etc. of the Troy trucks. I had to keep telling myself, 'They're trucks. They're supposed to be heavy, simple, ugly. Easy to work on. Hard to break. It's okay. Get over it.' But after seeing the beautiful OSCA mechanicals designed by the Maserati brothers, I could never get over it. A Maserati engine is a work of art.

Fortunately there were many tasks around the shop that I could do and was good at. I could polish intake and exhaust ports to improve gas flow in the engine head and manifolds. This was like sculpture or redrawing a design element to get it just right. I was precise at organizing and packing tools and spares needed for race days. And when a repair went long if I chatted up the waiting customer, he forgot he was waiting. I knew all the technical specifications of every model of every popular sports car. I mean literally everything—their SAE horsepower versus their DIN horsepower, the swept area of their front and rear brakes, their weights, their wheelbases. The volume of oil in their crankcases. Those oil-burning Jags in the 1950s had 12-quart sumps. I could compare every detail of the customer's car to every other car in its class. Every other car on the road. Did you know that the swept area of the brakes on a 1,900-pound Alfa Giulietta was more than twice the swept area of the brakes on a 4,000-pound Buick?

I Meet Erna Gunther

About the customers in the last paragraph, should I have said "making him or her forget?" Actually yes. Erna Gunther, the brilliant ethnologist trained by Franz Boas, specialist in Northwest Coast Native Americans, had her Mercedes Benz 190 roadster serviced at Scott Larsen. She was our only female customer. Prophetically, she preferred talking anthropology with me, not cars. I told her of my earlier forays into her museum and how awestruck I was by the Northwest Coast Indian materials. She explained "potlatch" to me, how local chiefs would amass huge heaps of blankets, ceremonial copper plaques, and food. They would then invite a rival chief and his followers to an enormous feast. The rival was required to reciprocate and throw an equally sumptuous potlatch in return. The idea was to humiliate and vanquish your rival by throwing a feast he could not match. If the guests were unable eat enough, or carry away enough of the gifted blankets, coppers and carvings, the host would ostentatiously burn a thousand or so blankets and carvings to try to guarantee that he could not be matched when the guest chief and band reciprocated. So it became an escalating war of aggressive generosity and waste until one of the chiefs had to admit defeat. He could not continue starving his people and working them to death in order to keep pace and save face. "Like the nuclear arms race between the U.S. and the Soviet Union," I proffered. "The way our leaders blow up any excess we create so it never reaches the common people." "Well, something like that," Gunther allowed. But she immediately cautioned me that anthropologists try to avoid those kinds of cross-cultural comparisons. "The meaning of the potlatch to the Kwakiutl is not the same as the meaning of the arms race to us," she explained. I understood her point but resisted accepting it completely. In the moment I understood without knowing it that I would always be a comparatist.

I "banked" what I did not understand in my conversations with Professor Gunther for later like I banked "ball bugs," and "a piece of tail" from my conversations with my Uncle Eddie.

A Lesson About The Power Of Prejudice

As a marketing gimmick, Scott Larsen put on a kind of racetrack clown show with a pair of the least impressive cars you could find. Fiat 600s, tiny Italian economy cars with an engine so small that the production model was classed with the lowest of the low. If you took a step down from racing stock 600s, you would find yourself nowhere. There is nothing lower.

The Scott Larsen Fiats were class winners, but that was not the point. Jack Larsen had invented and built an ingenious flatbed, four-wheeled trailer with hydraulic suspension that allowed the bed to be dropped all the way to the ground. To everyone's amusement, we would bring one of the Fiats to the races on the trailer like it was a modified, non-street-legal race car. We towed the trailer behind a late 1940s Dodge "Doctor's Coupe" that Jack had rebuilt from nose to tail.

The main point to the Scott Larsen racing program was to have that trailer at the races. It could accommodate seriously broken cars. Even if someone's suspension completely collapsed, we could push the car on by squatting Jack's trailer only a few inches above the tarmac. I would drive the Fiat that had arrived on the trailer back from the race. Our shop would earn a hefty (often more than 100 miles) tow fee, and sometimes a big repair job. The most frequent disabling incident in the "modified" classes was blown engines. "We can handle the rebuild and try to squeeze a few extra horses out as well if you're interested." We were the wrecker to the racers.

But we were not there only to offer a tow. Paul and Jack dramatically raced their two little Fiats against each other going door against door through the turns. They would exchange the lead multiple times a lap. It was all an act just to please spectators and the crowd ate it up. The act ended a few laps before the finish. Paul and Jack would align them-

Stock bodied Fiat 600.

selves going down the main straight and then really get into it. Jack won more often than Paul.

Almost everyone running "Production" had undertaken mild-to-radical engine and other modifications that were mainly invisible, the Scott Larsen Fiats included. There was always a chance that a sharp-eyed race inspector would notice your mods and bump you into the "Modified" class. It was my job to take the cars through technical inspection so they would have plausible deniability if they were caught cheating. ("Well, Red didn't

know. I guess he just assumed we were running unmodified.")
No one wanted to get bumped up to "Modified" where the competition was much rougher. We knew about many of the surreptitious modifications because we had done them at Scott Larsen for our customers.

With the help of Carlo Abarth, we made sure the Scott Larsen Fiats kept pace with the other "Production" cars in our class. Carlo Abarth, soon to be a famous name in the sports-car world, had a speed shop in Torino, Italy, the hometown of Fiat, where he sold performance-enhancing modifications. Before there was an internet and before there were credit cards, using an Italian-English/English-Italian dictionary, I was able to decipher the Abarth catalogue and foreign ordering instructions. Paul and Jack purchased speed parts delivered by air freight as fast as Abarth made them available for sale. While on the outside they were still the same little economy cars, on the inside the 600s were evolving into proper racing machines.

We kept running the Fiats in the "Production" class and with the extra horsepower and were able to show the other "Production" cars who was boss on the track. But we also let them win occasionally. We did not want to ignite a dueling teardown debacle that would have all of us bounced up to "Modified." The technical inspection scrutinizers were not knowledgeable enough about what to look for in the engine compartment to call us on our many visible Abarth speed parts. My blood froze when the first Abarth Zagato showed up at a race late in the season. It was a bespoke racing

Fiat Abarth Zagato. Aluminum bodied race car based on Fiat 600 mechanical components with the same Abarth performance enhancing engine and suspension modification we installed in our stock-bodied 600s.

machine on a Fiat 600 chassis with a beautiful, streamlined body by Zagato, one of my automotive-design heroes, and all our Abarth engine modifications. Fiat Abarth Zagatos were unambiguously classed as "Modified."

Sitting in line for technical inspection three cars behind the Zagato I knew we were busted for running as "Production." When you lifted the hood of my secretly modified 600, it would look like an identical twin to the modified racing version two cars ahead of me in line. The scrutinizer would surely note that my car's engine was identical to the engine in the Abarth Zagato. It would be fresh in his mind. We were busted.

As I moved ahead in the line, I tried to compose something to say about having obviously cheated. I suspected a life-altering moment was about to happened. And I was right. It just was not the life-altering moment I was expecting.

The technical inspector snapped open my engine cover and peered in. Watching his face closely, I noticed his look of condescension for our little Fiat economy car never wavered. It seemed to intensify. Out of his mouth came these words, "Sure is different from the Abarth Zagato."

The man was so intent on putting me down and showing his expertise as a scrutinizer that he failed to see that the engine he was looking at was the same as the one he had just seen in the Zagato. In the service of his prejudices, my engine had to be different, and he could only see what was in his mind, not what was before his eyes. There was a dollop of sadistic enjoyment as he insulted me for running a pathetic little production version of the real race car he had just inspected. He was literally blinded by his prejudice.

The experience taught me that everywhere, all around me, and all through life, there are similar moments of prejudicial blindness. I skated through inspection with an easy pass. Driving back to our pit I didn't even bother to minimize the giveaway "brapity-brap-brap" exhaust note that was also identical to the Abarth Zagato's.

When I arrived, Paul and Jack were looking at me with a combination of fear and guilt. They had seen the Zagato exit the inspection line two cars before me and assumed we had been kicked out of the Production class if not off the track. They were clearly ashamed that I was the one holding the bag when we got caught. They both rushed up. "What happened?"

"We passed."

"What about the . . .?"

"We're still running 'Production.'"

No, I hadn't bribed the scrutinizer. "He was so blinded by the Zagato gestalt that our mods did not register with him. He just waved me through with the usual condescension."

As soon as we got back to the shop I began working on concept drawings for a race car that we could build from the ground up around our Abarth modified Fiat 600 components and run openly and competitively against the Zagatos in H Modified. We already had the engines for it. It would be a relief to be able to stop pretending to be running Production. Our breach was not that great. Very few of the cars running Production at the time had not been souped up. We were cheating, but we took great care never to beat a car that was not also cheating.

That summer at the tracks I became confident that I could be a successful designer of racing cars. Without a degree in engineering? One might reasonably ask. That was not an issue then. John Cooper (1923-2000) was one of the most successful race car designers of all time. He was a high school drop-out at age 15 but that did not stop him from conceiving and executing the now universal rear engine configuration for high performance cars. And he did it with no further study beyond the experiments he conducted in his youth in a shop much like Scott Larsen.

I could assemble in my head the most effective types of engines, brakes, suspensions, wheels, body shapes, etc. and organize them in different configurations with predictably different driving characteristics. I began drawing transverse rear engine performance cars in 1957, eight years before Lamborghini offered the same radical configuration in its 1965 Miura. "Unheard of in 1965" according to Wikipedia. Paul Hanna, Jack Larsen, Paul Scott and others enthusiastically encouraged me to keep on drawing. Jack told me to chalk out my designs full scale on the

Concept drawing I made in the summer of 1957 for a transverse rear engine (Jaguar) special based on Fiat 600 components.

shop floor so we could discuss and debate their features. When we arrived at a design we liked best, Jack would bend and weld up chassis tubes right over my chalk lines.

My Plans Demolished

Sometime that Spring (1957), my father received an offer of an assistant professorship in Sociology at San Diego State College (now San Diego State University) beginning in the Fall.

I was aware of the offer but hadn't paid much attention as I had no intention to move with my family to Southern California. I did not discuss it with them.

I stupidly thought there was no need for discussion.

When my father demanded a meeting, I knew it could not be good. He had never before asked to meet or have a discussion with me. About anything. His opening gambit was to tell me I had to sell my Ford. Or he would sell it for me. It was his way of easing into his main point. "We can't be taking two cars to San Diego." I tried to explain: "No. No. No. I won't be going with you. I don't mind selling the Ford. (He was the insurer.) I never use it anymore. But I'm not going to California. My life is here. I have good jobs. I'm completely self-supporting. I'll behave myself as I always have and finish my last year of high school. The Hannas are looking after me. Eddie and Betty live nearby. There is no need for me to go to Southern California."

17

Forced Move to San Diego

MY FATHER'S FACE TURNED PURPLE, but he remained outwardly calm. He explained that I was a minor child and had no right to make my own decisions. If I refused to go, he would have me arrested. I was stunned by his declarations and demands and still, to this day, do not know what motivated him. He had shown no interest in my life up to that point beyond occasionally remarking "You've always had it too easy." My best guess is peer pressure. He did not want to show up in San Diego minus a son and have to explain why. One member of the San Diego State Sociology Department, Aubrey Wendling, knew me. He had been a graduate student with my father at Washington who finished his Ph.D. and left for San Diego two years before. Aubrey and I hung out together at Sociology department functions like the annual picnic. Aubrey climbed mountains--not as fanatically as Tom Steinburn, but seriously and competently, and we had formed a bond. Maybe my father was worried that Aubrey would ask, "Where's Dean?"

The overwhelming reality was that I had been raised with a military style chain of command in the family and as independent as I was, it was also unthinkable that I would ever disobey. Up to that point, the life I had been able to build for myself had not been warped by any parental direct orders other than the overarching "*18 and out.*" They had nothing to say when I got my first job; about any of my friends and associates, including girlfriends; when I moved out of their house; etc. But now came the crushing news that I was being forced to move with them San Diego where I would have no support and would end up back under their roof. The thought was physically nauseating.

Today I hear a lot about parents avoiding moves while their children are in high school so the kids' friendship networks would not be disrupted. Obviously, this was not high on my parents' list of concerns and, from my standpoint, it need not have been. Leaving my high school friends was not a problem. Except for my girlfriend, I wasn't close enough to any of them for there to be genuine sadness on either side. I had a couple of weeks to say goodbye to my girl, to sell my car, give notice at Troy and at Scott Larsen, bid a sad farewell to the Hannas and a number of my other car club friends. It was wretched. The one positive note was I would be back in nine months. In nine months, I would have finished high school, turned 18, and beyond the reach of capricious parental commands. It would be like a short jail sentence. I could not wait for "18 and Out." Except now I had to. My friends told me they eagerly looked forward to my return. My bosses at Troy seemed genuinely sad to see me go.

The only memory I have ever suppressed is how I got to San Diego in late August 1957. I know I did not travel with my parents and brothers in their now sad 1953 Dodge Meadowbrook with worn crankshaft bearings that were beginning to knock. I must have told them I needed more time in Seattle to wrap up my affairs. I know I did not hitchhike or ride the rails. I may have taken a "Drive-Away" car, the train, or the Greyhound. One way or another, I got myself to San Diego a few days before my senior year of high school started in the Fall.

In San Diego, I found my family settled into an abject lower-middle-class housing tract filled with US Navy, below-officer-grade, retirees. My new home in the belligerently tacky "Allied Gardens" sub-division had three tiny bedrooms and one bath. The bedrooms were smaller than the ones in the projects of my early childhood.

My brother Bill got a room of his own because my father said he had "something wrong" with him and he did not want him sleeping in the same room with John. As I write this, I am reminded of how much more harm my brothers suffered in the thrall of my parents than I ever did. If Bill had anything wrong with him, it was entirely a projection of my father's sick mind.

From this experience, I learned that in this life, one can lose everything almost overnight. In a matter of days, I went from earning good money to having no money at all; from having my own car and being able to borrow Jaguars and other interesting roadsters whenever I went out on a date, to having no wheels at all; from having a large network of helpful and generous adult friends to knowing no one; from work that I loved and looked forward to everyday to being unemployed. From living separate from my odious mother and father to being jammed into a tiny house with them day and night. From having an eager girlfriend to being involuntarily celibate. I was more diminished than I had been under Jens Aure's reign of terror.

A quick sketch I made soon after I arrived in San Diego. It is what I imagined my future would be like after forced reunification with my parents.

The most disgusting change I endured was having to share a double bed with my brother John. I don't know why they ended up with an old double bed for us instead of bunkbeds. But that was our lot. There was no room on either side of the bed for my sleeping bag and air-mattress. So I ended up sleeping with my tween brother. I did not care for physical contact with him, so whenever he rolled over or thrashed about, I squeezed myself ever closer to the edge, clinging on all night, almost falling out. If we had been a loving immigrant family with no other options, I would not have found the situation so creepy. But every time John touched me I was reminded that he could have had this bed to himself if only my father had allowed me to stay in Seattle.

And I was reminded that in Seattle I had life and in this dry, hot and ugly place I had less than nothing. The move had completely exhausted my parents' resources. We could afford nothing but food for several months. My mother probably suffered a dislocation as profound as mine. She had just been ripped from the arms of her lover, Tom Steinburn, with whom, until the move, she had been going off on dates and lost weekends at every opportunity.

On their arrival in San Diego, her passive-aggressive response was defiantly to refuse to look for work to make ends meet. With truckloads of drama and over-acted irony she expounded about how this is why we had sacrificed for all those years.

My father finally got a Ph.D., and this is how we ended up. In a hideous house in Allied Gardens, a quarter the size of the house in Seattle they just left. How do you like them apples Mr. Big, Fancy Professor Philanderer? His assistant professor take-home pay was about $400.00 a month. Barely enough to climb out of the hole they were in. But slowly. Not right away.

From the moment I walked through their front door at Allied Gardens, I refused to speak even one word to either of them. I ate in silence with the family because I would have starved if I did not. If anyone addressed a question or comment to me at the table, I just tilted my head back, raised my upper lip and glared. We had endured almost two decades of abject poverty looking forward to our reward and this was it.

In many ways, life in Allied Gardens was more wretched than the projects. No one had a garden or even watered their lawns. It was so dry not even weeds would grow.

The house in Allied Gardens. The total living area was equal to two single car garages. My mother is posing proudly on the front porch. I don't know why.

Our yard was hard, yellow-colored dirt.

Every day when I got home from school I went straight to bed. I got up briefly for dinner that I continued to eat in silence and went back to bed immediately after. When John came to bed around ten o'clock, I got up and went to the living room (it was also the dining room and kitchen) and did my school homework. Drawing and reading were my only outlets and solace. But I could not bring myself to draw another car. I got sick to my stomach when I tried. A few sketches from this period remain in my files. They are hastily made and depressive.

The school bus trip from Allied Gardens to 'Pervert' Hoover High School was about five miles zigzagging back and forth on freeways. I did not bond with anyone on my bus. I just sat in silence. I was half-depressed. At home with my parents, I maintained a full-on depressive attitude. It was not an act. They were the cause of it, after all. But it was not in my nature to be an alienated teenager in my own mind. I could not stop myself from studying my new surroundings looking for possibilities.

How far was the trip from school to home as the crow flies, I wondered? Could I walk it? I knew it was illegal to be out on the freeways as a pedestrian. Would they effectively prevent me from moving around on foot? My only free option. Do you have to have a car to get from point A to point B in San Diego County?

One day I did not get on the bus. I took off in the general direction of Allied Gardens, beating my way through the scrub chaparral in the canyons between the freeways. I discovered that the freeways did not block my passage. There were numerous drains under the roadbeds and between the canyons. The drain tunnels were four and six feet in diameter welded and corrugated steel and open on the ends. Easy to crouch down and clamber through. They were designed to handle the occasional torrential rains that could lead to flash flooding if the runoff was not contained and directed. As it happened, they effectively contained and directed my progress toward Allied Gardens. I plotted my course from drain to drain and got home in under an hour. It was my first taste of freedom in southern California. My spirits lifted. Somewhat. Not enough to get me speaking to my parents. But it was something for me to do. I started walking home every day.

The Drain Tunnels Were Infested With
Black Widow Spiders

On my first trip I used a stick to clear the webs in front of me and scatter the spiders from my path. On subsequent trips I carried a flashlight and a Mason jar to collect the spiders. Black widows are not particularly defensive creatures and are fairly easy to catch. My mother had emphasized throughout my child-hood that Western Washington had no poisonous spiders and no poisonous snakes. She often cited this as the reason she allowed me as a young child to wander unsupervised in deep woods. She was crazy afraid of snake and spider bites. When I was a little kid, Eddie told me that a tarantula bite would not kill you unless it bit you on the genitals, and that they lived under the seats in outdoor toilets. Even though I had no experience with poisonous spiders, I had been adequately forewarned. After our move to California, my mother often brought it up that we could no lon-ger be carefree out in Nature. There were venomous spiders and snakes everywhere. She was somewhat obsessive and paranoid about it. We had to be extremely vigilant.

I found what I was looking for in the garage jumble of half-unpacked stuff moved from Seattle. My father's large guppy breeding aquarium. It would make a perfect black widow zoo. I filled it with my biggest specimens and kept the ladies well sup-plied with grasshoppers, moths, and other insects to eat. I kept the aquarium in a hot dark corner of the garage. Was I making my collection as a favor to her, to show my mother that they could be handled safely and were actually quite interesting to observe? To allay her fears? Of course, that's what I would say. My true intent was to terrorize her. I got between fifty and a hundred big ones crowded together in the aquarium, crawling all over each other. Then I left them where she would accidentally discover them. Maybe, just maybe, I could give her recurring nightmares. With luck, a mortal fright. My project gave me something to look forward to every day after school. If you destroy my life without giving it a second thought, there will be payback.

This was the only time I ever lashed out at my parents. And yes, she chanced upon the infested aquarium just as I had planned. And yes, my act of terror was effective. And no, they did not believe my, "I wanted to show you how actually docile and sweet they are as pets." Not even for a minute. They were both furious. And, I think, a little frightened to learn just how evil I could be. There it is. My single open act of adolescent rebellion. I received no punishment for it. Just my parents shaking with rage and speechless. And showing me some respect. I may have postured that if there was a next time, I would not keep the lid on.

At home, from late August to mid-November my psyche festered like a glass box full of poisonous spiders. In school I quickly became my normal self. I did my work, answered questions in class, and was friendly to anyone who was friendly toward me. It was my first semester of high school that I wasn't working at least half-time, and I was getting top grades.

Pervert Hoover High

As a transfer student, on the first day of classes I had been sent to the main office to take a battery of aptitude and other tests. Later in the year when the San Diego Union newspaper asked each high school to send their brightest student for a meeting with a professor to discuss scientific breakthroughs' impact on the future, Herbert Hoover High sent me. Even though by then I was on speaking terms with my parents I saw no need to tell them of being driven downtown in a limo to the Union offices for the conversation with the scientist and a photo shoot. A couple of days later, there was a full-page write-up with large photo portraits of the four "top" students in San Diego high schools.

My mother and father became furious with me when their friends and associates congratulated them for having such an "incredibly brilliant son."

For about a day and a half, they had no idea of what their friends were talking about. They responded with vague, half-hearted agreement. When someone finally showed them the article, they really hit the roof.

260

"San Diego's 'Top High School Seniors' Interview Scientist.

"Why didn't you tell us about this? Imagine our embarrassment that everyone knew about this but us."

"I didn't think there was any need to tell you. It was nothing. It was some kind of fluke. There was a mix-up. The smart kid who was supposed to go was absent. They just grabbed me. I was the first kid they saw walking down the hall. I'm no super bright kid of the future like it says in the article. I'm just average. Remember? It was a total accident that I was chosen to go to the paper. There was no reason to tell you about something so dumb. I didn't want to make a big deal out of something that shouldn't have happened in the first place."

My enjoyment as I watched them swallowing all my lies was almost sensual. My excuse, made up on the spot, hit the sweet spot of their prejudices against me so precisely that it met with zero resistance on their part. They seemed relieved when they heard my explanation. They believed every word.

"Oh. Okay. But you still should have given us a heads-up." Yes!

I Was Adopted Into The Jewish Community In San Diego

In Seattle, Jewish kids like my friends Bill Moses and Janet Greenbaum were mixed in with everyone else. In San Diego, the Jewish kids were a separate category. They hung out together with almost no overlapping membership between them and the other cliques. I was a new kid arriving in the final year. No one knew anything about me. I wasn't a member of any of the long-established non-Jewish cliques. I was competing with the Jewish kids for the top grades. There was a natural attraction. Almost immediately, I was mainly hanging out with Adrian Cantor, Rena Barach, and Rafael Levine. They invited me home after school to meet their parents. Their mothers loved me at first sight. Rafael was the son of the Conservative Temple Rabbi. Rafael invited me to his father's Friday night services.

"Won't I look odd with my red hair?" I asked.

"Nah. There are three Polish women in the congregation with hair as red as yours."

Rafe's dad delivered the first sermon I heard that made sense to me. It was not at all preachy. Just an intelligent discussion of a contemporary issue. I loved the fact that everyone took care with the way they looked and were very stylish, not hard-bench Christian plain and stiff. I got nice smiles from the three Polish women.

My new friends never made me feel that I needed to be Jewish. No one ever tried to proselytize me, but they treated me with the utmost respect and kindness and made it clear that they liked having me around. I loved being with them and learning about their lives and experiences. But mostly their opinions. The feeling was mutual. A bi-directional curiosity bound us together. I especially enjoyed conversations with the parents. They were lively and unafraid to express their opinions and always interested in my different take on things. I especially loved the way they loved to tell Jewish jokes. Rena's mother introduced me to matzos. "Put a thin spread of unsalted butter on an unsalted matzo, then sprinkle a few grains of coarse kosher salt over the top. Delicious." Ten years later in graduate school, I told my friend Paul Kaplan about it. He said, "Yeah, we call it Yiddish temporary fillings." It is still one of my favorite go-to snacks today.

Country clubs were segregated in San Diego as in most of the United States at the time. A wealthy old uncle took me to his all-Jewish club. The club barber called us in and insisted on giving me a free shave and haircut. He wanted to get his hands on my red hair. It was the best hair cut I ever had before or since.

I felt like the first piece of Americana they were comfortable embracing.

In 1957, most of the Jewish parents of my classmates were from "the old country." And they all had harrowing and sometimes hilarious stories to tell about how they got to the United States in the 1930s. One elderly aunt who arrived after the war always held my hand very tight when we talked. She had the tattoo. When someone else in the room noticed my noticing of it, the looks I got and the silence that followed conveyed the weight of suffering and evil it represented.

In the beginning I did not date Jewish girls. Their parents would not have minded. But in a strong expression of peer group solidarity, their brothers made it clear I should not be poaching on their turf. Their sisters were for their Jewish pals, not for goyim. When I became strongly attracted to a brilliant and lovely girl, her brother brandished a .38-caliber long-barreled pistol in my presence. He pretended it was friendly, not menacing, like 'Get a load of my cool firearm.' I got the message. The following year he emigrated to Israel and joined the IDF.

A Different Meaning Of 'The Color Purple'

For dates I joined a Methodist youth group and discovered that most of the Methodist girls my age in San Diego had already had sex with a previous boyfriend. So there was no waiting. Things were looking up. My first serious girlfriend in San Diego was the daughter of a retired Navy Commander. Not quite San Diego royalty, but almost. You would have to be the child of a Captain or an Admiral for that. She was a tall thin, grey-eyed, ash-blond girl a year older than me.

We got on quite well for several months. It took that long for me to find out she was a racist. She did not sprinkle her everyday speech with occasional racist shibboleths or other revealing comments. It never came up until one day it all came pouring out at once. She was a racist at the level of her autonomic nervous system. She rushed up to me clearly agitated.

"I just had the most horrifying experience."

I was concerned. "What happened."

"I almost clunged."

"Clunged?" I wasn't yet familiar with Southern California teen-aged slang.

"It's when you get a turd caught in your aorta."

"Ugh. What happened?"

"I was waiting for the bus and this Negro girl came up to the bus stop."

"And?"

"It was sickening. She was wearing this sleeveless dress and I had to look at her arms."

"And?"

"Have you ever seen one of their upper arms? In the bright sunlight? They say they're brown or black, but they're purple. I got so sick to my stomach I almost hurled on the spot. I couldn't stay at that bus stop with her standing there. So I ran to the next stop. And when the bus came, I didn't get on. I waited for the next bus so I wouldn't have to see her. When I close my eyes I can still see her hideous bare arms. I'm still shaking all over. They should be required to wear long sleeves."

That was our last conversation. She called a few times and I got off the phone as fast as I could. At age 17 I learned that jiffy-lube, no waiting hot sex was not enough to bend my life around. Not enough to try to talk her out of her bigotry. Not enough to be hanging out with someone who had a deficient personality. It was one of those moments that stood me in good stead for the rest of my life. I did not know these things about myself until this incident. I was under the impression I would overlook anything for sex. I am thankful to the girl for effecting this self-discovery. From that moment foreword, I could smell a racist from a half-block away.

In those first months in San Diego, I visited a few foreign-car dealerships and repair shops. What I discovered was almost as soul-killing as having a racist girlfriend. In San Diego sports cars were a fad and their owner's primary interest was being seen in them. The racing scene was already saturated with big money, petroleum industry sponsorships, professional drivers. An Alfa owner I encountered did not know his car was among the few that had an overhead camshaft engine, exotic engineering at that time. He had never heard of overhead camshafts. When I started to explain, he shook his head like I was some kind of weirdo and walked away.

I thought I could start building models again. But one, I had no money to buy kits, materials and tools, and two, there were no model shops even if I had money.

It seemed impossible to me that there could be a region of the world so bland and bleak that the only interesting thing to do was collect black widow spiders in mason jars to terrorize your mother and date girls who didn't need to be persuaded.

Something happened at Thanksgiving that changed everything. I was able to come to terms with my transplanted life. It was not cars. But just beyond the edge of town there were antidotes to the conservatism and bleakness of San Diego and as compelling as a twelve-cylinder Ferrari—an international border with a completely different culture on the other side, and deserts.

18

Thanksgiving With The Pai Pai

MY MOTHER AND FATHER wanted to continue their weekend camping trips but were hesitant. They didn't know what to expect or how to prepare. And especially how to detect the possible presence of poisonous spiders and snakes. The deserts of southern California were so different from the woods of Washington. They joined the San Diego chapter of the Sierra Club. After a few trips with the Club, they reckoned, they would know enough to go out on their own.

The first trip they signed up for was epic even by Sierra Club standards. They had not yet joined the Club so we were not eligible to go on the trip. But Aubrey Wendling (my father's colleague who knew me from Seattle) intervened on our behalf and secured us a spot. As soon as I was told about it, I broke my silence and told them I was coming. My parents and my brothers were happy that I was no longer snarling, withdrawn, and possibly plotting terrorist spider attacks.

Over Thanksgiving weekend, we would travel way off road into Baja California and camp near a village of Pai Pai Indians. The leader of the trip was the legendary Edward Douglas ("Bud") Bernhard. It was more like an expedition than a camping trip. Bud scouted the route several weeks before, contemplating how to get American sedans through deep sand. He carried several dozen lids of oil drums to the worst stretches so we could lay out two tracks made of drum lids across the sand. We extended the temporary road by people on foot grabbing the lids at the back of the track and running ahead to place them in front of the slow-moving cars. It effectively turned the cars into treaded vehicles. Only it was the people outside the cars running alongside who were moving the treads. I felt I could breathe out for the first time in weeks. Bud Bernhard was not Paul Hanna, Jack

Larsen, or Ross Meskimen, but I was back in the presence of someone who knew what he was doing.

We made progress along more than 50 miles of the western edge of the Laguna Salada reaching the lower village of the Pai Pai after dark. The last times the Pai Pai had seen a white person was the small Henderson party six years before and a solitary hiker 25 years before that. Our party was 75 people in 27 cars, much larger than the population of the Pai Pai village. In addition to the San Diego Chapter of the Sierra Club, there were Sierrans from Berkeley, Los Angeles, and Riverside.

Before satellite imagery, there were no maps of the interior of Baja south of an imaginary line drawn roughly between Ensenada and San Felipe. The Sierra Club trip would cross that line dipping into more than a thousand miles of unmapped territory with indigenous people almost untouched by so-called "Western Civilization." This was something worth doing. By mid-day I was almost chatty with my brothers and parents.

To her credit, my mother wrote a detailed account "Thanksgiving with the Pai Pai." Many years later my brother Bill published an Island News Press limited edition of her account illustrated with the many photographs my father took. [I can make a copy available on request.]

As was true of almost all aspects of my life, except for the car rides down and back, my experience did not coincide with the rest of my family's. Friday morning, I got up just before dawn and found another guy, a high school teacher named Ben, up and pacing around. He told me that this place was not the main village of the Pai Pai. They were a semi-nomadic people who kept sheep and goats and hunted for a living. They wintered here but their summer village was at Santa Catarina high up on the San Pedro Martir mountain range. And the full tribe had not come down yet. The head man in the lower village, a caretaker really, was named Ramon. Ramon was the younger brother of the great chief, Juan Arvallo, who was still with most of the tribe up at Santa Catarina. Ben explained to me his disappointment that there were only a few Pai Pai in the lower village. He obviously knew quite a bit about them and had counted on visiting the whole group of Pai Pai. Usually, they would have come down off the Martir by now. I could tell what was on his mind. The Sierrans would be camped here two more full days and nights before starting back for San Diego Sunday morning. If we left right away, there was a slim chance we could reach the upper village by nightfall; at least get a glimpse of the main band of Pai Pai; and get back to camp Saturday evening in time for departure the next day.

Bud Bernhard was also up before the others and we told him our plan. He was not happy. He said we would almost certainly become lost. And even if we didn't get lost, we probably could not make the trip in a single day. It was more than 20 miles to Santa Catarina as the crow flies and almost straight up. We would be gaining 4000 feet in elevation. If we got lost, he would not be coming back for us until the rest of the party was safely on paved roads, probably Monday morning at the earliest. But in the end, it was exactly the kind of wild-ass adventure he liked to be a part of.

Bud asked me a few questions about my experience. He told us to make a rock duck every time we stopped to rest so he could track us easily. Then he said, "Get going."

There was no marked path. The Pai Pai knew their way between the villages. Each time their animals reached a flat spot, they spread out across it to graze. These natural pastures were beautiful hanging valleys usually about a half mile wide and a quarter of a mile across. They were separated by almost vertical rocky ascents of varying lengths, sometimes more than a mile. Sometimes much more than a mile. As we progressed, we figured out that the Pai Pai did not exactly follow the straightest of lines. They zigzagged between valleys to give their herds plenty to eat. Because the animals had been allowed to graze the entire valley, there was no clear trampled path across to where the rocky trail picked up on the other side. There were dozens of these pastures on the way up the mountain. When we reached one of them, we would have to make our way around the edge until we located what we hoped was the trail on the other side. We followed Bud's instruction and marked where the trails entered and exited the valleys with a rock duck big enough that he could see it across the valley with his field glasses.

Our progress was slow and about 3:00 in the afternoon we had to make a decision. We could turn around and make it back to camp at the lower village shortly after dark. Or we could keep going based on nothing but hope of reaching Santa Catarina. If we did not find the upper village before dark, we would spend the night in sub-freezing temperatures high on the cougar- and wolf-infested San Pedro Martir and have to turn around the next morning in defeat.

We kept going. It got dark and there was nothing. No cooking fires in the distance to guide us. Our trail was almost invisible by flashlight. Our batteries were giving out. It was time to give up. The terrain had leveled somewhat. It was possible that we had reached the top of the escarpment and were on the gentle western slope, the general location of Santa Catarina. But there were no signs of Indians or any habitation. And it was pitch black. We stumbled into what seemed to be a wide path and saw the impossible. Our flashlights revealed unmistakable car tire tread impressions in the sand.

This was beyond strange. Santa Catarina was not on or near any road. The nearest road to where we thought we were was more than 50 miles away across uncharted territory. We could not have traveled 70 miles in a day. We were really lost. Bud would never find us. But maybe a car would come along. We had no idea of which way to turn so we took a guess, turned right and began walking. After about a quarter of a mile we came across a Pai Pai house. It was a one room, sand floor, adobe with a thatched roof, fire pit, grinding stone. It was beautifully neat with dishes stored along one wall and bedding opposite. No one was home. Or so we thought. We were discussing spending the night there uninvited when I heard the unmistakable "thrap-thrap" of a Model A Ford engine coming toward us.

A car full of Indians pulled up. All men. The people of the house heard us coming and raced to the center of the village about a mile away to let them know that two white guys had just stumbled up over the edge of the escarpment. Out of the car stepped Chief Juan Arvallo dressed in a great coat, a Stetson hat and, incongruously, a pair of tan and white saddle oxford shoes. He spoke serviceable Spanish on almost exactly the same level as mine. He wanted to know where we had come from. I told him there were almost 80 white people camped in his lower village and we had walked up from there. He was impressed we had made it in a single day and insisted that we come with him to the schoolhouse to be fed. All the other Indians in the car except Arvallo and the driver faded into the night. We were ushered into the Model A and driven to the center of the village.

What about the car, I asked? It was our understanding that there were no roads into or near Santa Catarina. It's true, Arvallo told me. But the young men in his village love cars. They had walked out to Calexico, worked the cotton fields, bought the Model A, completely disassembled it, and brought it part-by-part to the upper village along with a good supply of gasoline in five-gallon cans. They put it back together and used it on special occasions like funerals and weddings. And surprise visits from white guys, evidently. The "road" we found was the track it made through the desert sand between Pai Pai houses.

The schoolhouse was a simple one room wood frame structure provided by the Mexican government. Mexico also sent a teacher who left a few weeks after his arrival. The Pai Pai insisted he teach the adults to read and write before teaching the children. That was not his mandate so he packed out. Every Pai Pai came to see us and touch my hair. I had run out of water on our climb and was extremely thirsty. A woman brought me water in an enameled tin cup. There were mosquito larva wriggling in the water, but I drank it (and the larva) with relish. One of the best drinks I ever had. They served us a simple but hot meal of goat meat in a tortilla, sang us some Pai Pai songs, taught us a few Pai Pai words, and left us to sleep before it got too late. They were very excited to see us but they also understood that we had to get up at dawn to make it back to the lower village.

As we packed up to leave the next morning, Chief Arvallo came to the schoolhouse and told us he would accompany us down to the lower village. He wanted to see with his own eyes this huge assemblage of white people. He told me that the Spanish Dominicans had chosen the territory of the Pai Pai to build Santa Catarina mission. He added, clearly still angry about it, that the Spanish enslaved the Indians, notched their ears for minor offenses, and branded their foreheads if they were caught trying to escape.

According to Arvallo, one hundred years earlier, a few Pai Pai youths escaped to what is now Arizona, recruited a small army of Keliwa who came and captured the missionaries and soldiers, locked them in the mission, burned it, then pushed the walls in to make a mass grave. He showed the ruin to me. It was a huge mound and had clearly once been an imposing structure. Animals had burrowed into it leaving a triangular spew of human bones at the entrance to each of hundreds of holes.

He told me the Pai Pai still hated Christians and practiced their own religion. As we left the village we passed the cemetery. Most of the graves were marked by crosses. I asked him, "If you hate Christians, why do you put a cross over your graves?" He explained that a Christian cross makes a very convenient armature for hanging things. The Pai Pai believe that a person's grave should be decorated with the things they loved most in life. When I looked closely, I saw it was true. A vain woman's grave had perfume and cosmetic bottles hanging from the arms of the cross. A man had car parts hanging. A drunk had whiskey bottles. Etc.

Juan Arvallo, Jefe of all the Pai Pai, 1957.

I do not know how old Juan Arvallo was at the time. Probably around 70. But he was incredibly fit and moved down the escarpment at a rapid pace. I kept up with him, but Ben could not. He was exhausted from the previous day and moving with difficulty. As a result, the old man and I had to stop and wait for him a number of times as we climbed off the Martir. Juan Arvallo and I talked non-stop as we climbed down.

You might think that there would be very little to talk about between a 17-year-old kid from urban America and an old Indian man who had never gone to school, never left his villages, did not know how to read and write, was disconnected from the rest of the world without electricity or radio or telephone, who had refused Christianity in favor of an animist religion. But you would be very wrong to think that. Because of the enormous difference between us, we had literally everything to talk about.

The night before in the schoolhouse Don Juan demanded that I tell him about Sputnik. Six weeks before, Russia had launched the first orbiting earth satellite. Without a watch or any other mechanical means of keeping time, Arvallo knew exactly when to step out of the school to show me its passing. Whenever I recall this moment, I am touched by the memory of the spectacle of seeing the heavens through clear air. With no auto, industrial or light pollution, every one of Carl Sagan's "billions and billions" of stars were visible in the night sky. They varied widely in intensity, with the stars of the constellations shining the brightest, but in their enormous totality the individual stars appeared to be no more than two or three inches apart, filling the entire universe, sparkling like diamonds from horizon to horizon. And, indeed, there was Sputnik on cue, cutting its swath between them.

Without having any definite idea about the shape of the earth, the chief had figured out that the thing must be travelling around us. I tell the story of my encounter with Juan Arvallo and the Pai Pai in a brief autobiography published by Dennison Nash in his volume *The Study of Tourism—Anthropological and Sociological Beginnings*:

"*The Pai Pai Indians' main village is near the ruins of Santa Catarina Mission which they destroyed in an uprising in the early 19th Century, killing all the missionaries and soldiers. They are classified as Hokan, Esselen-Yuman, Yuman Pai. When I made my first visit they had persevered for over 100 years in self-imposed isolation. They caught and trained wild horses, hunted small game, and raised some corn. Only two or three of them spoke Spanish with any fluency. They had no electricity, no telephone, radio, or even a road to the outside world. Nevertheless, on my unexpected arrival on foot in their upper village at Santa Caterina, the chief demanded a detailed technical explanation of the Sputnik satellite which had appeared in the sky a few weeks before. He told me that there was something new in the night sky and he believed my people put it there.*

We talked half the night about it and many other things. He knew exactly when Sputnik would fly past and was delighted to hear about rocket propulsion, orbital physics, and wireless radio transmission. His questioning tested my grasp of western science and technology. This was how I came to experience the beginning of the age of global communication and interpenetration—concretely, intimately, late at night on a high desert plateau in conversation with a 70-year-old Indian who hadn't seen another white man since he was 20. . . . The "primitive/modern" antinomy dissolved in that conversation. I had friends in high school in San Diego who were more "primitive" than the Pai Pai chief. The most we can hope for is to be tourists in each others' worlds."

As we descended toward the lower village, our conversation continued. While we waited for Ben to catch up, I drew rockets and earth orbits in the dirt of the trail. I told him about modern cars, how they had evolved from the Pai Pai Model A, and how he was about to see almost 30 of them. I told him about dating girls and the importance of money in my world and the difficulty in getting it. He told me that day-to-day the Pai Pai neither had nor used money. But the young men would seasonally slip into the U.S. and pick crops long enough to buy whiskey or parts for the Model A. He went into great detail about his forebears' grievances against the Spanish missionaries. He was clearly still angry about it.

On our arrival at the lower village Juan Arvallo was an instant star. Everyone wanted to meet him, shake his hand, and have their picture taken with him. Bud organized a major campfire circle in his honor and we sang songs for him. He insisted that I stay next to him and answer his questions about our strange ways. He was the anthropologist. I was his informant. He maintained an air of quiet dignity throughout the proceedings. Before we parted he told me he was planning to winter at the upper village that year to resolve some tribal issues. I told him that even if I had to walk in, I would devise a way to get to Santa Catarina from Ensenada and the west and come back to visit him in the next two or three months. And I did.

Remember the funk I was in up to the Wednesday before Thanksgiving? It was all gone. It was not foreign cars, but near the international border, on both the north and south side of it, was a foreign human and natural complexity that was as fully engaging as the internals of a Maserati. It was one of those transformative blows. I loved every new conversation across lines of cultural difference, the new sights, new tastes, and exchanges of glances could hold my attention for the rest of my life.

Thank you, Mother. I would be able to put my ill-gained Tom Steinburn mountaineering instruction to good use after all.

Chief Arvallo did not let me leave his side for his entire visit with the Sierrans. Like an anthropologist, he asked me to explain everything these strange people were doing, and why.

19
Adapting to Life in San Diego

FROM THAT THANKSGIVING WEEKEND and meeting Chief Arvallo, I learned that a bleak and barren place can have beautiful and complex secrets. On my return to San Diego I was full of questions that could only be answered by going back into the desert and into Mexico. I made friends with a kid my age named Chip Everett. He was the son of the band leader at the Hotel Del Coronado. "The Hotel Del," as it was universally referred to in San Diego, had been designed by L. Frank Baum before he changed careers and wrote *The Wizard of Oz*. It was an interesting place. The staff at the hotel knew Chip and we could explore all its strangely unmotivated nooks without being bothered. A half year later, the "Del" would become the location of the Marilyn Monroe movie *Some Like it Hot*. I would have liked to have been hiding in some of the Dell's nooks for that movie shoot, but I was already back in Seattle.

Chip shared my fascination for the deserts and mountains of Southern California and Baja. His father had given him a WW II Army surplus Dodge Power Wagon. He generously allowed me and several other boys to join him on his weekend explorations.

WW II Dodge Power Wagon ambulance like Chip Everett's

Once again, I had very specific reasons for needing money. While they were well-worn in, I still had my climbing boots from the Seattle co-op. But I needed desert equipment. A pith helmet. A snake bite kit. Lightweight coveralls. And cash to buy food when I was away from home. I pounded the streets looking for "Help Wanted" signs. Restaurant and small retail shop owners took one look at me and said, "Sorry." Whatever it was about me that made people like Walter Hagen, E.R. Nottingham, and Jack Larsen hire me on the spot, caused the business owners of San Diego to slam their doors in my face.

A local service club posted notice on the Hoover High bulletin board of a speech contest for high school seniors offering a cash prize for the best speech. It sounded like the possibility of getting money for no work, so I set about writing a speech on the assigned topic and sent them a letter of intent to compete. I do not recall the topic of my speech or the amount of the prize. I do recall winning. The experience put me into an information network of similar offerings of prizes for high school kids' speeches. Almost every service club, consortium of churches, civic organization, chamber of commerce, had one. I entered several and won first, second or third prize every time. Mostly first prizes. I had zero interest in public speaking. Only in the money which was pretty good. I won the local ($25) and regional ($50) contests sponsored by an African-American Church on the topic "My Hope for the Future." The speech I wrote and memorized for that one was generic JFK-style inspirational optimism even though Eisenhower was still president and JFK hadn't yet appeared on the political horizon. When I got to the state contest ($100!) in the basement of a Black church in the Watts neighborhood of Los Angeles, I was trounced by a 13-year-old girl. Representing the San Diego African American Baptist Church, I was the only white person in the room. I cannot begin to guess what the San Diego church was thinking making me their speaker. The girl who was about half my size gave a full-on Malcolm X-style Black Power call to the barricades. It had some of the older Black folks shaking their heads like "No, no, NO."

But she won and deserved to. I got second place (another $50).

One of the cups I won in a different contest was the biggest in the Hoover High trophy case. I do not know why Kiwanis or whoever it was went so big. It was ludicrous sitting in there dwarfing state football championships and the like. Remembering my fourth grade Halloween poster and my model planes displayed in the shop window, I made the principal turn the trophy so my name wouldn't be visible.

Chip told me that the pet shops in San Diego would pay up to $10 for large iguana lizards if we caught and domesticated them. I was all in. A couple of lizards would turn a weekend jaunt into the desert into a profit-making enterprise without intruding on the enjoyment of the trip. It could even add to the fun if the iguanas were not too feisty. After an iguana spent a week or two locked in my room and being well fed, it would come when I called and be ready to sell.

I was good with iguanas. A few of them bit me. But most took to me right after I caught them.

Continuing to search for regular employment, I had a better feeling as I walked through the door of Hillcrest Star News. It was a hot lead print shop that put out a weekly neighborhood newspaper and did a good side-business in offset (fancy raised lettering) business cards, wedding invitations, etc. The Star News paper was mainly a shopper, 80 percent ads for local stores. The co-owner was a WW II vet who had recently bought into the old and stumbling business with a VA loan. He drove a new Edsel and had ideas about how to modernize the print shop. He needed a part-time printer's devil and had a good sense of humor. He thought a skinny red headed kid had all the qualifications needed to be a devil and hired me not long after I walked through the door. It was minimum wage, but I would have taken anything.

At Hillcrest I went straight from school to my job and except the night before the paper came out, I worked two to three hours until closing time. One of my tasks was to fetch asbestos molds for the composers, printers and typesetters who worked in the shop behind the front office. We poured hot lead into the molds to make generic images of things like bunches of carrots for a grocery store ad, or Christmas trees for a card shop ad. The pressmen would say, "Go get me a couple of Easter Bonnets," and I would look through the files under "Easter," or "hats," or "fancy dress," etc. until I found something that would work. Once a press run was complete, I popped the lead print blocks out of the frames and melted them down. Then I returned the molds to the files-- or was supposed to.

The melting process was quite wonderful. We had a bathtub sized vat with gas flame jets underneath. The vat was kept hot enough to maintain lead at melting temperature. When I threw a used print block into the vat it would go soft and then dissolve. The boiling lead had to be stirred and the dross removed. The dross that rose to the surface was composed of smoking ink, now in powder form, and any other impurities the blocks had picked up in the printing process. They gave me a long-handled iron ladle to skim it off the top.

Stirring the lead was less intuitively obvious. Suffering the heat and fumes, no one could stand over that much boiling lead long enough to stir it thoroughly. The solution was to put a very large russet potato into the ladle, invert the ladle and force it to the bottom of the vat. The potato would instantly begin to vaporize, producing a pocket of expanding gas around itself. This gas turned the potato into a rocket that roared around randomly in the vat stirring the lead. Super-heated gas escaping boiling lead makes a horrendously loud farting sound and is a source of endless jokes and worker-to-worker accusations and insults in the print shop. Of course, if you actually had to fart, doing it when the potato was blasting its way through the lead was the best time.

278

The residue from the potatoes percolated up to the top as part of the dross.

I had other tasks at the News, including feeding the Address-O-Graph machine to print the labels on the newspaper for mail delivery. Every week, the night before the papers were delivered, half the crew, including me, worked until 2:00 or 3:00 am finishing the print run, addressing the papers, and bundling them in address order for each mail carrier route. The last task was taking the bundles to the downtown U.S. Post Office for next day delivery. About four hours after I got home and to bed, I got up for a full day of school.

None of the other tasks I had at Star News were as much fun as stirring the lead. The best part was when a partly vaporized potato would break the surface and fly across the shop at high speed with a contrail of molten lead. I got to yell, "HOT POTATO," and watch the shop crew duck or try to cover their delicate print job set-ups with their bodies.

Edward Douglas Bernhard

Over Christmas break, a few weeks after the Pai Pai visit, Bernhard led another trip into the Anza Borrego Desert. It was not as challenging but the last bits were off-road and we would be able to see some ancient Indian petroglyphs. My family signed on and I was enthusiastic to join them.

Bernhard was San Diego royalty. He was the son of U.S. Navy Rear Admiral Alva Bernhard, captain of the USS Lexington and Commander in Chief of the Coronado Naval Air Station. Bud lived with his widowed mother across the bay from San Diego in an enormous stone mansion right on the Pacific Ocean. He had been a tail gunner in the Mediterranean theater during WW II and was famously the strongest climber in the Southwest. He made the southern deserts and Baja California his special study and domain. He had tracked and located, both dead and alive, a number of lost climbers in Baja. Whenever anyone got lost down there (remember there were no maps) Bud was the first person called to the rescue by both U.S. and Mexican authorities and the lost souls' loved ones. He was one of the first non-Indians to reach the top of Picacho del Diablo, the highest peak in Baja. His route up the final pitch to the summit, known as the "Bernhard Slot Wash," became the standard for all subsequent ascents. His day-to-day transport was an army jeep, but on special occasions he would take out his dad's Duesenberg. Also in his garage, left

Not a small displacement sports car but an enormous masterpiece of engineering. A supercharged, Duesenberg SJ, similar to the one owned by "The Admiral."

over from his father, was a 1930's Lincoln dual cowl phaeton and an early 1950s Jaguar sedan. I never met "The Admiral" as Bud always called his father. He was long gone before my time. But I could tell he was a car person as well as one of the highest-ranking officers in the US Navy. That helped draw me closer to Bud. I wanted to get my hands on that Duesenberg.

Bud was generally soft-spoken and understated, but people would get drawn into his charisma at about 100 yards. Here is how my mother described our first sighting as the cars were assembling at the meeting point for the Pai Pai trip:

"A jeep pulled up in the finest Wild West fashion—as if it were a bronc from the chute! The driver dismounted and we had our first look at the expedition leader. His hair was long on his neck, his coveralls baggy, barefoot, he resembled the sketches one sees of the young Lincoln. This was Bud Bernhard."

See what I mean?

Except for getting his approval to hike to the upper village of the Pai Pai, I had not had any conversations with Bud. Every Sierra Clubber held him and his exploits in awe like he was not quite human. I could not tell from the way they spoke of him whether he veered off the human in the direction of the gods or the animals. After he got everyone lined up to go into the Anza Borrego, he poked his head into our car and asked my father if we had the required extra water and motor oil. My brothers and I were sitting shirtless in the back seat. When he looked at me, there was a flicker of recognition for what I had done on the previous trip. He asked my parents, "How did you end up with three teen-aged boys without a single ounce of fat on their bones between them?" He moved on to the next car without waiting for their answer. We slowly made our way across the desert to the campsite, set up the tents, messed about getting to know some of the other Sierrans, ate dinner and bedded down for the night.

Here Is How I Got To Know Bud Bernhard

The next morning I was up, sitting on a boulder, waiting for the sunrise. No one else was stirring. "Nice, isn't it?" I heard Bud speaking softly behind me as the first pink streaks appeared in the eastern sky. "You want to climb up there?" He motioned to a pile of boulders about the size of small houses stacked up to the height of a mid-rise seven or eight story building. We were down in a sandy wash. "You can get a good view of the whole desert sunrise from up there."

"Yeah, I'd like to see. Let me go get my boots."

"I prefer to climb barefoot," he offered. "You can actually get better grip that way. The soles of your feet fit the contours of the rock better than any shoe."

"OK. Let's go," I said. I knew I was being tested. The other Sierrans had over-credited me for bringing chief Arvallo down from the mountains, like it was a major physical feat and diplomatic coup rolled into one. Some thought I must have had to assist the frail old man to make the journey in one day. I repeatedly explained that I could not have talked the chief out of coming if I tried, and he was the one who guided me down and set the pace all the way. We might not have found our way back without him. The more I protested, the more they thought I was trying to be humble, and it raised my reputation a few more notches.

What was Bernhard up to, inviting me to join him on a scramble to the top of that pile of rocks, barefoot? Why was he even bothering to talk to a 17-year-old kid? Perhaps he intended to teach me a lesson in humility. Even though I was the hero

Climbing in Baja. Bud Bernhard in pith helmet. Frankie Bochacio seated with glasses. I've forgotten the name of the third guy. I think his first name was Pete. He held us back. When he stopped, Bud infuriated him by moving on and calling out, "To rest is not to conquer."

of the Pai Pai trip, I still had a lot to learn. If that was what was on his mind, I was in complete agreement. I had everything to learn. We moved off toward the rock pile with me following a few steps behind, fully prepared to come off looking like a damn fool. The climb was no more than 200 feet, but almost straight up.

Bud moved fast bounding up the boulders at a running pace. We could stand almost upright as we climbed but because of the steepness we could also reach out and grab the rock ahead and above us. Bud was using his arms and hands as much as his legs and feet. He was basically running up the pile on all fours. It was no different than had I been chasing a great ape. I now knew that he veered off from the human toward the animals. I stayed close behind and unerringly placed my feet and hands where his had just been.

The mountaineering lessons I got from Tom Steinburn were of zero value in that moment. The way Mr. Kerr taught me to change keys on the violin was more appropriately instructive, enabling me to follow and keep up. We reached the top together in under five minutes. I was no more than a half step behind and not at all out of breath. He did not try to hide his admiration. No one keeps up with Bud Bernhard. He said, "You're good at this." I told him he had done all the work, figuring out exactly where to place hands and feet on the fly. He said, no, he'd been up that pile many times before and this was the fastest. Without any more words, we bonded closely.

Hard climbs are as much a test of one's state of mind as physical ability. The mental dynamic between climbers of different capabilities can become ugly. Even if they are not in need of it, leaders always get a good rest while they wait for stragglers. When the exhausted slower climbers catch up, the impatient stronger ones get up and leave. This can be devastating. The slower ones are faced with a wretched dilemma. Do they stop and catch their breath and rest their lungs and legs and continue to fall behind? Or do they keep on going without pausing to rest and eventually fail completely? There is a consequential loss of reputation that goes with not being able to keep up. No one talks about it. Not to your face. You are just not invited back. What to do? Do you try to save face by going on exhausted to the point that you are about to pass out with your legs crumpling beneath you? That moment can completely undo the psyche of a slower climber. I have seen grown men go berserk. And matters are made worse by cruel leaders who turn to the stragglers and snarl the standard mountain refrain for failure to keep up, "To rest is not to conquer."

The mountains let you know right away what your capabilities are. You learn from observing yourself and others that 90 percent of your strength and stamina is in your head. It has very little to do with physical conditioning. It has nothing to do with competition. It has only to do with the strength of your desire to continue. We have all heard stories of 90-pound women lifting a car off a child it has just run over. From observing my fellow climbers, I have no doubt that this can happen. I saw men in their 20s sitting on a rock halfway up a mountain crying like babies because they could not go on. Often these were the guys who pumped iron, ate whey, took steroids, and did aerobic exercises several times a week. They are reduced to begging you to carry their pack for them. Sometimes to carry them. On the other hand, I had a college friend who chain-smoked, ate nothing but Coca-Cola, Twinkies, and Cheetos, and never did any kind of exercise. He invited himself on a climb over my objections. I tried to teach him a lesson by speed climbing an eight-mile 20 percent grade. It was not a technical climb, but I made it hellishly arduous. He matched me step for step all the way to the top. I don't know how he felt the next day, but it was evident that he had only one gear, forward—full speed, and it was all in his head. He'd never even been on a level hike before. His determination to keep up was simply the way he was mentally wired.

The San Jacinto Disaster and Our "Salvage Operation"

A few weeks after the Anza Borrego trip Bud called on the telephone. He wanted to know if I could help him. His request was an almost unbelievable honor. I help him?

The week before, a Sierra Club snow mountaineering class had climbed to near the summit of Mount San Jacinto towering 11,000 feet above Desert Palm Springs. They had come up the easy way from Idyllwild starting at about the 5000-foot level on the western slope. The plan was for the 20 students to prove their skills at making camp and spend the night in the snow. Would they be able to cook their meals and keep themselves warm, their boots dry, etc. in snow-bound conditions? This took place under the watchful eye of several instructors.

What no one had counted on was a horrendous wet blizzard that hit the peak in the middle of the night burying the students and the instructors under six feet of snow. Everyone woke up at the bottom of a hole filled with ice water, buried under soggy wet heavy snow. The instructors frantically dug the students out from under the drifts. The students were soaking wet, frozen, half-suffocated, and panicked. No one could get a fire started. Everyone's clothing was soaked and starting to freeze. Once all the students were accounted for, the instructors took turns pushing the deep snow aside to force a trail back down the mountain. They got everyone back to the fires and the brandy of Idyllwild with nothing but the clothes on their backs.

"Is everyone OK?" I wanted to know.

"Yeah. Some frostbite. But yeah. OK."

Here is what Bud claimed to need me for. The students and instructors had abandoned all their gear. Twenty-five sleeping bags, tents, food, stoves, lanterns, mountain coils, everything they took up with them was still up there except the clothes they wore coming down. Bud said, "Can you imagine when the spring thaw comes and the tourists begin walking up there what a mess they'll find? This is the Sierra Club. We are supposed to be dedicated to cleaning up the wilderness, not trashing it. We need to go up there and bring all that stuff down."

"Shouldn't the instructors and the best students be doing that," I asked.

"Yeah, I told them to, but they are still too traumatized."

I was all in. Bud went on to explain that we would undertake the "salvage operation" in two weeks. He would give the instructors and students notice that they could go get their own gear and bring it down before we went up for it. But once we retrieved it, it was ours to keep. Salvage rules.

"It seems like too much for two of us to carry."

"I got another guy. The three of us can do it. It's all downhill. It'll only be about 100 maybe 150 pounds each."

This is How I Got to Know Jerry Gallwas

The "other guy" was his friend Jerry Gallwas who a few months later would be the first climber ever to ascend the grade 6 (overhanging sheer rock) northwest face of Half Dome in Yosemite Valley.

Bud and Jerry had no intention of keeping any of the gear for themselves. They already had everything they needed. One of the instructors on the snow panic trip was a teacher in a middle school. He arranged for us to bring the stuff to his school gym. The students and other instructors were notified that, after we brought it down, they could come to the school and retrieve any of their belongings that we had not taken as salvage.

Bud told me to go through what we brought down and outfit myself. He knew I did not have money for good gear. He said most of the students were rich tourists who bought expensive gear and probably would never use it again. The law of salvage said if I brought it down, it was mine if I wanted it. I coveted a nylon, goose-down filled mummy bag. The kapok-filled cotton sack my parents got for our family camping outings did not keep me warm in the Mexican and California mountains and deserts. I had to get up several times during the night to re-build the fire. But I could not bring myself to expropriate one of the new high quality salvaged bags. What if the bag belonged to some kid who saved his newspaper route money for two years to buy it? No. I would just keep getting up to rebuild the fire. Bud was quite insistent that I take advantage of the situation and outfit myself properly. Finally, I backed him off with a compromise. I would not take anything of value, but I would take all the food. There was almost a hundred packets of expensive, Swiss-made freeze-dried instant meals and one frozen pork chop. I took them and a small Primus stove to cook them on. My 15 hours a week, minimum-wage job at Hillcrest Star News did not pay enough to get me the extra food I needed. Bud could tell I was hungry and accepted my interpretation of my scaled back salvage rights.

When we arrived at the disaster site, it was a real mess. We cleaned it up, gathered everything, bundled the stuff in canvas sheets that we formed into three bags, balanced the huge loads on our heads and shoulders, stooped over and headed down. The bags were so heavy it was like we each had a hundred horsepower outboard motor powering us. We had to work hard to keep ourselves from running out of control down the mountain. Somehow it was comical, and we laughed all the way down. We carried out nearly 400 pounds of equipment and garbage.

Jerry Gallwas was four years older than me and already one of the world's top technical climbers. He was the most gentle, understated, and generous person I had ever met. He had a number of world's-first, impossible climbs to his credit and it was like pulling teeth to get him to talk, even briefly, about them. We once hiked to a chalet high in the southern Sierra accessible only by trail. It had a wood burning stove, about ten bunks, and a small stream of water had been re-routed through its sink. There were already eight or ten climbers there planning to spend the night. Jerry was palpably relieved that no one at the chalet recognized him. He could be just Jerry, another hiker on the trail, and not Jerry Gallwas, one of the two or three most gifted and accomplished rock climbers on earth. Everyone settled down to playing cards and talking about their exploits. When someone turned to Jerry and asked him what his favorite climbs were, he said "Hey, it's almost dinner time. If everyone will give me what they planned to eat for dinner, I'll put it all together into a common meal and we can eat it together." The other climbers thought it was a strange idea, but Jerry exuded confidence. Everyone contributed something and he created a delicious stir-fry and several imaginative desserts. He earned accolades all around for his cooking prowess and was able to steer the rest of the evening conversation toward cooking tips. I wondered at the time, and still wonder, what they would have thought if they had known who cooked their dinner that night.

Jerry and I became friends even though I would never attain sufficient skills to accompany him on a serious first ascent. He was a patient teacher on challenging pitches and gave me a vantage point to witness some of his miraculous moves. He loaned me his equipment if he was not using it. And he loaned it again even after I brought it back damaged, and he needed to repair or replace it. He lived with his mom in a ranch house in a semi-rural area, and they always threw a steak on the grill when I came to visit. Christmas the following year he conceived of a seasonal business for us. We used a shotgun to blast the mistletoe out of the oaks in rural San Diego County. The pieces that fluttered to the ground were just the right size to tie with red ribbons and sell to local merchants. I was delighted that we could make good money off a thousand kisses.

As summer approached, I was recruited to be a "volunteer" (i.e., unpaid) instructor for the Sierra Club mountaineering course. I taught the sections on things that often go wrong with the human mind and body under the stress of expeditionary mountaineering. I did not choose my subject. It was among the least popular and was assigned to me. I read accounts of trips where everything went wrong, organized some observations from my personal experience, prepared my lectures, and supplied cartoon drawings for the written course materials.

My vivid accounts of mental and physical breakdown earned me the nickname, "Miserable MacCannell."

Picacho del Diablo

Picacho del Diablo is the most challenging climb in Baja. It rises 10,000 feet from the desert floor. Approached from the east, the last place you can get to by jeep is the entrance to La Media Canyon. Approached From there, you have to climb all ten thousand. The name "La Media" had no official standing. Bud called it that because it was the middle canyon of three that seemed to him the only plausible approaches to the summit. It led directly to the proven route up, the Bernhard Slot Wash, the last thousand feet of near vertical rock guarding the summit.

The first white man to climb Picacho found some re-arranged stones, evidence of a prior Indian presence on the summit. After the first ascent in the 1930s, no more than two dozen other climbers of European ancestry had made it to the top. Bud conceived of the idea that I should become the youngest (non-Indian) climber to stand on top of Picacho. We began planning our ascent for Spring Break. In addition to getting me to the top, he was possessed with the desire to find another route. His Slot Wash was widely regarded as a real "gut buster." Perhaps we could find an easier way.

Picacho del Diablo looking west from the San Felipe Desert. The desert is at sea level and there are no roads approaching the peak. All 10,000 feet must be climbed on foot.

On a previous climb, Bud sat on the summit of Picacho for almost an entire day studying the topography of the canyons below. He thought the best candidate for an alternate route was the next canyon over, one he named La Providencia. So our expedition had two goals—to get me to the top and to explore a new and better way up. It turned out that these two aims were at cross purposes.

La Providencia proved to be a bigger challenge than it appeared from Bud's vantage point on the summit. Wall to wall in the canyon there were impenetrable thorn thickets growing out of the creek banks to a height of about thirty feet. So we had to make our way for long stretches along the near vertical rock walls of the canyon, always at risk of falling into the bed of thorns below. What should have been an easy trip wading in the smooth horizontal bed of the creek turned into a technical climb clinging to near-vertical walls. This slowed our progress to the point where the final pitch to the summit was several miles of challenging rock. It was not straight up like the slot wash. It was stair step with thirty-to-forty-foot vertical rises, then more or less level, walkable, for 60 or 100 feet, then another pitch straight up. We were pushing hard

Climbing the Bernhard Slot Wash, the last pitch to the summit almost, 1000 feet straight up.

toward the summit that we could see in the distance, but time was running out. Then we got hit by a freezing squall and a brief blizzard that dumped about four inches of snow on us.

Bud was despondent. He saw my chance of summiting fading away. He said we could camp where we were, delay our return to San Diego, and keep trying the next day. "Camping" there would not have been a picnic. We had left our sleeping bags (Gallwas had loaned me a good one) in the base camp with most of our food and all of our cooking gear and Pete the laggard. We would have had to sit in front of a fire shivering and hungry through the night and finish the climb on empty stomachs the next day. Bud blamed himself for wanting to do too much on one trip. He was more distraught about my not summiting than I was. Missing the summit was perfectly fine as far as I was concerned. Every minute of the past five days were among the best minutes of my life right up there with sitting on a starting grid waiting for the flag to drop. Every step I had taken was filled with excitement and privilege at seeing things perhaps no one had seen before me. He told me the decision was mine. He would "gut out" anything we needed to do to reach the top. I told him we were turning back. I actually had to pretend to be more disappointed than I actually was so he wouldn't think I was weird.

Our failure festered with Bud. He kept his ear to the ground and two years later sent me with a letter of introduction to the leader of the next Picacho expedition. On his say-so, the group of 16 fanatically prepared climbers from Los Angeles grudgingly took me in, saying, "if you can't keep up you get left behind." I was the first in the party up the Slot Wash and the first to make the southern peak of Picacho. But I was not the youngest person to climb. On the trip was a rich kid from L.A. who was on the United States Olympic swim team. Every night he showed me the handful of performance-enhancing drugs his coaches made him take and asked me if I wanted to share. I declined. He was two months younger than me.

My first ("failed") trip to Picacho was in early April 1958. March, April and May 1958 I was teaching sections of Sierra Club mountaineering courses in the evenings after work at the Star News and going to the desert and into Mexico on the weekends. I was fully engaged in and intrigued by everything I was doing and very happy.

But I had not forgotten that I was now only weeks away from my eighteenth birthday, high school graduation, leaving my parents' home for good, and my planned move back to Seattle.

There is quite a lot of exposure in the traverse between the two peaks of Diablo. So everyone ropes up. On my second attempt to climb Diablo, I went across first, belayed from behind. I set up the forward belays for the rest of the climbers. This gave me time to frame this shot as everyone worked their way carefully across. The canyon we approached in is in the middle ground. The San Felipe Desert is in the background. And on the far horizon is the Sea of Cortez
RIGHT: Me, on top of Picacho del Diablo, finally.

As much as I was enjoying my adventures in Southern California, I was not conflicted. I was mentally prepared to leave all of it behind and return to the quite different life that awaited me in the Pacific Northwest.

18 and out At Last—Well, Not Quite

One of the friends I made at Hoover High was a goofy, hapless kid named Charley. He was an only child and even though he had not done anything really wrong, he was not much liked by his parents. When he turned 18 before me, about the middle of the school year, his father bought him a new MG, rented him an apartment of his own, paid his bills, gave him a generous allowance, and told him to get the hell out from underfoot. At first, we bonded over his car, which I taught him to drive much faster than someone like Charley should ever drive. We took "Movie Making" together second semester and I filmed his fast-driving lessons as our class project.

I told Charley that I, too, had to move out when I was 18 but without any parental support. He was eager to take me in for the two weeks between my birthday and graduation, the gap I had to cover before leaving for Seattle. I had been worried about how to cover that gap. The only thing I knew for sure was I would not be asking my parents for their help. Temporarily moving in with Charley was a good solution.

He told me he would like me to stay on as his roommate for as long as his parents kept paying his bills. I was getting similar messages from Bud—stay in San Diego. Why would I want to go back to Seattle? "Your future is here," Bud said. I made nice with everyone, Charley, Bud, Jerry, my Jewish friends, saying I'd love to stay but I had real work in Seattle, not part-time, minimum-wage as a printer's devil. Bud tried to pull some strings and get me a job as a copy boy at the *San Diego Union* but they did not like me. Not enough to offer me a job, anyway. I was relieved.

My future really was in Seattle, I thought.

During our entire childhood and youth, my parents never had a birthday party for Bill or me that involved inviting guests. My mother would bake us a cake with candles to blow out. The immediate family would hover around. That was it. After we turned 13, they did nothing to celebrate—no cards, no cakes, no presents. A smiling "Happy Birthday" greeting at breakfast was what we got. It is important to me that anyone reading this not get the mistaken idea that I regarded this as mean on their part, or sad. It was simply the way things were. I had no expectation of anything different. By the time I was 18, I would have regarded any pretense of celebratory emotional bonding around birthdays as unbearably hypocritical.

My birthday in 1958 fell on a Saturday. I got up and packed my clothes a few books and my art supplies in a large army surplus duffle bag. I wrote Charley's address and phone number on an index card and gave it to my mother, said goodbye and headed for the door.

"Wait. Wait. What's going on? What are you doing?"

"I'm 18. I'm leaving."

"Why? Why would you do that?"

"What do you mean? Why? You told me when I turned 18, I had to leave."

"Do you remember that? You weren't supposed to believe that. It was just so you would . . ."

"Look. I'm fine. I've got everything under control. I'm moving back to Seattle the day after school gets out . . ."

"Back to Seattle? What will you do there? How will you live?"

"Don't worry about me. I've got work. I'll be fine."

"Where are you going now?"

"I've got a nice place to stay until school gets out. I wrote it on the card. I'm okay. Goodbye."

My mother started to sob uncontrollably. My brothers were looking on with their eyes bugged out. My father looked almost embarrassed probably for the first time in his life.Through her sobs my mother managed to say, "You know you can always stay here. You can stay for as long as you want. We did not mean for you to believe that. It was so long ago. I'd completely forgotten about that. I can't believe you would remember such a thing."

She ran to her bedroom and came out with her old Argus C3 camera that she had recently replaced with a German single lens reflex. She held it out to me with both hands in a position of prayer. "Here. Take my camera. A birthday present." She was visibly shaking with emotion. Even though it probably was not an act this time—I had sprung it on them, so they were completely unprepared—I was revolted by her pathetic gesture.

My mother might have tried to hug me for the first time since I was an infant. If she did, I am sure I pulled away. I wasn't particularly surprised by their inconsistency, but I found it disgusting. They thought they could erase their earlier crass definition of my entire existence with one tearful moment. How could they imagine that I might wish to stay with them? Except for my brothers there was nothing to keep me there. And I felt powerless to help Bill and John enough to sacrifice my life trying to make theirs better. I knew I could not succeed at that. My only life-affirming option was to get the hell out on schedule.

They made such a scene that I called Charley and told him I would come for a visit, lunch at his place the next day. But I would not be moving in. I'd stay with my folks until I left for the Northwest.

The next ten days were weird. My parents did not treat me any differently, but now there was a new phony edge of them supposedly liking me. I didn't pretend to like them and the day after the last day of school, without waiting for the graduation ceremony, I took a few dollars I'd saved and treated myself to a train trip to Seattle. There were few passengers on the train, and I had an entire car to myself most of the way. This time, I was really free and my whole life was in front of me.

I was euphoric—so relieved and relaxed to have gotten my first 18 years behind me I felt like I was floating on a cloud all the way to Seattle. I was naïve enough to think that I would never have to put up with any of their crap again. My sense of the moment was true. The kind of happiness I felt then for the first time deployed itself over the entire rest of my life.

Of course, I had to put up with some of their crap again, especially toward the end of their lives. But it never weighed heavily on me. It was never consequential. Not negatively consequential.

Something my father did three months after I left would change my life completely. And not for the worse.

294

Sketches that I made, aged 18, for the 1958 Sierra Club
Southern Mountain Section's loose leaf *Mountaineering Course
Manual*. See page 286 for the story behind these.

20

A Race Car of my Own

BACK IN SEATTLE my life was waiting on hold for me. Paul and Valerie Hanna greeted me warmly and told me that Paul and Jack were expecting me back at work. My night job at Troy was gone. Valerie told me it was time for me to find a more permanent living arrangement. "You will be wanting more space and privacy," she diplomatically explained. Paul told me that the upper floor of his father's large house was available at a price I could afford if I wanted it. I eagerly agreed and moved in right away. His father was a grumpy old man, but I had my own entrance. Valerie renewed my invitation to drop in for dinner anytime, only now I would help out with the groceries and the cooking instead of providing free uniform cleaning service.

My girlfriend from the year before had gotten engaged to an older blond guy who owned a new American car. I had little desire to compete with that. There were dozens of attractive women hanging around the racing scene and their racer boyfriends were notoriously unfaithful, so about half of them were temporarily unattached about half the time. They were all several years older than me, but I did not count myself out.

After a couple of days settling in, I hopped on the Hannas' Lambretta and rode out to Scott Larsen, arriving just before the shop opened. The guys were friendly but low-key. The definition of the situation seemed to be that I was coming back to work almost as though I had only been away for a few days, not nine months. Everything around the shop was exactly the way it appeared when I left. My crayon marks on the floor were still there, but no frame tubes had been cut, bent or welded for our racing special. Neither of the "Production" 600s had been torn down for its suspension parts. Neither had yet sacrificed its modified engine to the project.

The guys did not attempt to explain anything to me, but I could sense some tension. They never discussed "business" with me, and I assumed it had to do with the business. The shop had gone through the winter hopping up and "prodifying" Austin-Healeys, etc. for wannabe boy racers. I worried that they were short of money, but they didn't hesitate to hire me back so they could not have been that short. Racing season had just begun, we fell back into the pattern of the previous year hoping we would not get busted for running modified cars as stock.

When I told Paul Hanna that I had hoped for more progress toward constructing a proper race car, he said "I have an idea. Come with me." We got into the Triumph and drove a few blocks to a duplex with a basement garage. He searched his ring for the right key and opened the garage door. Inside, under a tarp was a very small, two-seat roadster. It was up on blocks and its wheels, brakes, and some suspension bits were in boxes on a work bench. Its engine was completely disassembled down to the headless, crankless, block. Everything important—pistons, valves, camshaft, carbs, fuel pump, radiator, gearbox, etc. was in boxes or scattered on the bench and floor.

In the dim light, I didn't recognize the car. It was ugly. I'd never seen that make and model before. "What the hell is this thing?"

Paul really enjoyed that I was stumped. Both he and I thought I could recognize and name the year, make and model of every car that had ever been made in the history of automobile manufacture. He let me know right away, "It's a Crosley Hot Shot."

A Crosley Hot Shot. I had seen pictures two years before of this awful-looking, American-built, limited-production racing roadster with a tiny one-liter engine. It had been declared winner of the first Sebring

The winning Crosley Hot Shot at the first 12 Hours at Sebring

My first look at the Hot Shot

race organizers scaled their distance back proportional to the engine size difference between them and the Hot Shot. It got an immediate reputation as a "giant killer."

Paul explained that two years before he had purchased this disassembled Hot Shot as a project. It had all the racing modifications and spares. He rented this neighbor's garage intending

endurance race. It had not crossed the finish line with the most laps after 12 hours. But it won the race based on its "index of performance." It had done better than the Jags and Ferraris once the

My Hot Shot bits and pieces first see the light of day

One of many sketches I made for a new body for the Hot Shot.

to build the car there but had made no progress. He told me that if Scott Larsen would permit me to tow it out to the shop and work on it after-hours I could build it and race it until I got better offers. He would eventually get a running car. I would get to use it as my own in exchange for my re-building it and getting it into racing condition. A Crosley Hot Shot was potent enough if driven well to be competitive in G Modified. I was especially intrigued by its brakes—the first disks offered on a race car. I was certain that its Sebring win was because of its braking, not its engine power. With little or no brake fade, it could continue cornering at full racing speed, long after the heavier cars with overheated and failing drum brakes were forced to lift off early and coast through the corners losing much of the advantage of their more powerful engines. The Hot Shot was ugly, but conceptually it was my kind of car and Paul knew it.

Paul's offer was not merely generous, it was potentially life-changing. With a car of my own, I could race every weekend without having to hope some driver got sick, or his wife put her foot down, or someone broke their car in practice and told me I could race it if I could get it running with Jack's help—all scenarios I had experienced. If I worked fast on the Hot Shot, I could probably get it on the track before the last races of the season. Then I could use the winter ahead designing and building a beautiful new body. Pete Lovely had an English Wheel for shaping aluminum body panels. I would get the body man in Pete's shop to teach me how to use the wheel. Then someone in my family could weld the aluminum panels together—hell, my Grandma Fran could finish the car for me. If I could start the next season with the most beautiful car on the track my career as a designer-builder would be launched.

There were a few Hot Shots racing elsewhere in the United States. Most of them, like the Hanna/MacCannell machine, were extensively upgraded for racing and ran in "Modified" classes. None of them had been fitted with the kind of special body I was planning to build. I was happy to be running in "modified" because there were no rules beyond having an engine with no greater displacement than allowed by your class, two seats, fenders, working lights, and a minimum ground clearance.

About halfway through the summer, long before my car was ready, another Hot Shot appeared at the track, the first I had ever seen or heard running. It had a very kindly middle-aged owner/driver who was blind in one eye like my paternal grandfather. He explained to me all the different ways we perceive depth even if we lack depth perception. When I told him I was building a racing Hot Shot similar to his machine, he eagerly looked forward to the direct head-to-head competition between matching cars and he gave me hundreds of helpful pointers that sped my progress through the build.

Even though it was low key and in a low performance category, I was fortunate at age 18 to have a subsidized program to get me racing. Paul Hanna gave me a car, or all the parts I needed to build one. Scott Larsen motors gave me space to work with a grease pit and the free use of very high-quality examples of every automotive tool in existence at the time. Jack Larsen would advise me in the morning if I got stuck the night before. He told me how to fit the parts together correctly as I rebuilt the valve train, transmission and clutch. Finally, there was an "old" (he was probably in his late 60s) master machinist named Frank who hung around the shop most days because he liked our company and we liked his advice and occasional interventions. When I found most of the brackets that held the dashboard to the cowling had gone missing, he came in the next day with a full set he'd machined overnight from billets of aluminum. They were stronger, lighter, and far more beautiful than the Crosley factory brackets. It made no difference that they were not "stock." I could do anything I wanted because I would be running modified.

As the summer and the build progressed, I became increasingly concerned that my wages at Scott Larsen would not cover starting money or tires. There were no sponsorships that paid in kind like a tire store that would give you free tires in exchange for putting their name on your car. Nothing like that. In general, you were lucky if you could get two races out of a single set of tires that you bought at a tire store.

I had to find a way to earn a few hundred extra dollars by working at night. It would slow down the build, but I had nothing to be building for unless I could put tires on my car and put my car on the starting line. I asked around about night work. From several different sources, I learned about "The Filter Factory."

My Worst Blue-Collar Job

Not Jack or Paul at Scott Larsen, nor Paul Hanna, but almost every other adult male in the racing scene had at some point worked at "The Filter Factory." It was not really a factory, it was a cleaning and servicing facility, but the men called it "The Filter Factory," always followed by a knowing look. It was the only facility in the Pacific Northwest that had the equipment needed to clean and service the type of HVAC filters installed at the time in department stores and office buildings.

The filters were steel-framed, about four inches thick, and filled with fine, curly, steel wire squeezed into a dense mesh. They varied in size between about 18 by 24 inches to 36 by 48 inches and weighed between forty and eighty pounds each. There were no standard sizes. All the air intakes were architectural elements so each filter had been custom-built to fit its opening.

The wire mesh in the filters was covered with a fine coating of heavy oil to trap particulate air impurities. When they became clogged, they had to be brought to the "Factory" to be cleaned and re-oiled. Filters from department stores open seven days a week had to be done overnight. Office buildings could be serviced over a weekend.

The Filter Factory owner was a small-time crook who drove a Lincoln almost new enough still to be seen as a luxury car. The floors and passenger seats of the Lincoln were buried under a deep layer of trash. If I had to guess, it was the debris of four or five divorces. Stuff his wives might leave behind when he helped them move their belongings. "I don't want this old hairbrush. You keep it." There was a lot of that kind of stuff on the seats and floor. Toys a kid had outgrown, etc. He wore a gold chain around his neck before any other man did and he had a gum chewing swagger that announced before he spoke that he had a "really good thing going." And he did. If you wanted your filters cleaned, you had to go to him or to San Francisco. Since no building could go without getting its filters cleaned on a regular basis, he had a monopoly on a service that was an absolute necessity for wealthy clients—building owners and management companies.

The sleazy owner guy—I have suppressed both his first and last name—really, I have—scheduled the filter jobs and drop-offs. A truck load of fifty filthy filters, give or take, arrived at the Factory usually about 9:00 pm. The worker, whoever held the job I was applying for, arrived two hours before drop-off time to fire up the equipment and be there to greet the store service crews and help them unload.

Most buildings had between 30 and 60 filters that needed to be cleaned and re-oiled overnight. A crucial component of the Factory job was maintaining the order of the filters as they came off the truck. Filters that looked to be the same size varied by a few inches and none of them were marked with their size or proper location. They had to be cleaned, oiled and re-stacked in the exact reverse order of their arrival. When the buildings' crews re-installed the clean filters, if they had been re-loaded on the trucks out of order, nothing would fit. This was all hyper time-sensitive work. The HVAC had to be turned on when the building opened the next morning. If the store crew had to try three or four filters before finding the right one for the hole, the reinstallation would get bogged down. The store crews would become fighting angry at the Filter Factory guy for returning the filters out of order. Especially if it caused them to carry an 80-pound filter up a three-story ladder only to discover it to be half an inch too large for the hole.

Accordingly, the Filter Factory worker's priority was to maintain the stacking order of the filters even if the night's work was interrupted by accidents resulting in bodily injury, fires, explosions, sickness, exhaustion, or a visit from the police. There was no "even if" about it. Explosions, fires, etc. occurred on every Filter Factory worker's shift. A police visit demanding immediate shutdown and possibly arrest was a constant threat. The premises had been condemned and the Factory operated without permits or a business license. That is why no sane adult would take the job even though it paid $20 an hour, lawyers' wages at the time. Working at the Factory made you an accessary to several serious crimes. That is why I wanted the job (the wage rate), got the job (no one else would take it), and held the job for the rest of the summer, working between one and three nights a week as needed at the Factory, and never stacking the filters out of order or attracting the attention of the police or fire marshal.

Cleaning and oiling the filters involved heating three large (eight feet across, five feet deep) vats to the boiling point. They all had multiple roaring gas jets underneath. The first vat contained boiling water with detergent, the second, clean boiling water, and the third boiling 90 weight oil. There was a fourth vat with a drain and a large centrifuge for spinning first the wash and rinse water, then the hot oil, out of the filters. Overhead there was an articulated gantry crane with a grappling hand to lift the filters from tub to centrifuge to tub as they were cleaned, rinsed, oiled, and ready to be restacked.

The centrifuge had to be run with two filters of almost equal weight or it would shake itself apart. Differences of a few pounds could be compensated for using adjustable weights on the arms near the filter clamps. Since adjacent filters in the building were not necessarily of similar size, maintaining the "equal weight" requirement of the centrifuge was fraught with risk of losing track of the proper order of the filters. 'Let me see, there's a filter eight back in the stack that's about the right size to balance this one.' Now that one's out of order. Better not lose track where it belongs on the rack.

The hardest part of the job was dealing with the equipment breakdown and failure that happened on every run. It was up to the worker to patch it together and keep it going. It had been installed without permits and both the Fire and Health Departments had cited and "closed" the Factory for multiple violations. This did not stop the work from getting done. All it did was cause the sleazy owner to board up his front windows and door and hang a single dim bulb so no light was visible to the police who patrolled the street. The Factory was effectively sealed without ventilation for the run of a job. I knew the police would not bother me so long as there plausibly appeared to be no one working the Factory. They were aware that commerce in the Pacific Northwest would grind to a halt if not for the continued functioning of this place of Gothic horror. They would ignore it so long as nothing seemed to be going on, but not its flagrant operation. This nuance was explained to me in my job interview.

The work had to be done in semi-darkness in a closed room with giant vats of boiling detergent water and boiling oil. The build-up of steam and heat on hot Seattle summer nights was such that I could not see from one end of the room to the other. When I became exhausted from wrangling filters and lost my breath, I had to get down on my hands and knees to find a layer of breathable air and recover myself.

That was not the worst of it. The gantry crane to lift and lower the heavy filters into and out of the vats only worked intermittently. Sometimes it did not work at all. It didn't just break down and stop working. It fought back. It would get a half-grip on a filter and lift and start to move it, then let it slip and fall. Sometimes the dripping filter crashed to the floor between the vats. Other times it dropped back into the vat, splashing boiling oil onto the floor and onto me if I didn't move fast enough.

As the night progressed, the crane would begin dropping more filters than it successfully transported between vats. At this point I had to switch to a 100% manual labor mode of operation. The owner knew this happened and equipped me for it. I was provided asbestos lined long rubber gloves that came up to between my elbows and shoulders. And an asbestos/rubber bibbed apron that came down to my ankles. Wearing these, I could bend over the edge of the tubs, reach down into the oil or water, grab the filter and snatch-lift it out. The maneuver had to be done quickly before the heat from the boiling liquid penetrated the gloves and cooked my hands and arms. Once out of the vat, I carried the dripping filters to the centrifuge, bolted them in, spun them, unbolted them, and took them to the next vat. It was back-breaking physical labor but faster and more dependable than trying to use the hostile crane.

A few hours into the job, the entire floor of the Factory was covered with an inch or more of a slurry of filthy water, detergent, and hot oil. Standing or walking without slipping and falling was almost impossible. When I jerked a filter out of a vat, I would inevitably lose my footing. Both my feet would skid violently under the vat until my shins banged against the lower edge, stopping the skid, allowing me to stabilize myself and regain my balance by hooking my elbows into the vat. Then I would hug the filter in my arms and skate over to the centrifuge.

Starting about halfway through each night run, I had to snatch-lift every filter out of the racks, vats, and the centrifuge seven times. It took seven separate lifts to move one filter through the three-vat cleaning and re-oiling process: lift off the "in" rack, then in and out of the boiling detergent, in and out of the centrifuge, in and out of clean boiling water, in and out of the centrifuge again, in and out of the boiling oil, in and out of the centrifuge finally, then onto the "out" rack. If a 50-filter job broke the Factory half-way through, that meant 175 manual physical lifts of between 40 and 80 pounds. My reader will understand why I have never felt much in common with guys who pay to exercise in gyms. I got paid handsomely to exercise.

Every shift, late in the night, the goop on the floor got deep and flowed into close contact with the flame jets under the vats. A few fires were inevitable. My first recourse was to put them out with one of the many available extinguishers. If there were still flames after the extinguishers were empty, I would open the back doors and squeegee the flames out into the alley and stomp them out while praying that no one would call the Fire Department.

I soon learned that at midnight I should take a break and go outside. There was an all-night hole-in-the-wall, pre-7-11 convenience store in the next block. I bought myself a Twinkie and a quart of milk. I could not eat anything in the heat and stench inside the Factory, so I always consumed my snack in the alley outside. Early on I learned the hard way that if I took even a small drink of water in there, I would throw it right back up.

One night the owner of the little store said, "Here, Red. Have a beer." I told him that I was still a minor and couldn't purchase alcohol.

He said, "I know. But I can see you are working at the Filter Factory."

"Yeah, I work there. Don't tell anyone."

"Here. Have a beer."

"I can't. I'm only 18. You could lose your license. I'm not old enough to drink."

"Listen, kid. Anyone who can take the Filter Factory for

more than one night is old enough to drink beer. Have a quart on me."

And he pushed a quart of Olympia into my hand.

Some nights at the Factory ran so late I had to drive directly from there to Scott Larsen and begin my day job. Usually, I could get in an hour nap between.

Down for a nap. Is the job over? A job like that is never over. Remember those thin curly wires that made up the mesh in the filters? When I began shifting the filters manually, those protruding wires penetrated my rubber-asbestos gloves. Because they were sharp pointed and curlicue shaped, they twisted their way first into my gloves, then into me. At the end of every shift my gloves were screwed to my hands and arms by hundreds of fine steel wires. I could not simply remove the gloves at the end of my shift. I had to peel them off slowly and carefully so as not to remove too much of my flesh with the glove. Each glove removal left me with hundreds of fine cuts like paper cuts, and punctures like needle pricks or wasp stings. The pain was exacerbated by the hot oil, detergent, and asbestos bits that followed the wires into my flesh. My hands and arms burned like fire for the next day and a half before they healed enough to allow me to forget the Factory until the next job call.

Am I complaining? No. I have no right to complain. I was glad to have the job. And the physically exhausting, unsafe conditions were far from unique. That summer, I only had to do about a dozen nights at the Factory. I was lucky. Some workers face conditions as bad as these or worse day in and day out, year in and year out for their entire lives. And I was getting the equivalent of $175.00/hour in today's money. Those who do this kind of work every day are usually paid minimum wage. I have nothing to complain about, but I have one request. Those who do this work their entire lives deserve to be elevated to the status of dogs. You know, "All dogs get a free pass to heaven." They deserve to be let in no questions asked. They have already spent a lifetime in hell. And a lifetime in a hell like the Filter Factory is actually much longer than a pleasant eternity in which not much happens.

By the end of summer, I had over $500.00 saved, a sum that would get me through a racing season. The Hot Shot build had been slowed but not stopped. Every evening when I was not at the Filter Factory I would work into the night, sometimes until 1:00 or 2:00 am. Before the end of July, the transmission and clutch were done, and I had the suspension and brakes sorted. At least as much as I could without a test drive. The last week of August, I was a day or two away from being able to fire up the engine and take the Hot Shot out on the road. My car would be road-ready in a matter of days and track-ready soon after. Then something happened that stopped my work at the factory, stopped the build of the Hot Shot, and ended my tenure at Scott Larsen.

Not so fast!

The last week of August, the National Meetings of the American Sociological Society were held in Seattle. My father came to the meetings and asked to see me. As I was 18 and beyond his reach I readily agreed, thinking I might get news of my brothers and some Sierra Club friends. Any news he brought would be warped by his lies, of course. But I knew him well enough to be able to unbend his words into an approximation of reality.

He got straight to the point. "I need you to come back to San Diego and start college."

21

Return to San Diego

I DO NOT KNOW EXACTLY how fast I decided to go back to San Diego and start college. It was a matter of hours, maybe even minutes, not days. Looking back, it seems like an easy change of direction. Large, but probably something I had been preparing for all along. The first thing I needed to wrap my mind around was not whether I would go along with his scheme. It was why would he suggest such a thing?

What on earth possessed him? There was nothing at stake for me because I was 18 and clear of his influence. Even though I was about to decide I would go, had probably already decided, I restated all their previous arguments against me going to college. I would not be able to handle the academic rigor. Since I was on my own, what would I do for money? College in San Diego was out of the question for me. I had no job down there. How could I pay tuition and fees? I had not applied to any colleges and did not intend to. I did not need a college degree to pursue the line of work I was in. I had done exactly as I was told and made myself financially independent before I turned 18. I had good jobs and my own apartment. I liked my work. How would I get around in Southern California? I didn't own a car. How could he even suggest such an insane thing?

The previous year in San Diego I had grown closer to Aubrey Wendling through the Sierra Club mountaineering courses and had met several of my father's other faculty colleagues. They were bewildered and seemed a little bit embarrassed for me when I told them that after high school I would be going back to Seattle to work in a garage. I could tell they assumed I was college-bound. Were my parents having difficulty fielding questions about why. Why would I choose that life for myself? I doubt they told their friends and colleagues about "18 and out." Whatever it was, I knew my father's reason had to be more about him than about me.

He was prepared to meet all of my arguments. He told me if I went to San Diego State I wouldn't have to apply. All I needed was to present my high school transcript during registration showing I had graduated with a better than B average. At the time, only the University campuses like Berkeley and UCLA required applications. Not the State Colleges. I would not need any money. He would pay my tuition and fees and buy my books. Tuition and fees were $30 a semester. Half the price of "start money" for a race. I could live rent free "at home" with them. They had moved out of Allied Gardens to a rented two-story house on a large ranch near the Mexican border south of El Cajon. He anticipated how little I would like that part and told me I could live with them without having to live WITH them. He explained their rental house came with an outbuilding that would serve as separate living quarters for me. I would have a little house of my own and could come and go as I pleased. I would not need a car. They had recently purchased a new Fiat 600 (!) that they would make available for my occasional use to go out on dates, or to the mountains. As far as the commute was concerned, I could ride in and out to school with him every day. He had everything figured. Whatever his reason, he seemed highly motivated to convince me and to make it work.

On the face of it, his proposition was in bad faith and too absurd to even consider. But without buying into any of his reasons I thought, "Why not?" A semester of college posed absolutely no risk to my future as a designer-builder of racing cars. I could go with him to San Diego, take a few classes, fail out, drop out or quit, and be back working at Scott Larsen and wrenching my Hot Shot by New Year's. I had already missed most of the racing season campaigning my own car. It would not take an entire off-season for me to be ready. Under the terms offered by my father, the timeout would cost me nothing and slow my progress very little, if at all. I also perversely enjoyed the thought that I might fail and prove they had been right all along about my woeful intellect. I looked forward to being able to tell them, "You were always right about me—so why did you drag me back here just to be humiliated?"

Mainly I was curious to see what goes on in college classrooms. I had adult friends who wore their college educations well; who were both humble and generous with their learning; who made their knowledge a positive part of their character. People like Phil Freeman, Aubrey Wendling, and others were well-educated and also decent human beings, even exemplary. Paul Hanna was a union Master bricklayer, but he also had a Master's degree in psychology. Clearly college did not cause people to have toxic personalities and miserable relations with their children. Nor did it prevent this outcome. How does that work?

My father's education qualified him for a faculty position at a second rank institution, but did nothing to reshape him into a better, more honest and sympathetic human being. Had something gone wrong? Was it that the education my parents got somehow didn't "take?" They earned degrees but were otherwise just as odious as ever.

Maybe going to college for a semester would provide some clues to the mysteries of my childhood. If I never set foot in a college classroom, I would go through life having to guess about what went wrong with the education of my parents.

One thing is certain. Had my father not showed up at that moment, I would never have gone to college. I still do not know the reason he intervened in my life as he did on that one occasion and that occasion only. I am certain of one thing. His subsequent behavior made it clear that his true motive had nothing to do with concern about me, my education, or my future well-being. No matter what his reason, benign or malevolent, he had never been motivated by my best interests.

When I transferred to Berkeley two years later, he objected violently, growling, "You've always thought you were better than us." He gratuitously added, "You'll never be accepted, and even if you were, we won't be paying for your plans."

I had already been accepted and I never assumed they would pay.

Leaving Seattle And Arriving In San Diego

My departure from Seattle was unplanned, hasty and somewhat chaotic. I was not expecting to leave, nor was anyone expecting me to go. I told Paul and Jack that I was going only to humor my parents and would be back after Christmas. They said, "Fine, your job will always be waiting." The Hannas were completely supportive. They said, "We always knew you'd go to college. You'll do great." It seemed odd to me. Before that moment, they had never once mentioned they thought I would go to college. They gave me a lot of practical gifts, cooking utensils and the like, that would help when I was on my own as a student. No one thought I could live with my parents. I bought several large and sturdy wicker baskets with lids, put everything in them, tied them up with ropes and sent them ahead on the Greyhound. I took my racing fund that I'd saved from my Filter Factory job, wrapped it in wax paper sandwich bags and put it in my sock. Cecil Smathers taught me about the sandwich bags. He said if it was in my shoe outside my sock, the robbers would always find it. If it was inside my sock they might not, especially if I had filthy, stinky feet. I didn't have bromhidrosis, but I also did not want my father to know I had any money. If he had known, he would have tried to grift it off me. I followed Cecil's instructions, hid my money and pleaded poverty. My father bought us two one-way train tickets to San Diego.

When we got off the train, he called my mother to come and pick us up. Ivanhoe Ranch was located in a very rural area not served by any public transportation, about 25 miles from downtown San Diego. My mother told him she would come to get us right away. She did not. She took the phone off the hook and left us sitting in the train station. After about ten hours and repeated failed efforts to get through to her I understood exactly what was going on. She was pissed about a recent or current affair and this was her way of making him pay a price. I was collateral damage. I did not ask my father what was going on and he did not offer any explanation. He knew I knew. We slept on the train station benches that night.

She arrived the next day in the early afternoon, pulling up in a pretty red Fiat 600 with wide whitewalls and a canvas sunroof. She was so angry at him, she barely took notice of me. The three of us rode back in silence.

When I sat in the Fiat, I saw that they had gotten into a box of my belongings I had left behind. They found about two dozen small participation awards I had received club racing in the Northwest. They had shined up the brass and affixed them neatly to the dash. Each plaque was about one-and-a-half by four inches and engraved with things like, "Participant Third Annual Seafair International Sports Car Competition"; or "Second in Class HP Bremerton Invitational Races"; etc. They were awarded as dash plaques, but I would not have chosen to stick them on the dash of any car I might be driving. My previous experiences after winning the poster contest and the reaction to my model planes in the store window caused me to know better than to make any such displays.

When my mother turned off the hard surface county road on the half mile dirt path approach to their new rental, I took in the ambiance of Ivanhoe Ranch. It was old west, rustic original Mexican land grant and quite beautiful with rolling grassy hills and occasional large oaks. It looked like the kind of place where I would enjoy living if my parents didn't live there. The plume of dust kicked up by the 600 hung in the hot still air for ten minutes after we pulled to a stop. The ranch owner was the retired proprietor of the largest Chevrolet dealership in San Diego. He bought the ranch for his divorced daughter to breed and raise quarter horses. They lived in the main house surrounded by multiple barns and outbuildings and an Olympic-sized swimming pool that they let my brothers use. My parents lived half a mile away on the next hill in what had been the foreman's house. There were a number of smaller houses scattered about, occupied by Mexican ranch hands and their families. An empty one closest to my parents was supposed to be mine. I knew as we drove up that my tenure there would be short. My mother had started to harangue my father loudly and non-stop about his infidelities and failure to provide adequate support every minute they were in the same space together.

Even if not something I would have done, affixing my dash plaques to the Fiat seemed a nice gesture on their part. At least well intended. Or so I thought until a few weeks later. I chanced to give one of my new college classmates a lift in the 600. He was a year ahead of me and had taken a sociology class from my father. He admired the dash plaques and expressed his amazement that Dr. MacCannell was both a college professor and a successful race car driver.

"How did you know about the racing?" I asked. That's when I learned that my father had been telling his students about his fabulous racing career in the Pacific Northwest that he had to give up to join the faculty at San Diego State. His lie effectively erased that part of my life from anything I might have shared with new college friends. At first, I did not think anything of it. It was simply par for the course in my father's fantasy world. It wasn't very long before I discovered that his appropriation of my life could cause me some grief. A bizarre rumor had been circulating during my absence.

No, I Wasn't In The Cuban Revolution

It happens that my departure from San Diego in early June 1958 coincidentally occurred at the same time as the first major battle in the Cuban Revolution. It had been won decisively by Castro and the rebels even though they were heavily outnumbered by Batista's regular army. My friends in California sincerely believed that when I disappeared at the start of summer, I had gone to Cuba to fight on the side of the Revolution. It probably began innocently as in, "Where's Dean? I haven't seen him in a couple of weeks." "I don't know, maybe he went to Cuba to fight in the revolution."

Whatever the origin of the story, I was not surprised that it gained traction. Recall that I could not afford Abercrombie and Fitch style gentleman sportsman clothing and equipment for my desert and mountain trips. I outfitted myself in U.S. Army surplus gear that was already pretty much worn out before I bought it. Going about with Chip in his Army ambulance wearing patched combat fatigues gave me the look of an irregular revolutionary combatant. I had heard several remarks to that effect in the spring before I left. Bud teased me about my look, but he also reckoned that it had a completely authentic aura that no amount of money could buy. I told him that was about what I'd paid for it.

All my friends assumed it was true—Chip and the other teenagers in Sierra Club, the Methodist Youth Group, Rafael and my other Jewish friends. When I first encountered an old friend or acquaintance, the same set of questions tumbled out:

"Are you okay?"

"What was it like?"

"Are you injured?"

"What is Fidel like in person?"

"I heard you got shot."

"Did you get to meet Che?"

There was nothing I could say to squelch the rumor. When I protested, "No, I've been up in Seattle working in a foreign car repair shop," all I got was, "Yeah, sure. Come on. Tell us what it was like." It would have helped if I had some dash plaques to document my life in the Pacific Northwest. But no. The participation plaques were useless to me unless I also chose to reveal what a lying sack of horseshit my father was. Something I never did until now.

It Wasn't The Last Time My Father Stole From Me, Or Tried To

It would be nice to report that this was my father's most egregious theft of my accomplishment. But 18 years later he was still at it, going all-in on a major heist. At the American Sociological Society Meetings in San Francisco in 1976, an advance copy of my first book, *The Tourist: A New Theory of the Leisure Class,* was prominently displayed in the Schocken Publishers booth. Professor E.H. MacCannell wandered into the booth, introduced himself as my father, and informed the Schocken representative that he had written the book for me. He told the rep that he did not think I could make tenure without it.

Fortunately for me (not for E. H. MacCannell) the representative in the booth happened to be my editor at Schocken. He had volunteered to handle the exhibit at the San Francisco meetings so we could spend some time together. We had worked over the phone editing *The Tourist*. Had it been anyone else, my father's lie might have gotten some traction. He was always very convincing. My editor was embarrassed for him, thinking he had to warn me about my delusional dad telling preposterous lies. ("He was taking an inordinate amount of credit . . .") I reassured him that sadly it came as no surprise, and I was certain it would not be the last time he would try to take credit for my writing. I have never included my first given name ("Earle") or even its initial (as in "E. Dean") on anything I ever published precisely because I knew he would try this.

[Note: I am known as "Earle Dean" and "E. Dean" to the Federal Government, to bankers, and on my health insurance. This caused confusion after my father re-married a woman named Julie. A credit reporting agency mixed up the files of "Earle and Juliet" MacCannell with those of "Earle and Julie" MacCannell. Juliet and I were denied credit on the basis of my father's credit score until I was able to establish my separate identity.]

College Registration

A week later, high-school transcript in hand, I presented myself for registration at San Diego State. Except for those who left for more prestigious schools, all my Jewish friends were with me in the line. It felt good. Like some unseen sorting demon had skimmed the cream off the top of the San Diego high schools. I didn't think I belonged, but I could at least imagine being friends with the others on line who did.

As soon as I was registered I walked off campus and found a small house for rent two blocks away from the main entrance. Two bedrooms, one bath and a detached one-car garage. Peeling off part of my racing fund, I rented it. This was an important investment on my part. I had been wrestling with how I would approach my studies. At first, I thought I'll just screw off, flunk out and go back to Seattle. But with the image of my Grandma Fran looming over me, I came to terms with reality—I am not capable of doing anything half-assed. In the end, I brought myself around to "I'll give it everything I've got." If I fail out on purpose

I will never know what might have been. If I fail honestly, I will always know exactly where I stand vis-à-vis higher education. I would approach college the same way I approached a high-speed corner, or a mountain, carefully but with serious intent.

On our way into school on the first day of classes I told my father he could drop me and my bags off at my house and not bother to pick me up after school. "I'm out of your hair," I told him. I had not mentioned renting a house. He was befuddled but there was very little he could say. He asked me how I was going to pay? I told him I would handle it and not to worry. "I won't be coming to you for any money." I knew that was all anyone ever needed to say to my father to make him happy and shut him up.

The $30 they paid for my tuition that semester was both the first and last money I received from them in support of my education.

My New College Friends

The first week of classes I found two roommates to share the rent. Ronnie Wilson and David Crawford. They were both older than me in their late 20s inching their way toward bachelor's degrees that neither of them ever got at a rate of one semester of course work every other year or two. Here is what I said about Wilson in my earlier autobiography:

"My good friend and roommate in San Diego and later in Berkeley, where we went together, was Ronnie Wilson, a perpetually "returning" student ten years my senior. Wilson had been a child-prodigy pianist and was about to begin his professional career on the concert stage when he was drafted into the Korean War. He refused combat, so he was given the job of stringing communication wire to the front lines. I believe that seeing men shot and flopping around in their death agony did something to his sensitive soul. In any event, he had an awful time concentrating on his studies and, of course, he refused absolutely to touch a piano.

It was characteristic of the ironical quality of his life that he eventually played Carnegie Hall in New York, but as the drummer for the rock group Joy of Cooking. [Berger, 174]"

When they moved in with me, I was unaware that Ronnie and David were among the approximately forty people in San

Diego who might be classed as leftist, bohemian intelligentsia. My house immediately became the central meeting place for protest planning, impromptu experimental musical performances, afternoon trysts between married people not married to each other, and days-long, non-stop discussions of religion, evolution and every other topic intellectuals of the 1950s thought it important to debate. For the most part I simply waded through the hoopla to my room, stopping only if I needed a break or my opinion was requested. The non-stop action in my house did not interfere with my studies which I will get to in the next section. I hung out in the conversations long enough to meet some interesting characters, hear their stories, and become friends with a few of them.

This was my first time with people who became a part of my life more or less at random. Every other prior group of friends or acquaintances had a reason for being. We were related to each other, or in high school together, or we raced cars. Suddenly I was close to people that I had no basis for being close to. Some of those I stepped over in my living room were characters I could never be friends with. The most disgusting habitué was a guy in his early 30s named Gordon McClure. He was skinny and stereotypically unattractive—unkempt, semi-shaven, bad skin, DIY haircuts, pop-eyed and chinless. None of this disqualified him from my caring for him. It was his way with women that put him beyond the pale.

McClure never had a girlfriend, but he approached every woman he saw and asked her, "You wanna fuck?" Girls and women sitting on bus benches, waitresses in cafes, someone stopped beside him waiting for the light at a crosswalk, passing in the street, he would approach them all and ask. He didn't have a type. He seemed to have a cut-off at about age 50. Going out and about with him was singularly embarrassing. It was a constant refrain, "You wanna fuck?" "You wanna fuck?" "You wanna fuck?"

The first time (and one of the only times) I got stuck alone with him in a public place I drew him aside. "Gordon. What's the matter with you? That's abhorrent. You've got to stop that." But he didn't stop. The very next girl we saw, it was lean in and whisper— "You wanna fuck?"

"Gordon, why would you do such a thing? It's disgusting." I turned to the young woman and added, "I'm sorry for my friend."

He explained: "If I ask every girl and woman I see, everyone I pass by in the street, about every ten days or two weeks, one of them says 'yes.' And we go somewhere and do it. Some of the girls that say yes aren't even that bad looking."

If Gordon was still around today, he would be involuntarily celibate. If I may be allowed to hope that some things can change for the better.

Without knowing it at the time, I was running a kind of "safe house" for oddballs. One of the oddest, named Vladimir, was living in this country illegally. He was a child of the Bulgarian Counsel in San Francisco. In 1950 his family had to leave because Bulgaria broke off diplomatic ties with the US. He was about 12 or 13 when his father was recalled, and he had lived in California and gone to school here since 1947. He decided to stay and effectively executed his plan as his family trooped onto the airplane. He hung back and his parents did not notice until it was too late.

He made his living going from door to door in San Diego charging people for improving their TV reception. This was very easy to do in the 1950s by micro adjustments of the orientation of the antenna. Or by hanging strips of aluminum foil from the antenna. Anyone could do it, but most people did not know how or would not bother. Vlad had a knack for it and could rake in enough from a trip down a couple of suburban blocks to live on for a day or two. He told his customers there would be no charge for no improvement and they could pay him what they thought his improvement was worth. He was conventionally handsome and as he entered his mid-teens he told me that an extra bonus was getting to have sex with some of the housewives.

When I knew him, he was in and out of jail on a variety of offenses—never violent—driving without a license, speeding, vagrancy etc. They never held him for long because he had no official identity and always gave a different name when he was arrested. He once gave my name or a version of it that was not so garbled as to prevent the cops from knocking on my door and determining that the guy they had was not me.

At the time he was making his living as a dirt-track racer on county-fairground circuits. He had a souped-up BSA 500cc single cylinder bike and was good enough to become a local hero and get starting money just to appear. Like many others, he simply showed up in my life about this time. But we bonded. I liked his story and he liked mine. He lived rent-free in the projection room of an abandoned movie theater.

When he was in jail for more than a couple of days, he asked me to care for his bike until he got out. I did not have a car so, even though he was my friend, I looked forward to his arrests that provided me wheels for brief periods. I even dated on his BSA.

Once at the peak of the racing season he got locked up for a couple of months and insisted that I show up at the races in his place. I could imitate his Eastern European accent perfectly. He said if I showed up at the last minute with his helmet, goggles, and face mask on, no one would know it wasn't him. I could collect the start money ($25 - $50 / race) so he would have some funds when he got out. I said, 'Yeah, but then I'd have to race a motorcycle.' He told me it was easy. 'It's no different from racing cars.' He told me if I didn't want to do it, I could go around a couple of times at the back of the pack and claim engine trouble and withdraw. It was an ill-conceived plan. I admit to trying but crashed (without injury) in my first race, on the first corner, bending the bike pretty badly, and was out for the season. The start money for that one race didn't cover repairing his bike. He was really pissed at me when he got out. He told me that even after we straightened out his BSA, it 'was never the same.'

Out on the road at speed, the vibrations from the huge single cylinder were enough to give me tooth aches. I think it really did loosen my fillings. But it also cleared my sinuses. I preferred cars.

From the myriad of strange encounters my new housemates brought me, one other stands out. An American Indian artist of some renown named Leon Sarsoza stayed with us for several days. He sketched obsessively. Leon was based in Los Angeles but he had a number of friends in San Diego including my roommates, Ronnie and David. I enjoyed talking to him. On the third day he disappeared but I knew he would be back because he left his bags and drawings. That night at about 2:00 am I woke up feeling strange—unfocused and giddy. There was a gathering in my living room which was not unusual. I often had to stumble through whoever was there on my way to the bathroom. When I opened my bedroom door I was knocked over by a thick cloud of blue haze. I had barely even heard of marijuana. It was certainly not something that anyone I knew would be familiar with. Or so I thought. Leon was there along with my roommates, and an older guy probably in his late 30s wearing a cheap business suit with his shirt button open and his tie pulled down. Everyone had a pipe or an ostentatiously large marijuana cigarette—more like cigars. The smoke was so thick I could hardly see through it. When I stepped out of my bedroom everyone laughed uproariously and began clapping like I had just appeared onstage to do a comedy routine.

I figured things out pretty quickly and was not amused. "What the hell is wrong with you guys? Isn't that stuff illegal?" They thought my first line was even funnier than my entrance. Ronnie introduced me to the suit as Officer so-and-so, "SDPD narcotics division." The narc explained that Leon was the main supplier of marijuana to the art scene in Los Angeles and the police needed to keep an eye on him. He travelled to Tijuana every couple of months to buy several kilos of high-quality cannabis. The deal he made with the San Diego police was he would pass through without selling even a cap of it in San Diego County. In exchange for free passage and reporting his coming and going, the narcotics officers asked to be invited to party with him and his pals while he was in their jurisdiction.

Yes, the stuff was highly illegal. Cue the laughter. I suspect Leon was giving the narc more than just a few tokes. But nobody told me. This might have been another one of those moments that caused me to see things differently for the rest of my life, but it was not. My maternal relatives had carefully taught me to assume that all authority is corrupt until proven that it is not.

Anyone who "goes off" to college may run into a more diverse cast of characters than they routinely encountered in their pre-college days. That is part of the excitement of stepping up into a bigger league. Because San Diego was an ultra-conservative Navy town, the leftists, gays, weirdos, artists, sex fiends, etc. were highly concentrated. Everyone knew everyone. And they were all at my house at least once a week or more. Every Friday afternoon I made lamb stew (lamb's breast was the cheapest meat you could buy) with carrots, potatoes, barley, onions, and tomatoes. I had a huge Mexican clay olla that held about four gallons. Dozens of people trooped through to talk and play music and grab a bite. It was important to me. I remembered how hungry I had been as a child and could tell that some of my new friends and acquaintances were starving. As the weekends progressed, I kept adding water and barley to the pot. By Monday morning it had shifted from being lamb stew to barley mush.

The Settlement Coffee House

Because of my new accidental centrality in the San Diego hip scene, I met the notorious Jack Fourey, his wife and brother who were high up in the West Coast Longshoremen's Union. Jack was a gifted labor organizer, union boss, and proud card-carrying member of the American Communist Party. Only a few years after the McCarthy Hearings, his affiliation made him seem to be dangerous to befriend even amongst San Diego's tiny leftist sub-community. He liked the fact that I had been born into a union family.

Fourey had an idea to start the first European-style café in San Diego. It would be called "The Settlement" and he included me in his plans. I knew my racing fund would not last forever and was looking for work. Even though the term "barista" hadn't been invented, it was the job I needed as I entered college. Here is the origin story of The Settlement coffee house as told to me. I was not a witness at the beginning. I came in about a week before the grand opening.

The year before, Jack carried his infant son into a fancy restaurant at one of their busiest times, jumped the queue and demanded that the hostess fill the child's baby bottle with warm water. He looked scruffy, like a labor organizer, and the hostess refused, telling him to go elsewhere, thinking he would slink away from the well-dressed clientele whose attention he had just grabbed. Jack had no intention of slinking away. The whole thing was a set up and his child was a prop. He had researched the restaurant and knew it had deep pockets. He had researched the law and learned that according to California code, food service businesses had to provide water for babies on demand even if the parent was not a customer. He knew that few people who worked in restaurants were aware of the Depression-era law. As a labor organizer he knew how to cause a hostess to take an immediate disliking to him and refuse his request. He knew how to make her dig in her heels and call for the manager. He knew how to manipulate the manager into backing the hostess. Easy. He knew how to clarify the issues, escalate, and draw all the customers into the conflict. He knew how to collect statements from witnesses. "All I asked for was water for my baby. You saw the way they refused me." He knew tough-as-nails labor lawyers who would assist him getting "The Settlement" out of court.

In their dealings with the Chinese, United States trade negotiators today are learning what I learned from the Foureys in 1958. There is no one more materialistic than a dialectical materialist. When it comes to working the capitalist system, there is no one better able than a hardcore communist. With the money he got from the settlement, Jack leased one of the most beautiful retail commercial spaces in San Diego. A room large enough to seat 60 patrons with 20-foot-tall ceilings and floor to ceiling gothic arch windows making up most of the walls on two sides. Park-like lush landscaping surrounding. He ordered the biggest espresso machine Italy made, about the size of a coffin, with four pressure handles so we could make eight cups at a time if needed. This was the first espresso machine of any size south of San Francisco. No one in San Diego had ever seen one before. Probably not more than five people in San Diego County had even heard of espresso, much less cappuccino. He ordered 20 small marble-topped round tables and comfortable, very high-quality high-backed wicker armchairs. Everything matched and the ambience felt both elegant and welcoming. Jack taught me how to make the various exotic coffee drinks and how to use, clean and service the espresso machine that doubled as a tourist attraction, Before the grand opening he hired me as the manager. An important part of my qualifications for the position was I was the only one who had ever been able to control his older brother when he was raging drunk.

We were open from 6:00 pm to 1:00 am seven days a week and immediately became the place to come and be seen in San Diego. At a time when restaurants on the West Coast were in a coffee price war—ten cents versus five cents for a bottomless cup—we charged 60 cents for an espresso and a dollar for a cappuccino. The only food we served were bagels and cream cheese and homemade (Jack's wife) cheesecake. I hired a lesbian couple, two pretty high school seniors, to serve as waitresses on call for busy nights and I single-handed it when business was light. We turned the long non-window wall into an art gallery and put up rotating exhibits of local abstract expressionist painters. I tried to find painters who favored huge canvases. Five feet was good. Ten feet was better. I wanted our display of decadent art to be seen from across the street.

Wednesday was open mic, "free speech" night. It wasn't quite "free speech" because I made every speaker run their piece by me before inviting them. On the weekends in rotation, we featured a classical guitar player named Mike who favored J. S. Bach, a Swedish folk singer named Ebba. Also Judy Henske, who went to a national career, and a weird gay mime named Eliot who contorted himself to his partner's free-form surrealist poetry and bongo drum accompaniment. High bohemian culture in the 1950s. I brought all the acts down from Los Angeles. On nights when there was an opera or classical orchestra performance in San Diego, we filled to overflowing with crowds waiting on the sidewalk to get in.

For one of my first open-mic nights, I auditioned my father to speak. He wanted to give his standard sociology 100 classroom lecture on "nature versus nurture." He argued, marshalling all sorts of "evidence," that babies are not human until they learn to talk. Until they can speak, he claimed, they are the same as the other dumb animals. He was actually convinced that this was true and stopping short of infanticide for pre-verbal humans, he linked his thesis to an argument in favor of legalizing abortion.

In the late 1950s, the last time the U.S. was tightly controlled by politicians in the thrall of the religious right, you could go to jail for having or giving an abortion. You could go to jail for sitting in the front of a bus if you were African-American, for smoking marijuana, engaging in homosexual relations, pre-marital cohabitation, and possession of pornography. Having "pre-marital sex" in a state where you were not a resident was a federal offence covered by laws against "white slavery." In order to get a divorce, for example in New York, either the husband or the wife had to permit themselves to be photographed having sex with someone who was not their spouse. No other grounds for divorce, or evidence, were accepted by the courts. None of these were "political issues." They were simply the laws of the land. Everyone broke one or several of these laws routinely. And everyone cowered. If you did any of these things and got caught you could be tried, found guilty, and sent to jail sometimes for many years. Abortions were performed in unsanitary surroundings using un-bent coat hangers. When I was 18 I lived in the kind of country the religious right wants us to return to. We broke at least one of these laws almost every day while living in fear that the next knock on the door would be the police. This is not an exaggeration.

I tipped off my housemates and a few friends about my father's talk. I knew well my father's sick need to be loved and admired by everyone. Even if they might have agreed with him on legalizing abortion, I made certain that key members of the audience knew that I would not be offended if he was loudly booed for his views on human infants. His confusion and pain when the catcalls rained down on him was palpable. Sorry about my earlier claim that the spider incident was my only moment of adolescent rebellion. As I write this, I realize there were a few others.

The communist Foureys were very hands-off owners of the means of production. They showed up in their new Ford convertible to collect the money and drop off cheesecake, and gunny sacks of coffee beans. But unless there was a big crush anticipated, I rarely saw them. I worked for minimum wage but most nights I could double or triple my pay in tips. This was when dimes, quarters, 50 cent pieces and silver dollars were made of solid silver. Later when their bullion value vastly exceeded their face value as coins they became pot-metal sandwiches. I didn't know it at the time, but I was letting a future fortune slip through my fingers. I could sell one of those 50 cent pieces today for 20 dollars.

With my earnings and tips from The Settlement, I was easily able to pay my portion of the rent on my little house and repay my racing fund. I went to classes by day and worked at The Settlement by night. If I gave the Foureys sufficient notice, I could take an occasional weekend off to go climbing with Bud or Jerry. Beyond what school, my strange household, mountain climbing and my job provided, I had no need for additional social life. There was more than enough excitement.

For the other students, the square ones, social life at San Diego State College in the late 1950s was mainly contained within the Greek system. Every fraternity on campus tried to recruit me because my father was a professor and they thought he might give higher grades to the frat brothers of his son. I could not conjure a more nauseating thought than imagining myself as a member of a college fraternity. I let them know, slyly but truthfully, that joining a fraternity would put a serious damper on my social life as it had evolved.

My priorities were straight. My classes were the most important component of my new life. Before I get to them, there is one more thing. A complicated girlfriend. It would have been my first "grown-up" relationship if I had been a grownup.

My First College Girlfriend

In the foyer of the Humanities and Social Sciences Building at SDSC there was a gathering space and stand-up coffee and snacks concession. It was a good place to hang out between classes. You could hear gossip about every professor and almost every student on campus. I could not help but notice a very pretty girl who wore beautiful clothes like charcoal grey Harris Tweed slacks with a light pink silk blouse. She spent more time in the foyer than almost anyone else. Many of the older students knew her enough to say hi. But except for a couple of faculty members, she rarely conversed with anyone beyond a simple greeting. When I asked about her, I found out she was an exceptionally rare type—a graduate student. At the time, there were no graduate programs at SDSC. One exception, the Spanish Department, offered an M.A. degree.

Marilyn S. was finishing a Master's in Spanish Literature. I was told that she was brilliant and completely unapproachable. She was four years older than me and Jewish. She had a troubled relationship with her Jewish background and preferred to be identified as Mexican. In high school, she had been an exchange student in Mexico City and returned to spend every summer with her Mexican surrogate family. This was remarkable. At the time, Jews were openly denigrated by the Anglos of San Diego, but not nearly as mercilessly as Mexicans were denigrated. Still, in the presence of strangers, Marilyn spoke flawless, unaccented, every verb tense perfect, Spanish. When it suited her, which was often, she pretended not to understand English and passed herself off as an upper-class Mexican visiting on a shopping trip from Mexico, DF.

Marilyn had only one prior serious long-term boyfriend whom she described as a "dork." By her account their relationship had not progressed beyond a few chaste kisses. Even though we got well past that on our second date, I had every reason to believe her. In retrospect it seems probable that her boyfriend didn't know he was gay. She lived at home with her parents who she refused to discuss. She drove and gave me free use of her pretty 1955 Chevrolet hardtop convertible, not a foreign car, but the most tolerable of the Americans at the time.

Even though I never understood what she was getting from me, she ignored our age difference and became an enthusiastic lover from the waist up.

She was firm about making it clear that her virginity was not in play.

That was fine by me. She was a good, multi-topic conversationalist. And she made certain that I understood the ins and outs of performing well in college classes. She went over my papers and reports before I turned them in and made helpful editorial suggestions. "Professor so-and-so will give you a better grade if you mention Plato." She became my academic tutor.

A few weeks into my first term she told me, "The only thing you have to do to be a straight-A student is to decide you are a straight-A student. Once you make that decision, it will happen." I detected a slight emphasis on the "you" when she said "the only thing you have to do . . ." So, it wasn't generic cheerleading. She was expressing confidence in me personally. The Hannas told me I would do well in college. But Marilyn's was the first affirmation I got in situ. I felt ready to take on anything. It was a good thing. Because a few weeks later, I got my chance to take on an unusually big academic challenge.

Early in our relationship Marilyn came to me and told me she was sorry, but we had to break it off, romantically. We could be friends and she would keep advising me about my studies, but her old boyfriend had returned. She explained she had broken up with him a year earlier. He didn't interest her romantically. He had little to say in conversation. All his observations were stereotypical and bland. He had no real interest in anything. "So why are you breaking up with me and going back to him?" I needed an explanation.

She told me, "We made a deal. I agreed we would get back together if his parents sent him on an around the world trip and he came back with interesting experiences and observations he could talk about. If he had a more cosmopolitan outlook and could see and understand things and be interested in things beyond the end of his own nose."

"Oh no! His parents sent him around the world?"

"Yes, and he's back and I agreed that we would get back together when he returned. And he wants us to get back together. I'm really, really sorry about this, but I made him this promise so we have to break up. We'll still be friends."

By this time, while intercourse remained out of the question, she had been enthusiastically giving me access to her entire body. I told her that it's hard for a guy to give that up and I would miss our intimacy, but it was okay. I understood that she needed to honor her commitment. We could be "just friends."

One week later she called and asked to meet. She greeted me with a warm embrace and a lover's kiss. "Hey. Hey. Enough of that. What about your boyfriend?"

"We don't have to break up. He's just as boring as he was before he went around the world. I think he's more boring if that's even possible. Our plan of getting back together didn't work out. Can we just forget about this last week?"

"Of course."

Marilyn had a kid brother two years younger than me. We had little contact, but he hated me for dating his sister. He told me so. I never met her parents. We often hung out in her bedroom when they weren't home. They came home unexpectedly one afternoon to fetch some papers and Marilyn freaked out, sending me stark naked racing across her back yard like a striped-ass ape. Trying to get into my pants on the run. I had to walk barefoot and shirtless through middle class neighborhoods over two miles back to my house.

Marilyn broke up with me offering no explanation. We weren't right for each other. That was it. That was all. Our age difference was enough to make me feel I had no right to ask why. So I set about the lonely business of letting go.

A week after the breakup, she came into The Settlement at closing time. "There's one more thing you need to do for me."

"Yes."

Using the sexual slang of the day she said, "Take me to a motel and de-virginize me."

If I had been two years older, I would have tried to talk her out of it. If I had been her age, I would have refused to go along with her scheme. But I was 18 and horny and had been unsuccessfully trying to entice her into having sex for months. I ignored the fact that we had broken up. Her request made it seem like I had prevailed. So I did as I was asked. It was not the best sex, and I fervently hope that it was far from the best sex she would eventually have. Afterwards she told me, "Thank you. But this doesn't change anything. We're still broken up."

The last I heard of Marilyn was two years later in Berkeley. Her brother found me in the Mediterraneum Coffee House on Telegraph Avenue and came up snarling. "I hate you, you bastard. You are pure evil. You ruined my sister's life." I couldn't get him to elaborate. He left hurriedly, apparently satisfied that he had delivered his message. The one time I had sex with his sister I'd been careful, as always. Over the next year she and I saw each other on campus to say hello and occasionally chat. There was no pregnancy, and no 'you ruined my life' vibe. I couldn't figure out any other way I might have "ruined her life."

Obviously, there was a great deal more to the story of our relationship than I'll ever know. I am sorry for whatever went wrong. Marilyn was highly instrumental in smoothing my way into college norms and expectations.

22

Straight to the Heart of the Matter

DURING REGISTRATION I SIGNED UP FOR CLASSES—*Spanish 2, Art* (pencil drawing), *Health* (required of all freshmen), *Physical Education* (required of all freshmen), and *Anthropology 2* (Introduction to Cultural Anthropology).

Cultural Anthropology

One might think I would major in mechanical engineering. It never crossed my mind. I loved cars as art more than science. I preferred finding new combinations working with imaginative assemblages of existing components—engines, suspensions, brakes from different cars brought together in creative new ways. Bodies of my own creation. Later I would discover the renowned French anthropologist Claude Lévi-Strauss' distinction between the engineer and the bricoleur. An engineer attempts to design a way out of the constraints of the materials at hand. The bricoleur "builds up structured sets from existing materials." Exactly. I did not need Lévi-Strauss to tell me that bricolage is the opposite of engineering. There is a whole lot of engineering you must not know to be a creative, if not always successful, bricoleur. Sometimes things break and even blow up in your face. But other times, miracles happen. I learned this important lesson from my Grandpa Ross, Uncle Doc, Jack Larsen, Colin Chapman, and the African-American man who took informal control of the Seattle dump.

Anthropology was my choice of major. There was no dithering about this on my part. After Grandpa Ross's National Geographic magazines, after the Washington State Museum, the Kwakiutl potlatch, Erna Gunther, Juan Arvallo, the subject matter of anthropology had already installed itself in me alongside my other vital organs.

Assistant Professor of Anthropology,
Frank W. Young

My instructor for Anthropology 2 was a newly hired assistant professor, Frank W. Young. He was an oddity, a recent Ph.D. from Cornell who had just completed a year of post-doctoral research in Mexico. He was shocked by his very non-Ivy League surroundings. It was like he had just stumbled across the border from Mexico and responded to the first "Help Wanted" sign he saw. He had never heard of a four-year college without graduate programs and research support for the faculty. He certainly never imagined being stuck in one. I felt a certain kinship. I, too, was completely out of place coming in from the opposite direction.

Because Frank Young was in the same department as my father (Sociology and Anthropology were combined programs then at San Diego State) I heard all the gossip. An Ivy League Ph.D. was considered to be quite a score for the Department.

Professor Young had other distinctive qualities. First, he was young. Not just "Young" but younger than the other faculty, even other recently hired assistant professors like my 40-year-old father. If Young was 30 it was just barely. Plus, he arrived with his wife Ruth who also had a Cornell Ph.D. Ruth was the only other woman with a doctorate I had met after Erna Gunther. Unfortunately, it goes without saying that Ruth was not offered a faculty position. Equally qualified academic couples were so rare in the 1950s as to be unheard of and certainly not accommodated.

My father regarded his own appointment at San Diego State as something like a crossing over, his great reward for a lifetime of struggle and privation, a happy ending. With Ph.D. in hand, and an offer from SDSC, he could switch on cruise control, kick back, relax and enjoy the coeds.

Not Frank W. Young. What kind of a place is this, he wanted to know? He certainly wasn't about to relax. He could not believe he had senior colleagues no one had ever heard of. He had never been around full professors whose curriculum vitae didn't run to multiple pages of ground-breaking books, invitations to lecture internationally, and scores of articles in prestigious journals. At SDSC all you needed to advance through the ranks was a Ph.D. and some lukewarm teaching evaluations. The other faculty, including my father, thought it was cute. Like, "He's just a kid. When he learns to love to surf, he'll settle down and realize what a great place this is. No rat-race here."

Professor Young was good with us students. He was open and honest about what he regarded as his predicament without ever condescending to us. He told us that even without selectivity, the best students at State were just as good as the best students anywhere. Even Cornell. Even Harvard. We were simply not a part of a demographic that made it into elite institutions no matter how smart we were. One of my Jewish friends from high school, Frank Bardacke, did get a scholarship to Harvard, but they kicked him out at the end of his first year. Not for low grades. For blasphemy. Not against God. Against Harvard. Frank was not impressed by the Harvard mystique and let everyone know his views. Young was right. We just weren't part of the demographic that made it.

Professor Young reassured us that we stood a reasonably good chance of getting a decent education at SDSC. He told us that in elite schools the professors only assigned books they had written and those written by their close friends. In Bible Colleges and junior colleges, the faculty assigned textbooks that were, by definition, out-of-date and insipid. At least here, in a middling institution, there was some chance of being assigned a range of well-selected books—the best writings in the field. And he made his words come true by requiring us to read Durkheim's *Rules of Sociological Method* and Ralph Linton on *Status and Role* in freshman anthropology. More important, he taught us how to read and understand these and other seminal works and the reasons their insights into the human condition were so fundamental as to be indelible. Frank Young's lectures mainly consisted of helping us through these advanced readings, framing their insights, explaining their intellectual historical context and background issues, until we got sufficient footing to be able to handle them on our own.

As far as I know, my father never prepared a lecture. At least I never witnessed him preparing one. He taught "*Introduction to Sociology*," "*Marriage and the Family*"—yes, his colleagues actually assigned him to teach *"Marriage and the Family"*—by reading his student notes from when he took the same courses as an undergraduate. Then he sat on his butt in office hours with a goofy "empathetic" grin on his face making goo-goo eyes at his female students. He was in heaven. He would be happy to spend an eternity on that dingy old Steelcase desk chair. Late in his career I imagined his lecture notes crumbling to dust as he turned the pages.

From the moment he arrived, Frank Young was plotting his escape. He explained a process that he called "publishing your way back into the Ivies." This was long before the social sciences and humanities began producing rock-star professors whose public lectures resemble political rallies. Academic reputations in the social sciences then were based on the same thing that reputations in the STEM fields are today. You had either opened a new line of inquiry or solved an outstanding problem or puzzle in an existing line of inquiry. Numbers of publications was a meaningless metric. It was not enough to toss around buzzwords to make your reader or audience feel like they were "in" on something. A publication that changed or challenged your discipline was all that counted. Strong reputations could be based on a single journal article if it was a break-through.

Young explained to us, his students, how it worked: "You have to write an article or book that gets notice. You must show that there is something important going on in the world that, until now, no one has noticed or figured out. Or you must find something important that an earlier researcher purported to explain and show they were dead wrong about it." He added with a smile that it is best if the previous researcher who got it wrong was still alive and teaching at Harvard.

In the 1950s, if you were hired as an assistant professor at Yale, Cornell, Penn, Harvard, etc. you did not have to teach any courses for one or two years until you established your research program and finished preparing a new graduate seminar built around your research. Then you began teaching your seminar and two or three undergraduate classes a year. This was before higher education became just another industrial product. Working conditions at the elite schools guaranteed their curricula would evolve in real-time with the advancement of knowledge. Oh, and every full professor had graduate student teaching and research assistants and their own full-time private secretary to type their manuscripts and handle their schedules and correspondence.

At SDSC, Young was teaching four undergraduate courses a semester, some of them repeat sections of the same low-level class to reduce his preparation time if he was lucky. There were no teaching or research assistants and no secretarial help available to anyone but the department chair regardless of rank. Young was absolutely determined that this would not stop him from "publishing his way back into the Ivies." That is what prompted his scheme to build a research team from scrap, out of the dump so to speak.

Before the first mid-term he announced to his classes that he would select the top three student exam performances from all his classes and offer positions as his student research assistants. He could not pay anything, but he would excuse the top-scoring students from future assigned coursework and exams and base their course grades on how well they completed their assignments advancing his research. It seemed like a bold move. He was willing to upset the order of things to make something new happen. There were more than 100 students sitting for the first mid-term in Young's classes. I wanted one of those three positions and committed all my mental and physical energy to preparing for that exam.

Soon, I would know if Marilyn's confidence in my academic ability had been groundless.

My blue-collar experience prepared me for this moment. It was like I was competing for a rare opening for an apprentice on the shop floor. We took the mid-term. It was hard, with both multiple choice and essay questions. When Young passed the tests back, he announced the top scoring students: Rena Barack, my friend from high school whose mother introduced me to buttered matzos; a returning student named Bernice who was 40-something and taking time off from being an executive secretary; and Dean MacCannell.

Marilyn was right. All I had to do was decide. It did not stop me from thinking of myself as "average." But now, I was a very dedicated, very lucky average guy in college.

Since it was so atypical, I will try to follow the contours of the first few weeks of my introduction to anthropology. I did not take any more tests or write papers. I sat in the class and followed Young's lectures and I did the assigned readings. Instead of coursework, tests and papers, I met with Young and the other team members and was shown the inner workings of a high-level cross-cultural research project. Young gave us specific tasks with deliverables and deadlines. He was an impatient, "I only give instructions once," kind of boss. He warned us, "Two strikes and you're out." But his explanations were detailed and crystal clear so getting things right and keeping up with the pace of work was only a matter of paying attention and working hard. I knew how to do that.

"The Function of Male Initiation Ceremonies"

The study Young set his sights on was "The Function of Male Initiation Ceremonies at Puberty." It had just been published to much acclaim by Harvard Professors John Whiting, Clyde Kluckhohn and Albert Anthony, all giants in the Social Sciences at that time. They had done a comparative study of 56 societies in the *Human Relations Area Files.* They were interested in the relationship between the length of *post-partum* sex taboos and the intensity of male initiation rituals. Every society has a period during which sexual intercourse after childbirth is avoided. Ours is minimal. Two weeks recommended and it is not encoded in law. In about half of the so-called "primitive" cases in the HRAF the post-partum prohibition of sex is between two and three years and has the force of law. Hold it! Three years? No sex?

As I entered the ethnographic record, every shock was followed by a revelation. How does three years of enforced abstinence work? Fine, actually. At least for the adult males. The societies with very long post-partum taboos in almost every case, also practice polygyny, that is, each husband has several wives. If they time things right, at least one wife is usually available. The post-partum taboo can actually minimize squabbling among the wives over their husband's limited sexual resources. There are also long post-partum taboos in parts of New Guinea, where the adult men engage in ritualized homosexuality with underage (i.e. not yet initiated) boys as their main form of sexual activity.

If "the city has 8 million stories" the Ethnographic Record has a Quadrillion

In their article, Whiting, Kluckhohn, and Anthony focus on the "exclusive mother-son sleeping arrangement" that is usually a by-product of the post-partum taboo. Claiming to follow Freud, they argued that the longer a son gets to sleep exclusively with his mother the stronger the Oedipal bond between them. The Harvard authors further argued that as the boy grows into adulthood and becomes large enough that he may be able to challenge his father physically, the adult males in the group need to impress upon him just exactly who is boss. They need to beat any potentially disruptive jealous emotions out of him. Their wording was more measured, but it boiled down to this: the longer he got to sleep with his mother, the harder they must beat him or terrorize him as he transitions to adulthood.

Ritual recognition of passage from childhood to adulthood is very nearly universal. In our society, it is a matter of obtaining a driver's license, or high school diploma, or having a quinceañera or a bar mitzvah. Or, *"18 & out."* In the ethnographic record, as I soon discovered, some male initiation ceremonies are quite violent involving physical punishment, piercings, scarification, isolation, food and water deprivation, etc. As a part of the ritual, some societies perform male circumcision at puberty, a few of them by pulling on the foreskin and pounding it off with a rock. In several societies, male initiation at puberty includes subincision, i.e., slitting open the initiate's urethra sometimes the full length of the penis. In preparation for subincision, a few Australian societies separate the entire urethra from the penis before cutting into it. This is accomplished by carefully splitting the penis from tip to base and pulling the urethra free. No society that practiced sub-incision had any form of anesthesia—local or general—other than going into shock and passing out. The prospect of subincision is even more withering in those societies where the operation is performed using stone knives. The adult males who perform subincision at initiation are usually the youth's uncles who bind his wounds with medicinal leaves and send him alone into the bush to heal. Most initiates fully recover physically with their organs returning to functionality. Growing up knowing that this is what you must undergo as your rite of passage to manhood may be more nerve-wracking than growing up worrying about how well you will do on your SATs.

Whiting, Kluckhohn and Anthony hypothesized and found the following: the longer the post-partum taboo, the more severe the male initiation ritual. There is a strong and statistically significant correlation between the two. They interpreted this as upholding their Freudian-based hypothesis.

Young was having none of it. Durkheim taught us to "explain a social fact with another social fact." Psychological explanations of social phenomena were wrong. Crude, mid-20th century readings of Freud concluded he was wrong about everything. Anything that seemed to show Freud was right had to be wrong. Needless to say, I had not read any Freud yet. If I had I might have pointed out to Young how clumsily derived from Freud's work the Harvard hypothesis was. That would have to wait. For now, it was a matter of finding a third variable. There had to be something yet unseen, as yet unmeasured, that both initiation ceremonies and the post-partum taboo were correlated with that was creating the illusion of a relationship between them. If we could find the hidden third term and take it out of the equation, the correlation Whiting, Kluckhohn, and Anthony had found would crumble. That was Young's strategy and his gamble.

Our task was to find the third term or variable that was producing the spurious relationship between initiation and the taboo.

My first task was to read my assigned one third of the ethnographies in the Harvard study sample. Young wasn't content with accepting the Yale coding protocols of the HRAF. We had to go back to the original ethnographic reports, verify the HRAF data, and bring out whatever additional details had gotten lost in the Yale summaries. I loved reading my ethnographies. I did not need them to be assigned in a class or as a part of my job on a research project. Once I discovered them, I would have read them compulsively like I read my Grandpa Ross' *National Geographics*. And I wasn't just reading them. I was reading them with a purpose. We were in the hunt for the elusive third term that would prove Whiting, Kluckhohn and Anthony wrong. If we found it, everyone in the field would take notice and Frank W. Young would be on his way, maybe all the way back to the Ivies. To make a quick getaway from San Diego, he had to aim precisely and hit the field of anthropology between the eyes.

This was how I learned to read with a real purpose, not a false purpose, i.e., not just to pass an exam. The lesson was indelible and marked me for life. I had to find purpose in all my future reading. Otherwise, reading can be dull as dishwater. Reading with a purpose is reading on full alert. This is the secret of the appeal of mystery as a genre. When you are searching for clues, everything you encounter along the way appears in higher definition. It was like I was eating and breathing and touching the ethnographic details that make up the tapestry of human life in all its beautiful and ugly variations.

Reading my first cases I discovered that many "primitive" societies are organized into clans that trace their ancestry back to a mythical deity, spirit animals, or sacred objects like the moon and the sun. And these clans are either endogamous or exogamous. That is, in some societies you are required to marry someone in your own clan, while in others the rule is you must marry someone from a different clan. I wondered if endogamy or exogamy might be the hidden third term. But I had no reason for wondering such a thing and I have never wondered without a reason.

Descent groups trace their ancestry through either the male or the female lines. Ours is lightly patrilineal, with children taking the family name of their father but not much more. Jews, for example, take the name of the father, but their Jewish identity comes from their mother. Perhaps because humans always know who their mothers are but are less certain about their fathers, the ethnographic record is dominated by societies that are organized into matrilineal clans. Could the hidden third term be matrilinearity? Or patrilinearity? We might pause for a moment to consider patrilinearity—to impress on the male youth the importance of the male line. But if this was the third term, male initiations in patrilineal and female initiations in matrilineal societies would be similarly severe and they are not.

What else might account for it? Was male initiation associ-

ated with how warlike the society is and the men's construction
and use of specialized weapons? It wasn't. How about subsistence
patterns? Herding peoples tend to discipline their children at an
earlier age than hunter-gatherers. Perhaps male initiation is a part
of that complex. It wasn't. How does the acquisition of status and
fame work in the society? Are there no honorific roles for wom-
en in societies with severe male initiation? No. Not that either.
How about the importance of class and status differences? Some
societies are divided into high and low castes with no possibility
for movement from your position at birth while in others there is
little or no distinction between high- and low-status individuals.
Perhaps initiation is associated with class division? Nope.

Setting aside for a moment the question of the cause of
male initiation, the main takeaway from my first foray into the
record was that few societies leave the choice of who one may

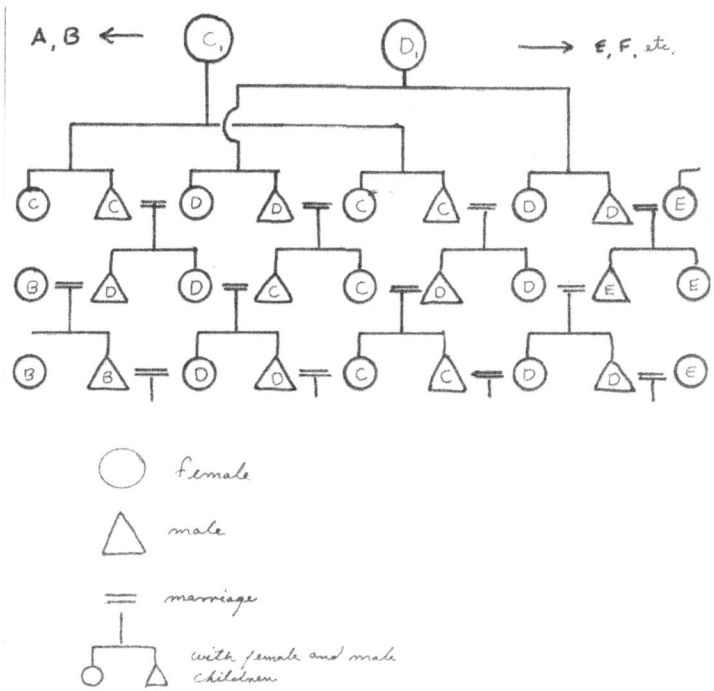

Kinship Diagram

marry up to the individuals who will make up the couple. Every case I read designated a specific category of relative as the only socially approved choice. The most common form is cross-cousin marriage. If you are a girl, you must marry your father's sister's son. Or your mother's brother's daughter if you are a boy.

If we extrapolate from our "primitive" contemporaries, first-cousin marriage was the statistical norm for several hundred thousand years of human existence. It still exists in some precincts of modernity—in the Muslim Arab world, e.g., and parts of China. But what about all those genetic defects that are supposed to occur if you marry a close relative? Apparently, cousins are biologically different enough that the transmission of defects is no more likely than the transmission of genetic advantage. But what if your mother's brothers don't have enough daughters for your brothers and you to marry? In that case, there will be a family somewhere that has a surplus daughter available for adoption by your uncle. Via adoption, well-formed marriages can continue to be made like moves on a chess board.

I loved prowling around in the ethnographic record and learning the creative solutions every society came up with to balance and repair itself and keep itself functioning. It became evident to me that humanity has been making itself up as it went along and, for the most part, we were brilliant at it.

Since I couldn't quite grasp the kinship patterns I was reading about, I began drawing diagrams of the variations. What would a society look like if it practiced cross-cousin marriage and was organized into matrilineal, exogamous clans? Is it even possible to have cousin marriage and require marriages to be between members of two different clans? How can my cousins be in a different clan from me?

Note that in the diagram, everyone belongs to the clan of their mother (matrilineal), everyone marries outside their clan (exogamy), and everyone marries a cross-cousin. Everything fits together better than the internals of a Ferrari engine. I was as fascinated by what I was learning about these societies as by any new (to me) exotic vehicle that crossed the threshold at Scott Larsen. Marx's favorite aphorism was, "Nothing human is alien to me." I had already taken the next step. "Everything alien is interesting to me."

Once I Entered The Ethnographic Record, I Was Unable To Leave

Once inside the ethnographic archive, it became clear to me that I was in the presence of an inexhaustible and intriguing dialectic—complex orders generated by norms of our own creation that give rise to the structures we inhabit day-to-day, moment-to-moment. Some of them are beautifully devised to be harmonious, weaving physics and genetics together with human enjoyment like the major and minor scales. Others, like the rules of grammar, seem to have been designed in the first place to produce suspicion, jealousy, and deceit.

It was not simply the beauty of the design of humanity that drew me in. I also took it personally. If my parents had been born 10,000 years ago there is no way they would have been allowed to marry. Which was good. But if they hadn't married, I wouldn't have been born. Which is probably not so good. If, however, by some chance I, or someone very much like me, had been born into a society like the one I diagrammed above, my father would not have been from my clan. He would have been an outsider and not well-regarded by my true relatives in my matriline. If I was a Cat person, he would have been a Dog person. My true relatives (all the other Cat people like me) probably would have assumed he was a lying son-of-a-bitch, and treated him like one, even if he was not. Fathers do not amount to much in matrilineal societies that practice cross-cousin marriage. He is just the lousy bum your mother was required to marry. The adult men in my life, the ones I should look up to, the ones who would assume responsibility for teaching me how to be a man, the ones who would initiate me into manhood, would be my uncles, my mother's brothers. Hmm, Eddie and Doc. A shadow of our ethnological past definitely hung over me.

Professor Young eventually argued that the function of male initiation was to dramatize male status in each society—to impress upon the youth how different becoming an adult male is from becoming an adult female. Little girls grow up to be women more or less automatically. No little boy automatically grows up to be a MAN! Men, real men, are a world apart. There can be no admission to the mens' club without painful tests and trials.

The passage from a childhood where the boys are mixed in with mothers, aunts, sisters, and female cousins, to a conventionally masculine adulthood can be a rough one for "Momma's Boys" even in our society. In those where the gulf between men and women is absolute, male youth need to have their distinctive and independent adult male identity ritually framed and forcefully impressed upon them.

The Harvard team found a relationship between the post-partum taboo and male initiation because they both tended to occur in societies with a high degree of separation of the sexes. When we re-ran the data to account for the fact that these traits both typically occur in sex-segregated societies, it canceled out what they thought they had seen. The post-partum taboo had no explanatory value when it came to severity of male initiation. Instead, sex segregation was the defining factor.

Young hit a home run. He was invited to present his results at the National Meetings of the American Anthropological Association where Whiting, Kluckhohn and Anthony publicly capitulated.

After Young read his paper, the one freshmen students at San Diego State at San Diego State assisted him with the research, Professor Anthony rose in the back of the room and said, "Whiting, Kluckhohn, and Anthony were crazy, crazy, CRAZY." In 1965 Young published his book, *Initiation Ceremonies*, based on our research; the study he hoped would open the door for a professorship in the Ivy League.

Most of the heavy lifting, i.e., the final coding of the ethnographies and hypothesis testing happened after I left SDSC for Berkeley. But this much is certain. My immediate exposure to the inner workings of seriously interesting research at the earliest stage in my studies changed my life. What would have happened if I had taken Anthro 2 from a journeyman member of the teaching faculty—or someone like my father? Would I have continued in college? Or would I have dropped out, returned to Seattle, finished rebuilding my Hot Shot, put together a business consortium and opened a Dealership? I do not know the answer to that question. But I strongly suspect I would now be a retired auto dealer.

This First Year Of College Foreshadowed
My Life's Work

From that beginning, I knew one thing for sure. Even if I dropped out, I would continue my study of anthropology. I also know that as much as I loved anthropology, I would never apply what I was learning directly to the so-called "primitive" case. I would never enter the classical domain of anthropology and write an ethnographic report about a group of hunter-gatherers. I had learned from Erna Gunther and from Juan Arvallo that there is no such thing as a "primitive" human being. What I was getting from anthropology was something quite different. How can I apply what I am learning about the Bororo, or the Aztecs, or Ashanti, Kwakiutl, etc., to our contemporary modern and post-modern situations? I could see fragments of what I had learned about male identity formation in the so-called primitive case scattered about all around me in the ways boys and men were expected to imagine themselves in my world.

From this starting point I continued to work just outside of anthropology, as a student of human cultural arrangements but in the empirical domain of sociology. What would the results be if the tables were turned, if a "primitive" ethnographer came and lived among us, and asked the same questions about us that we have been asking about them? That reversal is exactly what I experienced the day I spent walking down off the San Pedro Martir with Juan Arvallo. For the past 60 years I have very consciously comported myself as that "primitive ethnographer" among us moderns.

Out of San Diego

In the summer of 1960, my father, Frank W. Young, and I all left SDSC. Frank Young and my father departed their faculty positions at San Diego State under quite different circumstances. My father was asked to leave for "unprofessional conduct." I transferred to Berkeley where I completed my bachelor's degree in anthropology attending courses taught by some of the greatest in the field: Erving Goffman, Laura Nader, Robert Heizer, Del Hymes, Jerome Skolnick, Rene Millon, and Robert Murphy.

On the strength of his re-study of male initiation, Frank Young did succeed in returning to the Ivies. He was appointed to a tenure-track position at Cornell where I would join him three years later as his graduate student and research assistant—paid this time—tuition and fees and $160 ($1,400 in today's money) a month. My Ford Foundation monthly stipend was better (again in today's money) than what my father received from the G.I. Bill to support his family of five. It never felt like sacrifice. I could rent a nice one-bedroom apartment for $50 a month and have the equivalent of $1,000 left for food and incidentals.

Unraveling The Mystery of My Parents' Drive To Earn Advanced Degrees

After working on the *"Initiation Ceremonies"* research I began to understand that while my parents got the grades and degrees, they never quite got the idea of what it was supposed to be about. No one as dishonest as my father can be a scholar. He would not recognize the truth if it smacked him in the face. My mother could not have been trusted with the ethnographic record. She liked to make stuff up about Indians. Scholars search for the truth. My parents spent every moment of their lives running from the truth. Some of their friends like Phil Freeman had an infectious desire to share the excitement of their intellectual discoveries. Frank Young taught me how to embark on my own path to discovery. Neither of my parents could grasp any of this.

Here I am compelled to conclude that my parents were ahead of their time. They would be a near perfect fit with the university as it has evolved. Much better than me. Soon after my parents retired, universities in the United States began adopting a business model, emphasizing the production of degrees for profit.

They relentlessly promoted the asinine idea that no one could succeed in life without a bachelor's degree. To obtain these supposedly precious degrees, students were encouraged to take on crushing debt. Graduates today stagger under obligations for vast sums of money that they immediately and directly turned over to their colleges and universities.

Keeping costs down while increasing tuitions and enrollments is the formula for turning formerly name-brand colleges and universities into degree mills. They kept costs down by not hiring more faculty to handle the increasing teaching load. Permanent faculty at least. Today, San Diego State University would not hire Frank W. Young with a recent Ivy doctorate as an assistant professor of anthropology. It would hire five temporary, part-time non-tenure track lecturers to teach one course each.

When I retired from the University of California in 2008, if my salary was applied solely to my teaching responsibilities at the time, I would have been being paid $50,000 per course. We were then paying our temporary lecturers $3,000 per course. No wonder university administrations could not resist the temptation to shift to an underclass of temporary faculty. Plus the savings of not having to pay retirement and other benefits to part-time hires.

Increase the speed of the assembly line, pay the workers less, charge more for the product. The next step will be to video the courses and continue to offer them on-line after the professors retire and die. Eventually there will be no need to pay any faculty or even to maintain a campus.

The degree mill model is destroying every component of what higher education once meant: teaching, research, and service to the community. There are often highly dedicated and gifted teachers among the temporary faculty, but they are also trying to scrape by on starvation wages and are justifiably paranoid about their future chances for a stable academic career that will never happen. They may dream of a tenure track position someday, but their only realistic hope is to continue to string together enough temporary appointments to survive from semester to semester, often on several campuses requiring half-day commutes between them. Parents should be aware that their college-age children are being taught by one of the most exploited labor forces in the modern world.

On the research side, as they become degree mills, universities today are fertile grounds for new and highly suspect forms of research "success." Tenured faculty that are needed to process undergraduates through the system, as many and as fast as possible, are only nominally research faculty. Coming up through the ranks today is a wave of pseudo researchers and scholars who are forced to squeeze out one or two useless journal articles a year, who must write when they have nothing to say and find venues for articles no one will ever read. A new type of "high impact" academic journal will publish what you write if you pay them enough. We now have "renowned" professors who are the world's biggest experts in the world's smallest sub-field—i.e. in subject-domains where there is but one expert, they themselves. Famous professors go around the country giving lectures taking great care not to say anything that their audience does not already know. This mutual mirroring guarantees a reputation for "brilliance."

If I entered college today, what are the chances of my meeting and working with a Frank W. Young? Probably nil. If your child entered college today what are her chances of meeting and working with Dean MacCannell. Certainly nil. If I received my Ph.D. degree in the past five years, I wouldn't for an instant consider applying for positions in academia, permanent or temporary. I'd rather be a race car builder. I tell all graduate students and junior faculty, "I'm only interested in your Plan B."

Both Dr. E. H. MacCannell and Dr. H. F. MacCannell eventually squeezed through the rapidly closing gate to tenure leaving only scant trace evidence of their academic existence—two or three forgettable journal articles co-authored with their dissertation chair and, in my mother's case, co-authored with sympathetic senior colleagues. Neither of them published a single word after tenure and were consigned to a lifetime of teaching the same undergraduate courses over, and over, and over again. They bore up under this regime with remarkable good humor as if they expected nothing more. A dedicated researcher or teacher would regard the working conditions of their careers as brutal punishment, even torture. Yet, they would be a perfect fit for today's university as its mission has evolved.

I had the pleasure and honor of working alongside scientists and scholars who posed the right questions and solved complex problems, sometimes on matters of life and death. It is my greatest joy to read and to hear about work that is advancing knowledge. The mere co-presence of these serious, productive colleagues made the lives of the straggling deadwood a living hell. And vice-versa. Today the deadwood has successfully taken over administrative positions and re-made the university in its own image. Into the degree mill.

My parents plodded through academia seemingly oblivious to any professional responsibilities beyond classroom teaching. When I became Chair of Environmental Design at UC Davis, I mentioned it to my father's wife. She called to him, dying in an adjoining room, "Did you hear that, Earle? Dean's been made Chair of his Department." My father, honest this one time in his life, called back, "I hate department chairs." His feelings are understandable. If I had been his chair back in the day, one of my primary responsibilities would have been to hector him constantly about his lack of productivity after tenure. It was one of the worst parts of the job of Chair.

If they had been even more distracted as parents, had they been pursuing an education when I was a boy, I would regard them completely differently today. But it is now evident to me that they had very little interest in education, certainly not their children's, but also not even their own. They were pursuing degrees, something quite distinct. Then as today, it was possible to get a degree without getting an education. I suspect they were both so secure in their belief in their own brilliance that they were mainly uneducable. For them, it was only about cramming for exams, passing tests, getting grades, fulfilling requirements, and being awarded degrees. I do not recall either of them telling me about something interesting that they had learned. They liked demonstrating their knowledge as if they were born with it. But they never discussed the process of learning anything.

Still, I did not get to where I am today by accident. My parents had an important hand in it. From them I learned that a false life could be played convincingly as the real thing. As I witnessed up close the making of two ersatz scholars, an image of a real scholar or researcher must have been taking shape in my unconscious. Wordsworth said, "The child is father of the man." I always thought Freud said it. But it was Wordsworth, and I am proof.

A Startling Self-Realization

A few weeks into my first semester of college, I overheard a conversation about me. It was the final upset of my idea of who I was. I was waiting in the hall of the Social Sciences and Humanities Building for a professor to arrive for his office hours. Around the corner and out of my sight but well within hearing, Aubrey Wendling bumped into Frank Young.

AW: "How's your plan to create a research team using undergraduates going?"

FWY: "Great. I got Dean MacCannell."

AW: "You're lucky. He works like an animal. No one has been able to get him to stop working."

Aubrey's words shocked me more than anything I ever heard about myself, before or since.

Until that moment, my self-image was clear and uncomplicated. I thought I was a major screw-off; one of the laziest s.o.b.s who had ever walked the earth. I sincerely believed that my main tendency was to seize every opportunity that came my way to do nothing productive or worthwhile. It seemed completely absurd to me that someone who knew me quite well, someone whose judgment I respected, would say otherwise. And to go so far as to suggest that I was a good worker was beyond ridiculous.

Then, in that instant, I understood completely how a person's self-view can be, most probably always is, the exact opposite of their reputation. Everyone who works their ass off must think of themselves as laggards.

It makes perfect sense. If I went around patting myself on the back for having a strong work ethic, I would have grabbed every chance to back off and take it easy. Like, 'You work hard, you deserve a break.' For me, every moment of my life, it was, 'Get off your lazy butt and get that job done, you worthless lout.'

THE END
is
also
THE BEGINNING

* * *

Dean MacCannell's original field of study was anthropology. He was among the first to reverse the ethnographic gaze and study hyper-modern society and culture. His 1976 book, The Tourist, *has never gone out of print and has been translated into twelve languages. This memoir covering his childhood and youth tells the story of his improbable background for an evenutal career that brought him global recognition and respect.*

PHOTO CREDITS

All credited images are used with permission of the copyright holder.

Page 51 Photos by Dean MacCannell

Page 102 Photos by Dean MacCannell

Page 165 Photo: *Easimages.net*

Page 166 Photo: *Houtkamp Collection Fine Historic Automobiles, Amsterdam*

Page 182 Photo: *Davidsclassiccars.com*

Page 186 Photo: *Jalopyjournal.com*

Page 216 Photo: *Marc Vorgers Classic Cars*

Page 227 Photo: Dean MacCannell

Page 228 Photo: *Marc Vorgers Classic Cars*

Page 228 Photo: *Wikimedia*

Page 228 Photo: *Marc Vorgers Classic Cars*

Page 229 Photo: *Marc Vorgers Classic Cars*

Page 231 Photo: *Sports Car Racing Though Time, Grimeheel.blogspot.com*

Page 233 Photo: Dean MacCannell

Page 235 Photo: Dean MacCannell

Page 237 Uncopyrighted advertising image

Page 240 Uncopyrighted advertising image

Page 248 Uncopyrighted advertising image

Page 249 Photo: owner, Paul Coombes

Page 274 Photo: owner Glen Rummy, *barnfinds.com*

Page 281 Photo: *Wirewheels.com*

Page 282 Photo: Dean MacCannell

Page 288 Photo: Dean MacCannell

Page 289 Photo: Dean MacCannell

Page 290 Photo: Dean MacCannell

Page 296 Photo: *crosleykook.blogspot.com*

Page 297 Photo: Paul Hanna

Page 297 Photo: Paul Hanna

Made in the USA
Monee, IL
11 March 2023